Between God and Gold

Between God and Gold

Protestant Evangelicalism and the Industrial Revolution, 1820–1914

Robert A. Wauzzinski

Rutherford ● Madison ● Teaneck
Fairleigh Dickinson University Press
London and Toronto: Associated University Presses

Associated University Presses
440 Forsgate Drive
Cranbury, NJ 08512

Associated University Presses
25 Sicilian Avenue
London WC1A 2QH, England

Associated University Presses
P.O. Box 338, Port Credit
Mississauga, Ontario
Canada L5G 4L8

The paper used in this publication meets the requirements of the American National Standard for Permanence of Paper for Printed Library Materials Z39.48-1984.

Library of Congress Cataloging-in-Publication Data

Wauzzinski, Robert A., 1950–
    Between God and gold : Protestant evangelicalism and the Industrial revolution, 1820–1914 / Robert A. Wauzzinski.
        p.   cm.
    Includes bibliographical references and index.
    ISBN 0-8386-3481-8 (alk. paper)
    1. Evangelicalism—United States—History.   2. Protestant churches—United States—History.   3. United States—Industries—History.   4. Capitalism—Religious aspects—Protestant churches.   5. Economics—Religious aspects—Christianity.   I. Title.
BR1642.U5W388   1993
280'.4'097309034—dc20   91–58959
                                                                                          CIP

#26356231

PRINTED IN THE UNITED STATES OF AMERICA

Dedicated to the memory of Dr. Peter Steen:
A threefold honeyed Rock

and

to "Bucky,"
the love of my life

God wills that there be proportion and equity among us; each man is to provide for the needy according to his means so that no man has too much and no man has too little. . . . God sends us the poor as receivers. To give to the poor is to give to God.
—John Calvin

God gave me my money.
—John D. Rockefeller, 1915

Contents

Foreword   9
Preface   13
Introduction   17

1. Religion Defined   27
2. An Introduction to the Evangelical-Industrial Worldview   38
3. American Industrialism   65
4. Classical Christian Theorists   100
5. A Transatlantic Intermezzo   116
6. Case Studies   126
7. Exploring a Richer Life: Alternatives to the
   Problems at Hand   159
8. Conclusions   218

Notes   225
Select Bibliography   258
Index   269

Foreword

A State University of New York-based poll of 133,000 Americans found that 85% of us vaguely define our religion as "Christian." About sixty percent of the citizens of the United States describe their Christian faith in the broadest sense as "Protestant." Many of us see the vitality of the sector of Protestantism called "Conservative," a nexus that includes everyone marked "Evangelical," "Pentecostal," "Fundamentalist," "Southern Baptist," Missouri Synod Lutheran, Christian Reformed, and more. Still other opinion research indicates that a significant percentage of the Protestant populace describes itself as "born again," a core concept used to denote something of the heart of the Evangelical belief system.

Given this vast American, even global, phenomenon called "Evangelicalism," one is inclined to inquire into the origins and contours of the Evangelical identity. The historian advises a look at the past, because "born again" was not "born yesterday." And that backward glance shows Evangelicalism to have been even far more pervasive from the eighteenth century to the beginning of the twentieth century than it is today, though Unitarians, Universalists, and some small sects stood apart from Evangelicalism. The modernisms, liberalisms, and even moderatisms which characterize much of Protestantism developed during the twentieth century and were not strong cultural presences during the eighteenth and nineteenth centuries. It was during those two earlier centuries that so much of the ethos of the nation was formed; the shaping influences of those earlier centuries mold far more than churchgoing Evangelicalism today.

We have, in other words, a world-historical force on hand, one whose ethos and ideology, if we may call it that, have outlasted believed-in communism (as opposed to imposed, Chinese-style, communism), along with many other kinds of secular ideologies. The Evangelical ethos with roots in biblical (especially Pauline) thought, is a rich and varied tradition, traveling as it does through the thought of Augustine, Calvin, Luther and contemporary Reformed thought. This tradition has had much to do with attitudes surrounding economics, business, labor and social organization. As

9

everyone who has come close to the subject of Protestantism and capitalism knows, major theorists such as Max Weber and reasonably major elaborators such as R. H. Tawney have seen profound connections between Protestantism (at that time all of which could be coded as "Evangelical") and capitalism.

Given statistical, social, cultural, and religious bonds between American Evangelicalism and the industrial world view, one would expect libraries full of literature on precisely what those instigating and connecting elements are. Wauzzinski notes these connections. However, he goes beyond noting them to look at the "religious" roots of the Evangelical-industrial synthesis and to suggest alternatives to the problems outlined.

At the back of this book there is a bibliography beginning with A as in Abell to Z as in Zylstra suggesting that author W for Wauzzinski is not alone in the splendid idiosyncracy of crackpot theorizing about the tragedy of the relatively recent Evangelical-industrial liaison. A closer look at that bibliography shows that many of the titles are related only obliquely to the liaison per se, and a still more careful inspection will give the reader a more lasting impression (which will turn to realization): Wauzzinski is doing some fresh, even pioneering work. If I were a Japanese or Muslim businessperson, a survivor of Eastern European Communist regimes and now "starting up shop," or an entrepreneur in a developing nation, and knew I had to deal with the United States and wanted to understand the thought world of its secularized industrialists, financiers, and corporate leaders, I would want to read this kind of book to "get the jump on them."

Many things are done unreflectively in a culture; one is pushed unwittingly along by profound cultural forces such as the industrializing process. The Evangelical worldview in the early nineteenth century was the framework used by many to fashion a significant portion of the pre-industrial world. This influence was exerted while America was turning from a mentality of small businesses and regional agriculture to a culture stressing a corporate, universal, manufacturing, urban ethos. Elites of all sorts (everyone from small investors to Robber Barons) embraced the Evangelical view and had to grapple with the meaning of what they were doing. Their synthetic worldview affected subsequent struggles. Our world betrays the outcome of this struggle. The thought world and practices of Evangelicalism, which Wauzzinski takes pains to define, had a privileged position and role during those years. Thus, understanding the Evangelical role in industrial change is crucial. The industrializing process increasingly pulled Evangelicals even further from the Origin of their Sunday schools and Sabbaths, their sacred explanations and their churchly ties; certain ways of looking at reality kept alluring them, as this book makes abundantly clear.

America has not been a Jewish culture, though Hebraic, Old Testamental, and latter-day Jewish thought has been a significant complement to the Evangelical and Enlightened and Catholic outlooks; but Jewish terminology has made its way into the speech of non-Jews. So we seize the word *chutzpah* to describe an aspect of Wauzzinski's work. There is boldness and daring in his interdisciplinary venture. The historian who is writing this foreword keeps a watchful and even suspicious eye on the nonhistorian who is writing here about "classical Christian theorists" or one who makes "case studies" figures who belong on my, not his, turf: Finney, Wayland, and Conwell. The economic historian monitors the effort to tell how America "incorporated." Theologians whet their critical knives watching for mistakes in the treatment of the creation, the fall, and redemption. And, of course, economists will be watching, not spreading safety nets, as they see the author negotiating the high wires of definitions of land, labor, and capital.

However, a note needs to be clearly sounded. Wauzzinski does not slap several disciplines together like some academic pancake mix. This work is a multidisciplinary work molded into a coherent interdisciplinary piece through his core definition of "religion." Because of its several strands, it is not necessary, however, a completely safe or neat book. There is no other way to bring together what one needs to advance the argument than this interdisciplinary, somewhat risky way. Reality is coherent at its core. Therefore, the people who make decisions about the economy are not only majors in economics. They are citizens, family members, creatures who depend upon the natural environment, believers, walking embodiments of traditions which merged and fused and fought for priority in the cultures and minds of such people, the partakers of the world of 1820–1914. He glues this piece together through an examination of "presupposita," or basic commitments, in a manner that deepens his analysis. Continuous strains of clarity and practicality can be seen throughout this work, a necessary art in an interdisciplinary effort.

I have treated the Evangelical tradition, with due differentiations, as if it was whole, intact, continuous, and easy to grasp. This book does anything but that. Part of Wauzzinski's originality lies in the discovery of, and argument for, the notion that, because they drank deeply from the waters of economic secularization, Evangelicals *broke* with many parts of the tradition they claimed to represent.

But, as with the fall, the theological concept which receives due attention here, this lapse does not mean that there is nothing left of the creation and its products to retrieve.

The author, therefore, is engaged in some acts of retrieval, showing Evangelicals and their fellow citizens what was distorted in some of the industrial exaggerations and what might be revivified if rediscovered. There is a prophetic cast to much of what follows. In a time when partisans for the American free enterprise system or capitalist democracy often make it seem as if only one economic system could ever have belonged in the Christian lineage—as if God was sitting back, having created Adam, waiting for Adam Smith to set forth the divine purposes—Wauzzinski goes his own way with critique and suggestions for alternatives. They are not the tired ones associated with socialism or democratic liberalism. He finds resources in the Evangelical tradition itself, a tradition which can only be conceived, received, and put to work in complex ways by an informed and dedicated minority who must interact with a secularized, pluralized culture. This minority is not to be imperial, presumptive, or arrogant; Wauzzinski is certainly not. But it deserves to be given a hearing and to be encouraged—if, that is, it first can find itself. *Between God and Gold* is a critical work designed to help advance such discovery.

MARTIN E. MARTY

Preface

I have learned in my academic career that reality does not exactly comport with my theoretical models, as students are so quick to remind me. Our relatively abstract or separated disciplines are, at their best, pieces of a larger whole we call reality. That is, reality is far more interconnected than our individual disciplines suggest, or so I have come to believe.

In this study I am trying to discern what are meant by the terms "economic" and "religion"; in so doing, I am forced beyond these disciplines into related, but theoretically separated, areas of life. I am fortunate: having occupied an endowed interdisciplinary chair, having supportive colleagues as mentors, and receiving corrections from capable supporters have helped in this endeavor. Working on cohesion has the virtue of wholeness while possessing the potential academic vice of superficiality. I trust I will pursue the former and avoid the latter.

I have attempted to narrow the scope of this work by concentrating on the fusion between Protestant Evangelicalism and the Industrial Revolution. To probe the heart or bedrock of this interrelationship involves the study of religion or the "science" of ultimate commitment.

The knowledgeable reader will surely realize the dangerous waters I am entering. If I am wrong about religion as ultimate commitment and the interconnectedness of life, then my project is foolhardy. However, if I am correct—especially about religion's foundational importance—then my undertaking is not only (literally) radically necessary, but it affords a profound way to study and understand social phenomena.

I am constantly being reminded of the need for the help and the support of the professional academy. Professor Bob Goudzwaard of the Free University of Amsterdam—friend, confidant, and encouraging colleague—has paved the way by showing many of us how "religion," faith, and economics can and should be united. By exposing the ultimacies present in secular economic history, discerned in the context of Western intellectual thought, Bob has laid the foundation for an alternative economic science. The discipline has benefited from Bob's endeavors.

Mark Perlman, professor of economic history at the University of Pittsburgh, has also greatly contributed to this project. His suggestions about style, tone, and breadth have been valuable; they are only surpassed by his support for this project.

I am grateful to the staff of the Barbour Library—especially its director, Dr. Steven Crocco—at Pittsburgh Theological Seminary for providing me with excellent resources and generous amounts of space. Of particular help were the staff of the library of the Institute for Christian Studies in Toronto, Canada, at which I did much of my early research. The Faculty have always been an encouragement.

I must also extend my gratitude to Professor Martin E. Marty for his invaluable editorial suggestions and his belief in, and support for, this project.

I must also extend my gratitude to my colleague Dale Soden, a skilled historical specialist on the era under study. His suggestions about the necessity of nuanced historical facts have hopefully raised the quality of this work.

My wife and I are fortunate to have Bill and Karen Perkins as our friends. They allowed us to share their home while I worked on the revision of this manuscript.

I am in debt to my late parents, especially to my mother Annabelle, for their insistence that their less-than-academically-interested son pursue an education that circumstances had denied them.

I am grateful to the professional advocacy and roundabout encouragement given to me by Dr. James D. Bratt of Calvin College in Michigan.

Amal Tanas, Melissa Francis, and Terry Mitchell have contributed administrative and editorial skills to this project. I have been their student throughout this work—and beyond.

I owe a great deal of respect and gratitude to my colleagues and friends. While they have raised the quality of this endeavor, they have in no way contributed to its flaws.

This book is dedicated to the memory of Dr. Peter Steen and to "Bucky." Christy Buxton Wauzzinski, my wife, has been of inestimable help, comfort, and support in this effort. She has sacrificed much more than time and money so that this work could go forward. Christy, the academic community is much the "poorer" because of your sacrifice. Finally, the scope and spirit of this project would be inconceivable without the invigorating, troublesome, and herculean exhortations of Dr. Peter Steen, whose name means "out of the Rock" (Psalm 81:16b). It was Pete, in his own inimical way, who filled me with a vision of how life in its many aspects and at its depth should truly be called "religious."

This work addresses two of the crucial areas of our world: religion and economics. They have been, in spite of abuses, two pillars of "happiness" for the American way of life. Perhaps it is not too surprising that I have chosen these two disciplines to study. As the second-generation son of industrial workers and one who considers himself to be a part of the Evangelical family, studying them has meant studying the roots of my life. In addressing them, I have spoken in critical appreciation of two areas of life that have also decisively informed American identity.

Introduction

What does the study of "religion" entail? What is a religious act? Traditionally, cultic history, social and philosophical ethics, related theological matters, and topical issues have defined religious studies. Contrary to this rather fixed position, several theorists have come to identify religion as a complex of personal and cultural ultimacies. Many would argue, as we will see when we survey noted authors, that religion should focus upon ultimate concern and not be compartmentalized as merely an aspect of life. The study of religion, they say, should focus upon that which is believed to be foundational to theory and practice. I believe that to theorize in this way is to deepen our understanding.

This work will make use of the disciplines of theology, economics, church and world history, and philosophy to study one social movement: the fusion of Evangelicalism and Industrialism. While its methodology is to use an interdisciplinary approach, its disciplinary focus is that of ethics. I believe that this approach provides the most breadth and depth to the subject matter, permitting an analysis of the ethical, epistemological, and the ontological roots of the worldviews of Evangelicalism and American Industrialism. This study will attempt to shed new light on how social and religious change occurs by probing the consequences of the fusion of the worldviews of Evangelicalism and Industrialism.

This work differs from Max Weber's classic work *The Protestant Ethic and the Spirit of Capitalism* in the way that it defines religion. It is argued that not only Evangelicalism, but Industrialism[1] also, has ultimate commitments. Furthermore, this study will not deal, as did Weber's, with the Puritans. The link between Evangelicalism and Industrialism in the nineteenth century was significantly different from the link between Puritanism and capitalism. By exploring the interconnections between Protestant Evangelicalism and capitalistic industrialism, I hope to show how the liaison was of a profoundly religious, mutually defining character.

There are several other terms besides "religion" that need to be defined at the outset. I use the terms "Mammon"[2] and "Gold" simultaneously to refer to the many relationships and forces that surrounded Industrialism. Mammon and Gold are defined as money, wealth, or, more broadly, capitalism, but with the ethical implication that acquiring money and related activities is imperative. To use industrialist Andrew Carnegie's phrase, Industrialism suggests a "Gospel of Wealth."

The term "Evangelical" is somewhat harder to define. A common core of theological beliefs, with significant variations, can be discerned.[3] However, theology is not the sole component that defines Evangelicalism. This work will explore the additional social, political, and economic forces that went into defining Evangelicalism.

Evangelicalism seems to stress a more or less unified worldview. It centers on the need for personal conversion, the acceptance of a substitutionary atonement as the only path to salvation, and the evolving doctrine of an errorless Bible as the guide to Christian life. The desire for cultural renewal through an evangelistic or a para-ecclesiastical association and the desire for a "filling" by the Holy Spirit for witness and service in the world are also seminal. We will survey these beliefs and their connections with certain cultural presuppositions. Indeed, it will be argued that the link between Evangelicalism and Industrialism cannot be fully appreciated apart from an appreciation of more foundational presuppositions. Finally, the term "revolution" seems to apply to the changes brought on by Industrialism—changes that Evangelicalism helped to initiate.

I have chosen the time period of 1820 to 1914 for several reasons. In 1821 Charles Grandison Finney claimed to have had a conversion experience that was to radically shape the contours of his ministry and subsequent Evangelical history. One year before, Lowell, Massachusetts had become the first major site to have a large-scale assembly of machines and technical experts, and large-scale industrial problems. These two events changed the course of American history by changing our perceptions and ultimate commitments. By the First World War, both movements had become codified in American consciousness and were formative forces that even the horrors of a world war could not radically alter. Indeed, the war may have strengthened their force.

Interest in the relation between Evangelicalism and Industrialism is growing. Sociologist George M. Thomas concludes that there is an isomorphism between the worldviews of Republicanism and Protestant revivalism. That is, the structure and content of these movements made up a single, equal distillate or compound form. They exhibited similar commitments to the myths of the autonomous, self-determining individual, free will, and the belief in progress ordained by a Deity—democratically and mechanistically conceived. More profoundly, both shared a view of the person as a rational and moral agent who lives in a mechanistically conceived cosmos. By these criteria, Evangelicalism *should* have been oriented toward revival techniques that harnessed the mechanical forces of the cosmos so as to bombard the rational-moral sensibilities of people. A "born-again" experience was the determinable and manipulatable end.[4] In short, both the revival and the market synthetically helped define this era's view of the cosmos, a view that strengthened our national and personal identity.

But why a revival? Thomas traces the traditional reasons: class reaction to oppression, frustrated interest, loss of social control and hegemony, anomie, and deprivation. He masterfully adds a reason of his own to the mix when he argues that a crisis of meaning initiates the search for a new institutional order, complete with rules, a reconstituted ontology, and cultural programs.

Approaches such as Thomas' to the study of religion, however, marginalize religion and confuse faith and theology with religion. As a result, no foundational, transhistoric ultimacy can be discovered and no foundation for social change can be discerned. Since reality is seen to lack a fundamental meaning structure, such specialists are unable to provide a view that contributes both to a more radical understanding of our past and a more cohesive view of reality.

A theologically empathetic yet culturally critical examination of the interrelationships between Evangelicalism and Industrialism is obviously needed. George Marsden's work,[5] while admirably treating the Christ-and-culture problematics and the rise of Fundamentalism, fails to investigate the God-and-Gold liaison; the book tends to subsume economic questions under political topics. Ernest Sandeen highlights the theological origins of Fundamentalism but does not treat the capitalism link.[6] Conversely, William G. McLaughlin and Paul Johnson fully emphasize the link between Industrialism and Protestantism.[7] However, their sociological presuppositions tend to make religion overly dependent upon social forces, thus robbing Evangelicalism of its integrity and relative autonomy. On the other hand, Timothy Smith gives credit to the "supernatural" origins of the Evangelical religion, but fails to see that Evangelicalism must nevertheless interact with the forces of cultural change,[8] and thus become identified with them.

We may anticipate the role played by Evangelicals, given this interaction. "The [economic] system itself had no long-term disabilities that good-hearted people could not overcome."[9] And so Frank sensitively notes that Evangelicals salved the wounds and wounded of the market without seeking a surgical option—because no deep problem was discerned. It will be argued that an analysis of these forces as they pertain to, say, Rochester, New York, circa 1830, will reveal Charles Finney both changing proto-industrial culture and being co-opted by the tenets of a Whiggish worldview.

There are a number of works that parallel but do not exactly touch upon the thrust of this project. Henry F. May, in his classic work *Protestant Churches and Industrial America,* arrived at many of the same conclusions as this work. He remarks that in antebellum America, "organized Protestantism support[ed] the dominant economic beliefs and institutions even more unanimously than it accepted the existing forms of government."[10] He correctly sees that "clerical laissez-faire" opposition was directed against "radicalism" (thus that the two competing worldviews were matched against each other) and that the resultant conservatism became entrenched in many Eastern colleges through Whiggish worldviews. Moreover, he correctly cites Francis Wayland as an example of such a cleric; Wayland's unabashed laissez-faire commitments found fertile soil at Brown University in particular and in the antebellum curriculum in general.

There are many things about May's work, however, that are inadequate, if not disturbing. May fails to treat the interrelationship of theology and economics; thus, his work misses an important connection and fails to understand the rationale for this liaison. Secondly, by erring in some philosophical issues (he refers to Evangelical commitment in terms of "immutable laws" rather than in terms of "natural laws"), he misrepresents Evangelicalism. Finally, like many moderns, May casts all clerical laissez-faire supporters into a "conservative" mold. He is correct in assuming that such clerics wanted to conserve the traditions of laissez-faire, if not proto-Republican, America. However, by failing to penetrate to the roots of conservatism, he misconstrues the theological tradition by failing to see that belief in God was equated with belief in the natural laws that allegedly formed market operations.[11]

I will propose that a deeper, more integral view of religion can help us discern the contours of this "isomophism" more fully. Insofar as industrialization was a revolution of total proportions, changes in our ultimate commitments, faith stances, authority structures, and biological and cultural environments occurred.

The work of Aaron Abell, *The Urban Impact on American Protestantism, 1865–1900,* purports to deal with how Protestantism came to struggle with the forces of Industrialism in and around the urban complex (here meaning the Eastern establishment). But the strengths of this work are lost in an avalanche of mischaracterizations and sweeping generalizations. Typical of the latter is the following: "Protestant reformers overlooked in their readings of the New Testament its imperative injunctions of brotherly kindness . . ." Abell says, "the Reformation supported intense selfishness which is manifested in the pursuit of wealth and power."[12] The reformers, especially John Calvin, would directly and emphatically deny this charge. In surveying the socioeconomic thought of classical Christianity, the present work represents an attempt to expose the error in Abell's thought and show how far nineteenth-century and contemporary Evangelicalism have moved from their own religious roots in the Protestant Reformation.

One crucial factor, then, seems to be lacking in the literature. The scholars, while doing excellent work in their own fields, do not evidence formal training in the two most essential disciplines: religion/theology and economics. Hence, very important scholarly elements are omitted.

This work will also entertain, to a lesser degree, some conventional theses about the relationship of Evangelicalism with American culture. Contrary to some prevailing theories, Evangelicalism (with Fundamentalism being an exception) never went through a large-scale socially inactive phase.[13] Antebellum and postbellum social concern was often manifest. Nor did Evangelicals, à la David Moberg's *Great Reversal,* experience a radical shift in social commitment around 1890. The issue may better be defined by looking broadly at the interrelationship of nature to grace, individual to social or collective, and gospel to consequences. In other words, we need to identify the priorities and the hierarchy of emphases to ascertain why social commitment waxed and waned. It will be argued that individual salvation and its attendant phenomena, such as the "filling of the Holy Spirit," were of *primary* importance and that cultural (or natural) renewal was ascribed a *secondary* status. It is not that Evangelicals did not care about culture (although we will note the few exceptions); it is rather that cultural renewal was often thought to proceed through a mass of individual conversions. Individual conversion was central; cultural results were thought to follow as a matter of secondary consequence. The distillate was to manifest a nonradical, nonintegral, and truncated gospel message that too deeply separated the individual from society, religion from culture, and the kingdom of God from historical development.

Finally, this work will attempt to demonstrate that Evangelicals, in the main, cannot be characterized as anti-intellectual, since many were fully conscious of, and active within, their primary philo-

sophical tradition, Scottish Common Sense Realism. The challenge
of this work will be to explain how many Evangelicals could be
rigorous in thought and accomodating to capitalism.

This work attempts to explore the main currents that flow
between Evangelicalism and Industrialism. Scholars will follow
who will find side tributaries that move in contradictory directions. Such analysis and finding are necessary, for traveling on
these side currents may lead us to more verdant scholarly land-
scapes. For now, the mighty torrents that flow between God and
Gold must command our full attention. It is our hope that this
work helps focus our attention on the weighty matters that will
appear before you.

This book, though written for a scholarly audience, can have an
impact on the lay reader as well. Not only must the academic world
come to see the place of values and foundational commitments
within theory, but academics must also admit their own ultimate
(and, as yet, largely unconfessed) presuppositions and the place
these play in everyday life and theory. For the Protestant Evangelical laity, as for all Protestant laity, this work raises the great question of purity of worship: can one serve both God and Gold? If not,
what difference would single-minded loyalty to God make in the
world of moneyed affairs? Indeed, is such commitment even possible in business today? These questions can be asked because they
are part of the Evangelical tradition. In this book, some basic reasons will be given for the enduring, pliable, and steadfast character
of Evangelicalism and capitalism.

To take these worldviews seriously is to fully realize their limitations. At the same time, by lessening one's own biases, one can
hopefully appreciate more the contribution both movements have
made to American identity.

This work is divided into eight chapters. Chapter 1 will define
religion; chapter 2 will introduce the Evangelical-capitalistic synthesis in a survey of nineteenth-century history and worldviews. In
chapter 3 I will attempt to explore the religious depths of the Industrial Revolution, being careful to review all the pertinent facets.
Chapter 4 will present the classical Christian ethical-economic positions of Augustine, Aquinas, Luther, and Calvin. In looking at them,
I intend to show how much Evangelicalism has currently accommodated itself to the forces of capitalism. In chapter 5, I will explore
the British-American economic and theological liaison in an intermezzo. I hope to show that the political, economic, theological, and
cultural similarities between Britain and America were strong and
contributed to the industrial-capitalist synthesis. In chapter 6 three

revelant case studies will be presented. The attempt here is to locate key concepts in key figures. The mission of antebellum evangelist Charles G. Finney, the theory of the mid-century ethicist-philosopher Francis Wayland, and finally the postbellum contributions of Russell Conwell will be surveyed. In chapter 7 some alternatives to the system will be outlined. A more far-reaching gospel will be suggested as a corrective to the problems noted. The forces surrounding land, labor, and capital will be addressed from a reformed Christian perspective. Chapter 8 will present the conclusions. The language in these last two chapters will of necessity be straightforward, though hopefully not nonacademic.

I will use the evaluative paradigm suggested by the Amsterdam school of Christian philosophy. I believe that this position has all of the strengths of American Evangelicalism without many of its philosophical and cultural liabilities. Having established a long history of theoretical and practical excellence in social-philosophical affairs, the Dutch Reformed faith has manifested a theologically sound tradition while overcoming the difficulties surrounding Industrialism. Moreover, given their full and rigorous philosophical exchange with European intellectual leaders, the members of this school are qualified in all respects to speak on the matters outlined in this work. This school of thought is not, furthermore, restricted to a European context; many of its adherents live in North America. Having been educated at two seminaries and one secular graduate school, I have not found a scholarly tradition that can articulate a worldview with as much depth and faithfulness to the historic roots of the Christian faith as can the Amsterdam school of Christian philosophy.

Reformed Christian scholarship, like all scholarship, must be guided by humility. Christians have not been the primary ones who have contributed to the common betterment of humanity in the last 150 years. Therefore, we must be on guard against a religious chauvinism that paternalizes the contributions of other "religious" traditions. Christians are, after all, an offshoot of the Jewish faith, and secular humanism has contributed mightily to the arts and sciences. Muslims were adding to our Western technological tradition even before we had identified ourselves as "Protestant."

Having said this, a different note must be sounded. The Judeo-Christian tradition is one of the core traditions of Western civilization. If its intellectual voice is paternalistically ignored because of secular chauvinism, then the academy, the factory, and the pulpit are losers. The very use in secular philosophy of words like "com-

mitment," "depth concern," "internal steering fields," and "paradigms" tells us that knowledge is related to ultimate worldview
concerns. We live in a pluralistic age where many voices need to
be heard if the crucial problems of the day are to be meaningfully
addressed.

Between God and Gold

1

Religion Defined

This study will attempt to establish the universality and depth of religious commitment as it manifested itself in nineteenth-century Evangelicalism and Industrialism. Its approach is decidedly different from one that would relegate religion to a compartment or an aspect of life. We will look at the more practical manifestations of the industrial and Evangelical worldviews as well as the theoretical underpinnings of both, to substantiate this claim. To understand more fully what religion is, however, we must first discuss what it is not.

Religion is not to be equated with theology. Theology is a discipline, derived from confession, that eventuates into systemized thought, the philosophy of revelation, the history of creedal and faith development, and related hermeneutical concerns. To equate religion and theology is to confuse systematic creedal reflection with the basic stance or vision that undergirds all of one's reflection on life and practice.

Nor should religion be reduced to a sphere of morality. When science and other social and secular forces vied with traditional religion in the nineteenth century, many people turned to Victorian social mores for support. It was thought that critical reason dictated that nonsectarian, rationally valid facts should influence public discourse, while persons such as the clergy and institutions such as churches could augment these facts with subjective, personal values. "Faith" and religious commitment became a more private, moral affair[1] as the nineteenth century progressed.

A prominent nineteenth-century view held that religion is primarily psychological in nature and therefore to be associated with feeling and sentiment. Accordingly, the individual's religious experience was studied, and then attempts were made to generalize from one's unique experience to more universal religious beliefs and actions. Thus, people believed universal religious sentiments were the sum of individual, psychological experiences. This congruence functions as an unadmitted grid. While exhibiting the strength of the essential humanness of religion, this view made the psychological aspect of the personality the fundamental point of departure for study.[2] Like its moralistic counterpart, this view was profoundly circular and uncritically accepting of the foundational importance of individual experience. Charles Sheldon's popular nineteenth novel *In His Steps* manifests this psychological definition of religion.

Moreover, religion is often defined in terms of a dichotomy between nature and supernature and between "profane" and "secular" worldviews. Accordingly, religion is limited to a fixed set of human functions and often placed "above" the world or inside a "sacred" arena like the church. Society becomes secular by definition, and church and religion are correspondingly set at odds with the world and, say, science. Sociologist Peter Berger makes use of a version of dualism in his theories about religion and the origin of society. However, when he attempts to explain society's origin through this scheme, his dualism is derived from the monistic conception of a universal social embryo. He says: "Society . . . is a human product and nothing but a human product. . . . Society is a product of man. It has no other meaning except that which is bestowed upon it by human activity and consciousness. There can be no social reality apart from man."[3] Thus, religion as a social act may be designated as "sacred"; but in fact, its origin is totally due to people, and hence it is really secular.

Evangelical Protestantism has also manifested a version of a dualistic worldview. By considering nature and culture as autonomous, institutions like business, the state, and schools were set in tension with grace and associated institutions and practices. Religion was accordingly segregated from the world. It was associated with ecclesiastical structures, pious acts like prayer or benevolence, and mediated through evangelists, ministers, or theological experts.[4] In compartmentalizing religion in this way, nineteenth-century Protestant Evangelicalism was unable to penetrate to the root of secularizing cultural development, while at the same time it often remained blinded to the de facto religious presuppositions that guided industrializing culture.

Such dualisms, whether conceived from a secular or a Christian viewpoint, never seem to integrate or find the common root of parallel spheres or areas of life. One province of life always seems to be in tension with the other. R. H. Tawney describes such dualism as

parallel and independent provinces, governed by different laws, judged by different authorities. It is based on an attitude which forms so fundamental a part of modern thought, that . . . its precarious philosophical basis . . . [is] commonly forgotten.[5]

This form of compartmentalization readily adapted itself to industrializing culture and robbed nineteenth-century Evangelicalism of much of its potential culturally transformative power. Historian Samuel P. Hays says of traditional religions, and of Evangelicalism in particular, that after the Civil War they became "confined more and more to Sunday and then to Sunday morning. . . . [Evangelical religion] became for many more a social affair than a moving experience . . ."[6]

A tension arose in this era within Evangelicalism between those who stressed a more theologically exact definition of faith and those who, in a desire to be "born again," wanted a more practical religion. Revivalism desired to define religion as "warm," "immediate," and "active," and was not therefore creedally preoccupied. Given the century's "cult of busyness," revivalism in its antebellum form stressed, through supraecclesiastical mass meetings, surrender to a "loving Savior" who in turn empowered enthusiasts to "witness" and, in certain cases, to be active in social reform. Therefore, religion was defined not by its ability to inspire a deep theoretical critique of Industrialism, but by its reaction to cultural immediacies, by compromises, and by fervor.[7] Indeed it was Moody who said, "godliness must be measured primarily in terms of ceaseless action."[8] As we shall see shortly, such "ceaseless activity" was necessary for the growth of Evangelicalism and Industrialism.

I have maintained that religion means ultimate commitment. Religion should be concerned with how, and upon whom or what, our worldview is founded. Like a wellspring, religious commitments are found at the depths of our lives. Religion attempts to anchor and direct life's many aspects in meaningful ways. It is, therefore, all-embracing. These aspects are called "modes"[9] and cohere, according to the reformed Christian view, in one Origin. Because reality coheres, we can study the interpenetrability of, say, religion, faith and economic activity.

Each mode or area of life manifests its own meaning; we should not attempt to make it subordinate to another meaning. If we do, as in the case of the economics of this era, it is just reductionism. Arguably, the so-called "incorporation" of America represents a kind of American cultural reductionism. Nature, humanity, history and culture are modally diverse, manifesting different structures or realms of distinct reality,[10] which should not be distorted because of an overprescription of economic matters.

Both Evangelicalism and Industrialism became more reductionistic as the nineteenth century progressed. Evangelicalism was too narrowly preoccupied with the faith dimension as well as the moral or familial aspect of life. Thus, the revival, the church, and individual and familial morality too often became the objects of "redemption." When social legislation was pursued, it was meant to save these primary entities. This myopia is symptomatic of its underlying conservatism.[11] At the same time, Industrialism was increasingly preoccupied with various economic affairs to the detriment of a fuller cultural development, due to its obsession with profits, nature domination, expansion, and progress. It was fueled by what has been called the "horizontalization of life," a process stressing the mundane, the profane and the equation of material progress with human happiness. Economist-philosopher Bob Goudzwaard says that when this process of horizontalization replaced the verticalism of the Middle Ages,

> the legal order, the prevailing public morality, as well as the organization of socioeconomic life granted unobstructed admission to the forces of economic growth and technological development; and these forces subsequently manifested themselves by way of a process of "natural selection" as it is given shape by a continual competition in the market between independent production units organized on the basis of returns on capital.[12]

This is not to say, however, that the movements were unrelated. Though Evangelicalism seemed to focus on the "spiritual," the "otherworldly," the sacred areas, while Industrialism concerned itself with the "material," the affairs of this world and nature, they were united at a deeper level. Such a unification came about precisely because religion is not one function among many. Rather, religion is the function that unites the depths of life's activities.

> What does this metaphor "depth" mean? It means that the religious aspect points to that which is ultimate, infinite, unconditional in man's life. Religion, in the largest, most basic sense of the word, is ultimate concern.[13]

Therefore, though Evangelicalism and Industrialism seemed to be unrelated, they were in fact united at a deeper level. This represents a crucial axiom of this entire book. Moreover, to compartmentalize religion into one aspect of life, and to have it subsequently "penetrated" by economics, is to beg the more ultimate question of unification. That is, if religion and economics are simply mutually penetrating aspects, what unites these aspects with meaning, purpose, and ultimate direction?

The attempt to locate the fullness of life in one or two aspects is due in part to the unwarranted claims of autonomy. Speaking of industrial autonomy, theologian and philosopher Paul Tillich says,

> Personality and community . . . lost their intrinsic powerfulness and depth. Thus, personality, community, and things became instruments of autonomous secularism; they became merely objects for control and calculation in the service of man's economic purposes. Indeed, religion itself lost its sense of immediacy of the origin and became one sphere among other spheres . . .[14]

In autonomously rejecting the divine Origin, those having an industrial worldview attempted to offer another origin, and attempted to locate human happiness in economic activity. The richness of life's many modes was subordinated to the creation of wealth. As Samuel Hays says, "The American people subordinated religion, education and politics to the process of creating wealth. Increasing production, employment, and income became the measures of community success, and personal riches the mark of individual achievement."[15] Following the New Testament usage, we shall call this phenomenon Mammon (to be equated with the term "Gold").[16]

Our claim that Industrialism was at root driven by a religious imperative contradicts conventional wisdom. Sociologist Roland Robertson presents a more conventional view when he speaks of religion as "a set of beliefs and symbols pertaining to a distinction between empirical and super-empirical or transcendent reality."[17] He links this definition to an "exclusivist," "substantive," and "real" definition of religion. Although this effort has considerable merit, I believe that even by Robertson's definition the phenomena undergirding the development of modern capitalism can be called "religious." Was not, for example, Adam Smith's deistic "unseen hand" supposed to be a super-empirical reality? How else could it "control" market forces? Was Andrew Carnegie being merely poetic in entitling his most successful work *The "Gospel" of Wealth*? Do not capitalism's principles of self-interest, efficiency, "Manifest Destiny," and "happiness" function as ethical imperatives?

Why did this age (and why does ours?) manifest so much restlessness?[18] A religious analysis can help answer such questions. Reality is relative, limited, and interdependent. Beliefs and actions change, are subject to error, and are defined by other areas of life. The history of the production process, malleable as it has been, is proof of this point. Therefore, when cultures attempt to tie the meaning of vast areas of life to such shifting sands, restlessness and anomie result.

Religion not only anchors life's aspects, but its force directs culture to a true—or a false—Origin.[19] Thus, the term "industrial society" represents perhaps a deeper reality than previously conceived.

Few thinkers would deny the operative force that a worldview has upon life. However, disagreements arise when we look at the interrelationship of the notions of religion and worldview. A worldview is a more or less comprehensive way of viewing the world. Sociologist Berger refers to "cosmization" as the attempt to build a meaningful world. There can be secular attempts (science, for example) and sacred or religious attempts (such as theology) at this worldviewing process of cosmization.[20] Both, according to Berger, are humanity's attempt at self-externalization. Both, surprisingly, are founded upon the human need for "ultimate ground".[21] So, while Berger talks about ultimate ground, he locates that ground in the human attempt at self-externalization, the consequences of which are the worldviewing process of cosmization.

Axioms, ultimate presuppositions, and fundamental assumptions act as reference points for theoretical analysis as well as for cultural development. As such, they form another aspect of the definition of religion. We shall call these fundamental presuppositions "presupposita" because they are religiously rather than logically rooted.[22] John M. Keynes seems to make use of such presupposita when he says that "avarice and usury and precaution must be our gods for a little longer still. For only they can lead us out of the tunnel of economic necessity into daylight."[23] And what shall we see when we arrive in the light of day? "I see us free . . . to return . . . to the most sure principles . . . of traditional virtue[:] . . . that avarice is vice . . . and the love of money is detestable."[24]

Metaphors like depth and directedness and presupposita lead us to a fuller discussion of the category of ultimate concern. I mean by ultimate concern that response which is either tied to an origin—a god if you will—or is believed to be an unconditional object, itself conditioning all else. An ultimate concern is the bedrock of basic commitment and the foundation of various presupposita. As various secondary presupposita are united by faith into cultural expression, they inform the various aspects of life under a more dominant ultimate concern. Speaking of that which is of ultimate seriousness (and hence, that upon which life is built), Tillich says, "Is there really nothing at all that you take with unconditional seriousness? What . . . would you suffer and die for? When one answers this question, one will discover that even the cynic takes his cynicism with ultimate seriousness, not to speak of others, who may be naturalists, materialists, Communists or whatever."[25]

Evangelicalism and Industrialism shared the ideal or norm of progress as a presuppositum. Increasingly, Evangelical revivalism's millennial expectations were linked with economic and technological progress and development, thus causing a wave of optimism to sweep antebellum America. Christ would return to a economically progressive social order, according to this scheme. This optimism was founded in part upon the democratic notion of the perfectibility of people and their environment.

Furthermore, the progress ideal became tied to a materialist-naturalist worldview. Especially after the advent of Darwin's discoveries, Western humanity began to reject the "supernatural" and turned to the material world as a place of self-contained meaning and development. The ideal of economic progress became linked in theory with the evolution of the species. Just as organic life was moving to higher, more sophisticated grounds, so economic life was thought to be expanding and progressing to a greater plane of material abundance and thus of social good. The linkage of evolution and economic progress became an all-encompassing industrial worldview, and the combined product, as seen in Social Darwinism, had a profound effect on this era. Hays says, "The history of America is, above all, a story of the impact of Industrialism on *every* phase of human life."[26]

Is the meaning of faith different from that of religion? While the two are definitely interrelated, they are to be separated analytically: "Faith is active and dynamic . . . a way of moving into and giving form and coherence to life . . . or to one's ultimate environment."[27] Faith or certainty is the specific force behind the religious directedness of life that opens itself to some ultimate concern, that in turn affects one's environment. Thus, faith directs and gives specific content to cultural forces by unleashing the possibilities and content of a given culture's ultimate concern in a direction that a culture takes to be ultimate.[28]

A variety of metaphors have been used to suggest an ultimate environment. Utopia, Nirvana, the kingdom of God, the Worker's paradise, or, in Industrialism's case, "The Busy Beehive," represented such an environment. This last metaphor comes from Bernard Mandeville's famous poem "The Fable of the Bees." Mandeville was writing for the proto-capitalist English society of his day. Although greedy, acquisitive, selfish, and lustful, this society managed to demonstrate a remarkable degree of cohesion—just like a beehive. The apparent realism of the poem cannot hide the utopian imagery of the work:

> Millions endeavoring to supply
> Each other's Lust and Vanity;
> Whilst other Millions are employ'd
> To see their Handy-works destroy'd.

Nevertheless:

> Thus every Part was full of Vice,
> Yet the whole Mass a Paradise.[29]

The lack of conscious identification with this ultimate metaphor does not eradicate its operative power for industrializing England or America.

Augustine maintained, in contrast to this metaphor, that the world was divided into two kingdoms, each demanding absolute loyalty.[30] The *civitas Dei* or City of God stood in sharp contrast to the *civitas terrena*. Faith determined the fundamental direction and possibilities of each kingdom. Both kingdoms developed because creation possessed inchoate meaning. Augustine believed, however, that if any entity was directed to an origin other than Christ, such potentially meaningful things as economic trade would become provisional, distorted or even "demonic."[31] The struggle between these two kingdoms pervaded culture and nature and ran through history. "The struggle between *civitas Dei* and *civitas terrena* is carried on through the whole of the temporal creation in all of its many aspects. It finds its pregnant and dramatic expression in the temporal course of world-history . . ."[32]

Modern science, replete as it is with demands for empirical, logical observation and universal verification, became accepted as universal discourse, while religion was relegated to being a private affair. According to Harvard etymologist Wilford Smith, the word "faith" evolved into the term "belief." "There was a time when 'I believe' . . . meant, 'given the reality of God, as a fact of the universe, I hereby proclaim that I . . . pledge my love and loyalty to God.' In the nineteenth century it came to mean 'given the uncertainty of modern life . . . the idea of God and faith is a PART of the furniture of one's mind.'"[33] Given the evolution of this term and its acceptance, especially by Evangelicalism, faith was becoming a more private affair.

Dutch philosopher Herman Dooyeweerd, following the Dutch

statesman/theologian Abraham Kuyper, says, "Therefore . . . the meaning nucleus of faith is . . . an original transcendental certainty . . . related to a revelation of the Origin which has captured the heart of human existence."[34] Such a continental definition of faith stands in sharp contrast to American definitions. Kuyper's statement, and the analysis that stands behind it, is all the more remarkable when one stops to consider that Kuyper was speaking at the dawn of the twentieth century about worldviews, religiously-based presupposita, and the artificiality of the compartmentalization of religion to an area of life.

The all-encompassing dictates of religion suggest a way of viewing the core of human identity. Humanity at the depths of our life has been defined by Industrialism as *Homo oeconomicus* or the materially self-interested person. Gain, economic progress, profit and economic growth have often determined not only the patterns of culture, but its self-identity as well.[35] Certain nineteenth-century forms of the ideal type of *Homo oeconomicus* equated self-interest with societal well-being. Benevolence and a deistically-based market structure were supposed to be the natural mechanisms that prevented self-interest from degenerating into anarchy.[36] Evangelical economic theorists like Francis Wayland fused the concept of natural law and a market structure, otherwise dependent upon Ricardo's analysis, with the laws of supply and demand.

We now turn our attention to a fuller, more concrete historical discussion of the Evangelical and industrial worldview. The terms "world" and "view" are intentionally linked to emphasize the integrality and cohesion manifested by a culture's basic orientation to the world. Some clarity must be added before we fully define a worldview. A worldview is not the product of scientific theory. A worldview's influence is felt prior to investigation; it is not based upon a methodological and systematic foundation, nor qualified by scientific abstraction or detailed definition. Rather the components of a worldview form a bridge between the theorizing of science and the force of religion. Worldviewing is the first religiously based push toward comprehensive clarity, of which science is but the final flower.

A worldview is a more or less comprehensive orientation to the world, as I have noted. Coming from the German word *Weltanschauung,* a worldview is "a vision of the totality of man's life and the world in which he finds himself."[37] A worldview presupposes all of the contours of religion just mentioned. However, one of its distinguishing features is that a worldview allows one to take a more measured, reflective stance in the world and thereby give religious presupposita enculturation. This is not to say, of course, that one cannot be conscious of one's religious convictions. At the moment of movement toward enculturation, however, one begins to form a worldview with the components of his religion.

"Religion" also differs from a "worldview" in that the first is involved with depth and direction, the second with breadth and comprehensiveness. Adding yet another component to the definition of a worldview, Wolters maintains that a worldview is "the comprehensive framework or pattern of one's basic beliefs about life."[38]

The term "framework," as it appears in Wolters' definition, suggests a certain (but not rigidly systematic) cohesion or unity. A worldview attempts to be consistent. However, consistency is not always possible. One may, for example, profess to love God and one's neighbor as one loves oneself, while practicing gross economic injustice. Such an inconsistency may signal the operative presence of a conflict within a worldview. If this conflict between opposing worldviews is culturally powerful enough, the resultant tension may indicate the force of a kind of dialectical or conflict-ridden tension.

Worldviews are interrelated with many factors. A worldview both influences and is affected by climate, geography, ethnicity, social position, political patterns and economic standing, to name but a few factors. While incorporating these factors along with religious commitments, a worldview also helps give concrete expression to religious commitment. Concrete worldview expression represents the beginnings of the enculturation of religious presupposita.

Some nineteenth-century Evangelicals attempted to define Christianity in worldview terms. Statesman-theologian Abraham Kuyper was one of the first thinkers to use the term "worldview." Kuyper called Calvinism a "life-system" or "life-conception." In the 1898 Stone Lectures delivered at Princeton Theological Seminary, Kuyper attempted to relate reformed Christianity to many aspects of culture. He maintained that a worldview should include studies of ontology, ethics, theology, concepts of social happiness, and politics.[39] A worldview consisted accordingly of a related system of all-embracing principles which, when properly applied, would demonstrate the organic and interrelated character of life and history.

Kuyper disagreed with Kant's artificial compartmentalization of religion. Speaking of the effects of this Kantian reduction, Kuyper said,

> And the result is that . . . religion, once the central force in human life, is now alongside of it; and, far from thriving in the world, is understood to hide itself in a distant and almost private retreat.[40]

This limitation of religion, according to Kuyper, simultaneously reduced the effectiveness of Christian religion and enhanced other emergent worldviews.

Kuyper, following Calvin, used the term "religion" more generally than we are using it; he tended to equate religion and worldview.[41] Kuyper placed Calvinism over against "Modernism" as two fundamentally different worldview movements. Although he drew the lines between Calvinism and modernism too sharply, he maintained, nevertheless, his hatred of Mammon. Updating Christ's call, Kuyper said, "Come to ME, richest century that ever was, which is so deathly weary and heavy laden, and I shall give you rest . . . [by] overthrowing the idol of Mammon."[42]

Having discussed the contours of religion, faith, and worldview, as well as our working methodological assumptions, we will now turn our attention to the growth of the Evangelical-industrial fusion.

2

An Introduction to the Evangelical-Industrial Worldview

The Evangelical worldview and the industrial worldview and their fused parts changed during the Civil War. Prior to the war, Industrialism was in its infancy, while Evangelicalism soared with anticipation of Christ's return. After the war, Evangelicalism became more culturally pessimistic and increasingly accepting of American economic values, while Industrialism dominated life in America. The fusion between these movements became more pronounced as the century progressed. Therefore, both movements demonstrated a degree of identity continuity, and as both evolved they demonstrated a mutual adaptability and interpenetrability.

This chapter will be divided into four sections. In regard to the antebellum era we will discuss Industrialism's notion of "progress" and Evangelicalism's notion of a "revival." In connection with the postbellum era we will survey the contours of Evangelicalism as Fundamentalism and Industrialism's increasingly incorporative powers. The analytical distinctions of antebellum and postbellum must not suggest that epochs can be rigidly demarcated; there are ideological consistencies and inconsistencies within and between eras.

The Rise of American Industrialism

In 1854 Herbert Spencer published his now-famous work *Psychology*. Five years later Darwin, acknowledging his debt to the social theorist Thomas Malthus, published his *Origin of the Species*.[1] Both works were to have a profound impact upon the nineteenth century. Although these works were published before the Civil War, their full effect was not felt until the decades following the war.

Both men claimed to have discovered the "universal principle" of evolution. The basic presuppositum, soon to evolve into a worldview, was that life moved from "the indefinite, incoherent, homogeneous, to the definite, coherent and heterogeneous."[2] This principle came to function as an ideal to which people aspired.

An optimistic faith was placed in a secular providence in Spencer's worldview.[3] Gone was the older supernaturalistic view of providence in which God was thought to control the cosmos via various natural laws. The transcendent dimension was eradicated; natural law and human purpose allegedly resulted from autonomous laws which in turn guaranteed the survivability and potential perfectibility of the species.

This evolutionary worldview was popularized in America by the social theorists John Fiske and Edward Youmans. They applied this evolutionary postulate to the realm of economic thought. The linking principle between the theory of evolution and economic thought was the notion of "progress." A contemporary of Fiske and Youmans said of this notion of "progress," as it applied to society and economic practice,

> Social progress is in fact viewed as a natural evolution, in which human beings are molded into fitness for the social state, and society adjusted into fitness for the natures of men . . . until an equilibrium is reached.[4]

The reference here to adaptability and equilibrium is a portent of Social Darwinism's and classic capitalism's laws of supply and demand that were to characterize a portion of the nineteenth century.

Unlike some in this era, Youmans and Fiske were conscious of their religious starting points and worldview commitments. Youmans maintained that "science is the revelation to reason of the policy by which God administers the affairs of the world."[5] Moreover, Fiske argued that

> the doctrine of evolution asserts, as the widest and deepest truth which the study of nature can disclose to us, that there exists a power to which no limit in time or space is conceivable, and that all . . . material . . . or spiritual phenomena of the universe are manifestations of this infinite and eternal power.[6]

Here is a manifestly deistic faith in autonomous natural providence. Fiske optimistically maintained that evolutionary laws would, of their own power, lead to the "spiritual perfection" of humankind. Accordingly, such laws were inherently ethical. Indeed, it would not be long until humanity would be purified and redeemed.[7]

A more thoroughly secular naturalism emerged with the thought of William G. Sumner. He was one of the first Americans to attempt to ground all the social sciences in the scientific method.[8] He waged a verbal war on traditional metaphysics and "a priori speculation." Sumner believed that the notion of the "power of ideas" was a relic of the savages and that ethical data must be kept out of scientific analysis, as such data was not amenable to empirical verification. Therefore, any religious thought must be completely eliminated from scientific discussion because doctrine is "something which you are bound to believe, not because you have rational grounds for believing it, but because you belong to such and such a church or denomination."[9] To eliminate religious dogma from scientific or "truly critical thought" was to discover simultaneously the liberating force of "factual" data.

Sumner believed that all areas of thought and practice should be built upon the same methods, laws of cause and effect, and interpretations that have proven effective in science. This scientific methodology functioned as an imperative in Sumner's worldview.[10] He consistently applied his version of Comtean positivism to economic theories while writing on Industrialism. Economic analysis was to be neutral and value-free, obeying only inexorable natural laws. Natural law supports industrial culture, according to Sumner's reductionist view.

> Industrial organization creates the conditions for our existence, sets the limits of our social relations, determines the conceptions of good and evil, suggests our life philosophy, molds our inherited political institutions and reforms the oldest customs like marriage and property.[11]

This encapsulation represents Sumner's belief system, his confession of life. Indeed, Sumner's style is, from start to finish, driven by powerful religious imperatives.[12]

Sumner linked the force of natural law with social reality as it existed in that era. Because natural law was thought to be inexorable, social manifestations were considered to be predetermined. Monopolies, for example, were considered natural and divinely sanctioned. Moreover, what was considered "natural" was deemed to be "moral" by Sumner, while the "immoral" was equated with the "unnatural."[13] Thus, large aggregates of individual wealth owed their origin to the evolutionary, moral process, argued Sumner.

Sumner's worldview "actually deifies natural changes and makes [them] the object of moralistic praise."[14] The goal of economic evolution was an environment of freedom that allowed the sovereign individual to bind and loose as determined.[15] The central virtues of work, temperance, thrift or savings, industry, and self-denial were canonized by this form of capitalism. The good life (or happiness) was believed to come about through economic gain, which in turn became a secular sign that one had indeed "arrived."[16] However, Sumner failed to acknowledge that such virtues and achievements were themselves developments of a secularly enlightened middle-class conscience that, à la Locke and Smith, was trying to replace the mercantilist and aristocratic worldview.

Sumner's application of natural law, stressing as it did humanity's attachment or inexorable obligation to such laws, was to stir debate among American social theorists. Some stressed that humanity was bound to natural law, while other theorists believed that freedom could be achieved through the free exercise of science and reason over nature. Progressive-era economist and social theorist Lester P. Ward argued the latter.

Ward agreed with Sumner that the notions of evolution and economic progress were universal imperatives. Ward could not allow, however, such natural processes to dominate man; he felt free people must rule these processes to show their mastery. Ward could not concur with Sumner's implied mechanistic view of the universe; to him culture and history seemed to be more than a product of mere natural inevitablity. Thus, "Society . . . should seriously undertake the artificial improvement of its conditions upon scientific principles . . . to adopt an aggressive reform policy . . . as guided by scientific foresight rendered possible by an intelligent acquaintance with the fundamental laws of human action."[17] Prompted by an optimistic trust in science, Ward maintained that society could be improved through a reformist, progressive zeal.

The ultimate goal of social planning, and indeed of all of life, is happiness. The discipline of economics is defined, according to Ward, by its ability to organize happiness. Because happiness can be organized, humanity is no longer left to the dictates of nature; natural laws and society can be molded to suit our needs. This notion of the progressive spirit will be developed more fully in the next chapter. Suffice it to say here that Ward, like many other "progressives" of his day, did not deny the basic tenets of capitalism; he altered them and adapted them to fit the needs of the day.

Ward's thought was increasingly accepted by many Americans because he concurred with several of the fundamental notions of American progress which had already been accepted in the early antebellum era.[18]

By 1828, indeed, virtually all of America subscribed to a belief that the history of the world was a progressive phenomenon ... that had brought the human race closer to realizing the ultimate ideals of humanity.[19]

This faith in economic progress was bolstered by scientific and technological innovations, increasing amounts of wealth, and a jubilant national Protestant morality. American social theorists and popular sentiment supported the voices that argued for nature domination, wealth accumulation, human and material evolution, and progress.

The term "Americanism" signified America's self-understanding and economic identity. In 1824, Henry Clay coined the phrase "the American System" to designate his goals for domestic supply and manufacturing. In an attempt to gain more economic freedom and identity, American manufacturers and consumers, contra Britain, were supposed to increase domestic trade, thus enhancing the national wealth by a national transportation system.[20] More explicitly, this system was engineered to increase prosperity, develop natural resources and military advantages and establish, for example, the Second Bank of the United States. Thus, loyalty to the economic creed of Americanism and economic progress became synonymous.[21]

Americanism contributed to the identity of America's alleged Manifest Destiny. America began its expansionism propelled by a belief that only oceans should be its borders. Given its alleged divine mandate, America felt compelled to grow through the annexation of Texas and later Oregon. The South claimed to need more fertile soil for cotton, while border states felt the need to protect their boundaries from the threat of invasion; many Easterners moved west as population grew and opportunities grew. How the "Indians" fit into this scheme will become more apparent in subsequent analysis.

The term "enterprise" became a symbol around which many people could unite. Originally, the term simply meant "heroic undertaking," but gradually it grew to signify private wealth, and the process of enterprise did not carry with it any public responsibility.[22] An enterprising individual could gain status simply by accumulating wealth. Public welfare was thought to emerge from the aggregate wealth created by enterprising men.[23] Progress became equated with each individual's economic self-improvement. Summing up the then-popular sentiment, Rush Welter has said:

A young man who makes his way in the world in full reliance on his *own* power stops at nothing, shrinks from nothing, finds nothing impossible, tries everything, has faith in everything, hopes in everything, goes through everything and comes out of everything.[24]

Here is the Promethean myth of individualistic self-reliance.

The self-made person was eulogized during the antebellum era, in spite of less-than-grand adventures. Accordingly, "good" people became wealthy while "bad" people fell to ruin. Discipline, hard work and success were the secular virtues that helped transform the Calvinist concept of "calling" into egocentric notions of personal distinction.[25] This economic and socially mobile gospel was legitimized by preachers, evangelists, and secular theorists alike, so that "by 1830 the secular and religious ideas of progress were fused."[26]

Whig doctrine readily accepted and expanded upon such notions. Calvin Cotton, a Protestant apologist and Whig advocate, gave the now-classical conservative definition of this notion of progress when he said,

> Ours is a country where men start from a humble origin and . . . rise gradually in the world as a reward of merit and industry and where . . . they can acquire a large amount of wealth, according to the pursuits they elect for themselves. This is a country of SELF-MADE men, than which nothing better could be said of this society.[27]

Cotton strengthened his claim by looking to contemporary Protestant mores. He said, "Within one's own soul lies the capital, the productive power with which to trade. All wealth lies in abeyance to these physical powers and comes into hand at their summons."[28] This statement reveals a crucial part of the syncretistic self-understanding of Evangelicalism and Industrialism, as we shall see when we study the life of the evangelist-pastor Russell Conwell. It is a view conspicuously lacking in grace: all wealth is earned. One wonders how applicable these presupposita were for blacks, immigrants, poor whites, and Native Americans in this era.

Showman P.T. Barnum affords another, perhaps more secular, mid-century example of this syncretistic worldview. This adulated showperson turned moral pundit[29] owned a museum, built a "Persian" villa in Bridgeport, Connecticut, and was honored—in spite of himself—by the Queen of England.[30] With evangelistic-like sincerity Barnum would urge any eager listener on to success in his now famous "The Art of Money-Getting" speeches. These lectures were well-received because the virtues he outlined were thought to need no justification.

However, Barnum was no hedonist. He repeatedly used biblical analogies in his writings, suggesting a knowledge of current Protestant mores. He often entreated his audience, "Advertise your business. Do not hide your light under a bushel."[31] Success became his gospel and reward his heaven.

Barnum took advantage of an era that witnessed the emergence of the frontier as another important American symbol. The frontier represented, among other things, a place of confrontation between Liberty and the Devil.[32] The frontier was supposed to be a place of fruitful democratic opportunity for a free people. Beckoning opportunity and inexpensive land drew, circa 1850, those who were fleeing the crowded industrial centers.

The West became a natural outlet for those seeking wealth, opportunity, and liberty. A belief system arose to support this expansion. Industrious stewards were thought to be virtuous because they were cultivating Eden, the frontier.[33] Americans believed they were duty-bound to subdue the earth in God's name. Such was the beginning of America's manifest destiny. This manifest destiny, aided by missionary zeal and "progress," evolved into a millennial expectation.[34]

There was, however, a serpent in Eden. As slavery extended westward, especially after the Compromise of 1850, Northerners feared the shift in the balance of power. Such virtues as voluntarism, benevolence, and revivalism's ability to insure social control flowered more slowly in the West than in the Christian parts of the East. Moreover, far from being an orderly paradise, the West was accused of being a place of greed and lawlessness, characteristics Americans found contrary to their self-image.[35]

As the Civil War approached, a faint voice could be heard crying out in the wilderness, lamenting its oppression by the tyranny of Mammon. Gone or fading were the optimistic demands that prompted laborers, industrialists and missionaries alike to help settle the Garden. Now voices began to speak of greed and exploitation and class hostilities. The West became an extension of the North-South feud.

Emergent Evangelical Protestantism

Now we turn our attention to antebellum Evangelical revivalism. Evangelicalism manifested a growing preoccupation with the revival as opposed to Protestant orthodoxy's "theologism."[36] A revival, usually a well-organized, regional event, consisted of a series of informal meetings in which enthusiasts were encouraged to "renounce their sins," invite Christ to enter their lives and "let Him take control." Moral perfectionism was often attached to these doctrines. As one of the day's celebrants maintained, "God intends to perfect the human soul; to purify it from all sin; to create it after His own image, and to fill it with His own Spirit . . ."[37] Both the individual and society were to benefit from this experience.

Perfectionism became one crucial aspect of antebellum revivalism. Perfectionism is defined as "the absolute obedience to the law of God—declared attainable in this life."[38] Revivalists intended to perfect or sanctify the passions of the individual who, as a central agent of revivalism, was to be the leading force for social righteousness.

Perfectionism, like democracy and Industrialism, did not originate in America. Englishman John Wesley stressed that moral perfection was possible through the combined influence of the Holy Spirit and a voluntarily surrendered free will. Perfection enabled one to control one's temper, to maintain a consistently loving attitude to God and neighbor, and, especially, to manifest works of charity for the poor.[39] Like Industrialism and democracy, revivalistic perfectionism found secure roots in America's antebellum optimism.

Finney emphasized free will and rejected Puritanism and Protestant orthodoxy's stress upon the human inability to autonomously secure salvation. He sought to insure salvation by maintaining that the human will was not radically corrupted and thus could cooperate freely with God in salvation. Finney cried, "Make yourselves a new heart and a new spirit, cleanse yourself from all filthiness of the flesh and spirit."[40] Just as the adolescent nation began to develop its own identity by asserting its will and breaking away from the "mother country," so revivalism lessened the Christian's dependence upon divine grace for renewal and perfection through emphasis upon free will. This fact, in part, helps explain Finney's popularity and Calvinism's lessening influence in America.

New England New School Presbyterianism and expanding Congregationalism incorporated this notion of free will into their teachings to form a Protestant concept entitled "New Divinity." They maintained that at the "fall" or the inception of sin, humanity had not lost the ability to do what God requires. What was lost was the requisite disposition, intent or moral desire that enabled one to be "born again." Thus, the only quality that stood in the way of salvation and perfection was the desire or resolve,[41] a quality in abundance in early America.

The revitalization of the individual provided by Evangelical revivalism was the Protestant answer to the threat of unrestrained social passions. Revivals secured personal perfection or "holiness," the result of which enabled many Americans to voluntarily submit to the canons of morality. Lacking many of the external church-state constraints that Europe had developed, America needed a universal internal principle of self-restraint.

"What should religion rely upon?" thundered a revivalist of the day. "Only under God, upon efforts of its friends. . . . America must depend upon energy, self-reliance and . . . spontaneity."[42] These principles, which contributed to a rather homogeneous consciousness in antebellum America, also became the basis for later secular and Protestant (and Catholic and Jewish, for that matter) voluntary associations.

As revivalism grew in power, so did its millennial optimism. Individuals, while being transformed by Industrialism, were being reborn as a result of revivalism's fervor. Protestant hopes became tied to industrial optimism:

> If the physical resources of the country are becoming so greatly developed, the more the necessity then that those of man should be brought forward and carried to perfection.[43]

Perry Miller characterizes American society around 1830 as industrially and morally fused and optimistic.

As the capitalistic-commercial spirit grew in this era, so did the requisite moral prohibitions.[44] People involved with ownership, wealth accumulation, and trade needed to be disciplined by moralistic conversions. The full effects of a person's acquisition of wealth were to be mitigated by Christian compassion and sanctified by an Evangelical charity. How this tension of riches and salvation was resolved will be more fully explored when we talk about the "gaingive" principle.

Thus, freedom of economic choice was being tempered by moral conversions; Jacksonian America was witnessing, in part, the blending of free will and free trade.[45] The optimism of this age came about in part as the result of expanding economic possibilities tied to revivalistic hopes that Christ would soon return, thus establishing a literal one-thousand-year reign of universal peace on earth.

Perfectionism, however, was not simply a tool to preserve the capitalist order; it promoted social responsibility. Timothy Smith has demonstrated how antebellum revivalism spawned many socially responsible movements.[46] Antislavery societies, women's suffrage and rights movements, laws protecting the poor from economic exploitation in housing, unemployment assistance and political efforts to counteract political corruption were revivalism's legacy to America. The fact remains, however, that while revivalism did achieve certain humanitarian ends, it remained wedded to the American enterprising spirit. Like Industrialism, revivalism stressed unceasing activity. Finney's activistic "do it, don't think about it" philosophy made him attractive to a burgeoning middle class that found the enterprising spirit rewarding.[47]

Private enterprise and public piety were fused in an era that easily confused enterprising inventors and pragmatically active revivalists. American revivalists, like their British counterparts, were busy attempting to sanctify individuals who would industrialize society.[48] Technological discoveries were often trumpeted with pious phrases that had little to do with the purpose of the inventions. Thus Samuel Morse's rhetorically telegraphed question: "What hath God wrought?"

The revivalist-industrialist worldview was never crassly materialistic. Benevolence or charity was a cherished virtue. Indeed some considered it immoral to critique benevolent capitalism.[49] Benevolence involved more than mere financial gifts; it involved social reform on many levels.[50] Many believed God had given America a "sacred trust" that involved the demands of stewardship and justice, and a mandate to subdue the continent. Of the three virtues, stewardship increasingly occupied the thoughts of many Americans and was seen as a remedy to the greed of "freedom-loving" Americans. "First of all stewardship meant that God had given America a sacred trust of freedom, liberty and a special place in the world's life to fulfill her mission of freedom."[51] Early in the antebellum era, a steward was defined by the virtues of self-denial, tolerance, fraternity and patriotism; sectional claims and selfishness were to be eschewed. The operative force of an alleged special identity and a benevolent cooperative spirit help explain revivalism's success in social reform and in ecumenicity.

The notions of progress and benevolence became crucial presupposita for the antebellum Evangelical-industrial worldview.

There is growing up a spirit of missionary enterprise the effect of which is benevolence, which pervades the churches, just as much as the spirit of commercial activity, the result of a desire for gain, is taking possession of the mercantile world.[52]

Money and mission became key metaphors of this age. Much of America hoped that as voluntarism, piety and progress increased, so sectarianism, "sloth," moral laxity and poverty would decrease. This hope became especially prevalent in the Northeastern and Middle Atlantic cities where revivalism concentrated its efforts.

Because of this symbiotic relationship, the financial depression of 1857 spawned a revival on Wall Street in the same year. Dozens of businessmen gathered to pray, to rededicate their lives to Christ, to promote ecumenicity, and to provide relief work for the unemployed and poor in the area.[53] This urban business revival was organized by Wall Street laymen. The unique aspect of this revival was the conjunction of millennial expectations with specific technological innovations and finance capitalism. As the Civil War approached, America was in need of unity. The synthesis of piety, benevolence, and progress became a symbol for such mid-century attempts at national unity. The completion of the transatlantic cable and evangelist Stephen Tyng Sr.'s expectation of Christ's return were seen as two sides of the same optimistic coin. "Nor could it only be fortuitous that the movement should coincide with the Atlantic cable, for both were harbingers of that unity which was supposed to be the forerunner of the ultimate spiritual victory."[54]

I have used the term millennial to designate the Evangelical optimistic outlook in antebellum America, for many thought that Christ's return would culminate a literal thousand years of peace. Such optimism was bolstered by expanding economic prospects and new technological marvels. Postmillennialism, one form of millennial theory, believed that history was a battleground between Satan and Christ, with the forces of Christ gaining ascendancy. Increased economic and technological marvels, successful revivals, a declining papacy, and the truculent but beleaguered Islamic nations signaled a bright tomorrow. It was thought that America would surely lead the world into this golden age. There was coming a time when Satan would no longer trouble the nations, evil would be judged, the righteous would be rewarded, and peace would reign throughout the earth.[55] At the end of this one-thousand-year reign of progress, Christ was to return to earth, securing the triumph of grace over all destructive forces. The prefix "post" in postmillennialism refers to Christ's return *after* the golden years of peace, a return that was to consummate antebellum progress.

As mid-century America approached the horrors of the Civil War, an element of the American spirit remained committed to fighting the evils of slavery and Mammon. Since the inception of the republic, a small but significant voice could be heard at public gatherings, in Congress, and in churches, warning against avarice or the myopic influences of self-interest. Jefferson, for example, called for a republican "faith" as a deterrent to the myopic effect of "enlightened self-interest."[56] As the war threatened the Union, this plaint grew louder; sectional rights and self-interest seemed to be whittling away at the unity of the nation. Many Evangelicals such as Francis Wayland joined the abolitionist movement, hoping to eradicate Mammon as it manifested itself in slavery. In one of their last united national political struggles before temperance, some Evangelicals attempted to use the powers of various governmental agencies to restrict or eliminate slavery. Here, at least, Mammon was attached to something obviously abhorrent. The protests were short-lived, however.

As Evangelical revivalism's voice grew increasingly shrill, the major political parties resisted its influence. By the advent of the Civil War, the Democratic and Whig parties openly quarreled over the place "religion" should have in American life; the former wanted religion restricted to a private affair, while the latter wanted to use the legislative process to insure a national Protestant morality. As the Whig Party began to dissolve, so did its case for a national morality. In the place of Protestant mores, the republican virtues of "liberty," "freedom," and "conscience" gained ascendancy.[57] The churches were assigned the guardianship of private morality and order, while the public schools were commissioned to engender a public morality, or at least a conscience, that was nonsectarian, rational, and faithful to the dictates of economic progress.[58] As various Evangelical-revivalist political alliances fell apart due to increasing moral cynicism caused by slavery, Evangelical revivalists accepted a more privatized form of religion.[59]

The fear that the Democratic party provoked in these Christian enthusiasts was exceeded by Democratic dread of other legislative chauvinists. Northern Democrats feared the rule of the white Southern aristocracy, especially after the Compromise of 1850 and the Dred Scott decision. However much the abolitionists and the Southern aristocracy may have disagreed over the issues of slavery, they remained steadfast in their desire to use the legislative process for their respective causes. In rejecting a national Protestant morality, Democrats and (later) Republicans looked for a national ethos that could help solidify American identity. Thus, it is not surprising that civil religion was invigorated on the eve of the Civil War.[60]

A variety of groups and individuals condemned the evils of slavery and Mammon during the Civil War. Oliver W. Holmes, Sr. hoped that America would abandon its money-making lust and return to the brave deeds and noble thoughts that, he thought, inspired the Founding Fathers. Sacrifice for the nation and benevolence were the Jeffersonian virtues that America had lost. Protoliberal Protestant

Henry Ward Beecher asked, "What is slavery, but one way in which lust, avarice, ambition and indolence have sought to enthrone themselves?"[61]

Evangelical women during this era condemned slavery and Mammon, saying that if America would "lose herself" (i.e., her sectional claims and "selfish interests"), "she" would find herself again in repentance and newness of life. The nation had to once again discover her sense of moral stewardship to survive the "hour of trial." Stewardship would destroy the dynasty of Mammon, confiscate the possessions of his mercenary courtiers, and establish the reign of the excellent: the majestic rule of the good. Even President James Polk, while eulogizing the benefits of the Oregon Territory, cautioned Americans not to lose the sense of simplicity, frugality and conservation.[62] However, all such rhetoric did not hinder the advent of wage-slavery when Orientals, Eastern Europeans and the newly-freed Negro took their places in American society after the war. Deeply enculturated religious practices are hard to surrender; being naturally "born again" seems to exceed human effort.

Industrial Incorporation

Americans emerged from the Civil War temporarily chastened but more hungry than ever for economic progress. As often is the case with wars, the struggle prompted vast industrial changes that some called "progress." Indeed, it was said of the war that it was the perfect "symbiosis of modern war and modern industry."[63] Having expanded and modernized the small, semi-autonomous industrial worksites that existed before the war, America came to develop a commercialized scientific and industrial base that kept pace with her increasing geographic size, rising population, and rapidly advancing technological culture. A commercializing, practically oriented, scientific ethos helped secure the development of medicine, mass production, semi-automatic weapons like the Gatling gun, wholesale purchases, interchangeable parts and, of course, in 1862, Cleveland's Standard Oil Corporation. The revivalist was replaced in the postbellum era by the industrialist as America's new hero.

> Now individual activity, not philosophizing; the application of science to the material world and not civic virtue; entrepreneurship on a national and international scale, not industry and frugality in the corner dry goods store—these were the changes in value that were to characterize a new epoch.[64]

If America and Evangelical revivalism had flirted with Mammon before the war, they paid full homage in the postwar years.

The "gospel of applied science,"[65] the antispeculative, activistic, materially minded, scientific worldview, captured much of America's attention and efforts following the Civil War. This gospel was the energizing force behind the labyrinth of postbellum technological marvels. As science became more concerned with technology, America discovered a means of perfecting the subjugation of its resources and increasing its profits. In 1867, the celebrated inventor-philosopher Jacob Bigelow said of postbellum technology:

> More than any science, it will enlarge the boundaries of profitable knowledge, extend the dominion of mankind over nature, economize and utilize both labor and time, and thus add indefinitely to the effective and available length of human existence.[66]

This implied objectification of human labor and nature became a crucial article of the postbellum industrial worldview. This objectification was justified by the presupposita of utility (i.e., human happiness and efficiency) as we shall see when we survey the thought of Evangelical Francis Wayland and economist David Ricardo.

Postbellum industrial enthusiasts carried on the activistic, energized spirit of their antebellum ancestors; indeed, some have characterized this as "the age of energy." "Energy means the exploitation of human and non-human resources as well as the expression of . . . the personality of the prime movers."[67] According to Howard M. Jones, the term "prime movers" meant those machines responsible for capital development or upkeep. So thoroughly had the machine captured the energies and imagination of this era that this age has been designated the "machine age." The machine began to transform the "Garden" into the "City" (another biblical symbol), and the change in emphasis relegated some of America's most famous spokesmen to secondary roles of importance.[68] The machine became a religious metaphor in a worldview that was transforming the American experience.[69]

This metaphor represented the practical intellectual energies of the now-legitimized disciplines of technology and physics. As the machine devoured natural resources it spit out an abundance of goods and services. As the steam engine was replaced by the more powerful dynamo, postbellum excitement grew into almost a reverence for its power. Even Henry Ward Beecher came to sing the praises of the machine and its contribution to American progress.[70]

The machine and the energy that it produced added another element to postbellum American identity. Mobility necessitated not only a rapid and vast conveyor system designed for mass production and "interchangeable parts"; it also dictated that workers' life cycles be adjusted to its demands for efficiency and speed. Indeed, to be modern was to be mobile, and to be mobile was to be modern.

Progress required increasingly expensive machinery. Capital-intensive machinery required greater capital investments, larger money markets, capital upkeep and careful planning. Marketing research, sales and advertisements had to be developed so as to prevent the onslaught of gluts or depressed periods of consumer demand. "Consumers had to be carefully conditioned to want these blessings of planning"[71] if economic progress was to be maximized.

But what about employment in an industrializing era? Although unemployment was not a serious problem, capital intensity signaled the advent of labor displacement. Increasingly, "laborsaving machines" literally took the place of human labor. As long as America experienced expanding markets, however, this displacement produced no immediate massive problems. The introduction of newer machines coincided with the emergence of more jobs for the qualified. However, the patterns of progress were set. Americans increasingly demanded industrial modernization, which would come to mean worker displacement as modernization evolved. By "1880 it took a unit of about 20 manpower hours to harvest an acre of wheat; by the opening of World War I this figure had been cut to 12.7%."[72] Tragically, the reduction of manpower hours needed for agriculture meant a diminished need for human labor, thus forcing workers into burgeoning urban centers. As we shall see, these disenfranchised lower-middle-class workers became a crucial segment of urban Fundamentalism.

Industrial apologists promised order, social stabilization, and progress, but increasingly society experienced disorder, social confusion, and a preoccupation with, and dependency upon, economic matters. Typical was Carnegie's statement in the *Gospel of Wealth:* "It is to businessmen who follow business careers that we chiefly owe our universities, colleges, libraries and educational institutions."[73] Carnegie's benevolence did in fact help to bring about the emergence of the modern scientific university. However, Carnegie's own words betray a dependency of the university on the business corporation.

Furthermore, attempting to fulfill a secularly inspired cultural mandate, the journalist, pre–Civil War presidential advisor, and railroad apologist William Gilpin said in his book *The Mission of the North American People* (1873), "the untransacted destiny of the

American people is to subdue the continent."[74] Evangelical Josiah Strong repeated Gilpin's theme in his book *Our Country* (1886):

> Like the star in the East which guided the three kings with their treasures westward until it stood over the cradle of the young Christ, so the star of empire, rising in the East, has ever beckoned the wealth and power of the nations westward, until it stands over the young empire of the West.[75]

What was true of the commonwealth of nations was also true of the new commonwealth of America; the star of economic progress was moving west.

This star led men and women west on the rail system to a land of wealth being developed by the modern corporation. Like the dynamo upon which it was predicated, the modern corporation manifested a socially incorporating energy hitherto unknown in America. Speaking of this power, Jones says,

> these new creations, expanding horizontally and vertically, took the nation, the continent, and the world for their empires, swelling rapidly into institutions that rivaled government, the church, the courts and the schools as instruments of social energy.[76]

The vertical and horizontal incorporation represented the modern corporation's ability to absorb relevant companies. It also represented the modern corporation's ability to circumscribe human functions and cultural artifacts, a phenomenon that we previously referred to as "horizontalization of life."

The modern corporation's influence grew, in part, because the postbellum industrial worldview maintained an element of continuity. The Civil War did not dampen the ardor of Social Darwinism, individualism, or a secularized Protestant spirit. "To the Capitalist . . . and the business genius, the corporation was the last fine flowering of the secularized Protestant spirit and the philosophy of individualism; it was the inevitable outcome of what came to be known as Social Darwinism."[77]

Postbellum industrial development was not a conspiracy by one class or geographic section against another. Moreover, Evangelicals were not the only faith community to be deeply affected by Mammon; all followed it to some degree. Rather, as America grew in euphoria, it seemed natural to equate antebellum economic progress with optimistic and millennial expectations. As the effects of the Civil War passed, it often seemed the most generous and benevolent people were industrialists. It is hard to bite the hand that feeds one; thus, any theoretical critique of capitalism was difficult for money-conscious Evangelicals of this era. There were certainly antebellum words of protest voiced by Evangelicals; they even grew in intensity during the war. However, the increasing marginalization of the Evangelical worldview within American culture did not lessen the Evangelical-industrial synthesis; rather the liaison grew in intensity as Evangelicals clung to vestiges of respectability.

Cultures and persons change because of religious commitments. Evangelicalism lost the ability to transform culture because it failed to see the ultimate demands of Industrialism. This affected its own "incorporation". The term "incorporation" means

> the reorganization of perceptions as well as of enterprise and institutions ... and the concomitant expansion of the industrial capitalist system across the continent by an ever-tightening system of transportation and communication ... the result of which means that hardly any realm of American life remained untouched: politics, education, family life, literature, the arts; all experienced profound alterations.[78]

I am suggesting that the process of "incorporation" meant something more than merely granting businesses a certain legal status. While incorporation certainly had a legal side to it, its effects can be likened to that of a wholesale worldview change for America. Industrialism changed the presupposita of the rugged individualist to those of the incorporated individual. A "corpus" of associated individuals could, through corporate voluntary association, considerably expand their power base. The concept of the individual did not cease to be the primary presuppositum; rather, the individual simply found a more efficient means to insure his dictates through the sociolegal entity of the corporation.

America did not lose her faith in economic progress in this era, despite the occasional depressions. Autonomy seemed to define mechanical, industrial progress. The alleged autonomy of the machine placed demands on the worker for speed, efficiency, and routinized movements. However, many regarded the products of the machines as just compensation for any sacrifice rendered.

Americans grew in their industrial fervor following the Civil War. Carroll D. Wright, chief of the Massachusetts Bureau of Labor Statistics, was an ardent, enthusiastic supporter of the factory system. In 1882 he argued that the long-range practical results of the factory would be analogous to "human benefactors," "great emancipators of men from hard labor," and would therefore be a civilizing force insuring both culture and progress. Moreover, Wright tied the factory system to the Spencerian notion of cultural evolution. The factory process allegedly demonstrated that an untrained worker could evolve into a complex machinist and an independent home-steader could become an interdependent modern agriculturist, while a village jack-of-all-trades could progress into a production line specialist.[79]

Some of the popular novels of that day spoke of the Evangelical-industrial synthesis as if it were a matter of course. In Edward Bellamy's *Looking Backward* (1888), one finds a hero, Julian West, who is bored, nervous and generally unhappy with his upper-middle-class life. West passes through several economically related life crises, ending in a "born again" experience. He awakens one night, after bouts with insomnia, to find himself in Boston, circa A.D. 2,000. To his surprise, modern life, while still producing ubiquitous consumer goods, has solved the problem of anomie and unhappiness that characterized industrial society. This transformation was accomplished through the synthesis of the rational dictates of the machine system with the moral dictates of religion. The synthesis enables the hero to enjoy considerable leisure and material comfort while at the same time benefiting from the religious joys of "solidarity" and a personal inner peace. All of the communal associations in life—friendship, family, church and business—are perfected in the state system known as "nationalism." While few Evangelicals argued for such implied socialism, they, like Bellamy's hero, were willing to accommodate their religion to this narcotic.

Cities were often thought of as places of "brotherly love," charity, and hope in early American consciousness. It is not surprising, therefore, that John Bunyan's classic novel, *The Pilgrim's Progress,* has enjoyed the success it has in America. Bunyan's lonely individual pilgrim, having left all, including family, sets off for the beautiful city of Zion. The pilgrim journeys through such towns as Carnal Policy and Vanity, where the zesty fair displays many goods which have come to be associated with commercialized civilization. Like the Pilgrim, many Evangelicals attempted to avoid such lusts only to have their efforts foiled as the city became one of the crucial centers of postbellum life. Instead of being places of "love," "freedom," "unity," and "charity," cities increasingly became similar to Bunyan's City of Destruction.[80] The "Garden of God" was becoming the city of the Great Harlot.

Emergent Forms of Modern Evangelicalism

Following the war, Evangelical antebellum cultural optimism began to turn to postbellum cultural ambivalence for a variety of reasons. After following the star of Western progress, Evangelical Josiah Strong said of the Eastern and Midwestern cities that they were "a most serious menace . . . a place where Mammon held sway . . . where luxuries are gathered and where discontent and Socialism are bred."[81] The evangelical mission was, consequently, increasingly concentrated upon the city in the postbellum era.

Because of the Evangelical determination to counteract the forces of sin and human destruction, such organizations as the Salvation Army were formed. Simultaneously, however, the Evangelical attack focused upon sin as an individual and locatable act as opposed to a state of being. Sin could be more visibly seen and therefore more effectively fought, many Evangelicals thought, by addressing the drunkard and the prostitute, as well as the now-burgeoning Jewish and Catholic populations. Circa 1880, Industrialism was demanding more immigrant labor, which in turn threatened the Protestant majority gained during the antebellum era. As the definition of sin narrowed, redemption took on a more restricted scope. Evangelicalism increasingly equated its social agenda with patriotism and socioeconomic conservatism.[82] Moreover, because the individual was the primary social unit, sin was considered primarily an individual phenomenon. A large corporation's sin, at best, amounted to the sum of the sins of the individuals who made it up. Sin was not primarily a structural phenomenon, that is, transmitted to the fabric of social institutions by responsible persons.

This symbiosis of economic conservatism and Evangelicalism caused a growing division in the postbellum Evangelical consciousness. The actual symbiotic relationship was, of course, not new; however, the reasons for such a liaison were changing. A portion of Evangelical consciousness wanted to remain progressive by renewing and updating its social ministry. However, as the forces of secularity grew, some forms of Evangelicalism grew more reactionary. Reacting to the growing critiques of the Social Gospel movement, secular Darwinism and socialism, a portion of Evangelicalism mutated into Fundamentalism. Increasingly, defensive evangelists like Billy Sunday came to define his preaching and ministry vis-à-vis his Social Gospel counterparts. Fundamentalism's defensiveness was matched by its cultural despair as the shock of the Civil War, urbanization and non-Protestant immigration grew.

Although the postmillennial view dominated Evangelical eschatology in the antebellum era, premillennialism played a strong secondary role.[83] Premillennialism became predominant after the Civil War. Many premillennials believed that Christ's reign upon earth through his kingdom was totally discontinuous with human history.

During the present epoch all faithful believers were to concentrate upon personal salvation, because the earth was thought not to be the context of Christ's redemption. At the end of the epoch all, including newly converted Jews, were to meet Christ "in the air" at his second coming. Then a great persecution or "tribulation" would ensue, after which Christ would return with his Church to establish a millennial kingdom of peace. Finally, Christ would destroy the earth in judgment, thus consummating this age.

This scenario suggests several reasons why Evangelical Fundamentalism became so culturally pessimistic. First, the hermeneutic overreacted to cultural fragmentation, pluralism and corruption. Secondly, as a "way of escape" from this vale of tears, Fundamentalism too often longed for a literal flight from culture and the earth. Rather than being a place of Christian witness the world became an entity to be rejected because of its evil. The legendary statement of evangelist D. L. Moody best represents this attitude: "I look on this world as a wrecked vessel. God has given me a lifeboat and said to me, 'Moody, save all you can.'"[84]

Premillennial Fundamentalism drew much of its inspiration and theological wisdom from Dispensationalism. All of human history was sharply divided, according to this system of thought, into seven dispensations or unique periods of redemptive activity.[85] There were the periods of innocent, conscience, the promise delivered to Abraham and the Jews, law as given to Moses, the Church, the reign of the Anti-Christ, and the consummate kingdom of Christ. The Dispensationalists segregated these historic periods, unlike their Calvinistic ancestors. They thought that those in the church age did not need to focus upon the law given to Moses, because the "church age" was marked by grace. As a result, many Dispensationalists became ambivalent about law and government's authority, restricting its function to that of protection and capital punishment.[86]

An "Anti-Christ" was supposed to emerge from this present church age. He was to come, more specifically, from present-day Europe or parts of the old Roman Empire. The "Anti-Christ" would be an ecclesiastical dictator who would make alliances with various secularized church groups and political agencies in order to accomplish his demonically inspired purposes. At the same time, the Jews were to return to Palestine, with some being converted, while a "great tribulation" or world persecution was to begin. This persecution was to include any believer faithful to Christ. Prior to his millennial reign, Christ was to return to wage war on a combined army of world political powers and various additional rebellious factions in a valley in the Near East called Armageddon.[87] As Christ would return "prior" to his one thousand years of peace, this position is called premillenialism.

One can understand Fundamentalism's fear of the increasing influence of ecumenical Protestant liberalism, given the ecclesiastical and theological views of this system. Southern Baptists forced out Crawford H. Toy for his questionable views on Genesis. Southern Presbyterians arranged the dismissal of James Woodrow from Columbia Seminary for similar reasons. Northern Congregationalists removed Professor Egbert C. Smyth for maintaining that the Bible contains errors. On both sides of the debate, positions were becoming more confrontational.

Fundamentalists often supported economic and political individualism owing to their increasing overreaction to various collectivist tendencies in politics. Some, like J. Gresham Maschen, an influential Southern-born intellectual who left Princeton Theological Seminary because of doctrinal disputes, became an able defender of sociopolitical individualism.[88] Although Machen was not a reactionary and was well-educated, by supporting the principle of individualism he tended to defend a form of laissez-faire capitalism. Capitalism seemed more in keeping with the natural laws of voluntary benevolence, freedom of conscience, and a divinely controlled universe.

The modern Pentecostal movement emerged in the late 1880's as yet another facet of the Evangelical-Fundamentalist worldview. The term "Pentecostal" is taken from the second chapter of the Acts of the Apostles. According to this account, forty days after Christ ascended into heaven, the apostles were filled with the Holy Ghost for witnessing, miracles and the establishing of the Church. The Holy Spirit was "filling" current believers in a similar fashion, according to modern Pentecostalism.

This movement recaptured some of the earlier revivalist-Holiness emphases. Complete sanctification or moral perfection was believed to result from a "second blessing" or second encounter with the Holy Ghost. Following this experience, which was marked by a perfect love for God and a loving service in the world, a believer could have subsequent fillings in which "tongues" or a speaking in "God's language" would demonstrate the forceful presence of the Spirit.

By 1895, however, the Pentecostal movement split. The perfectionistic emphasis was dropped by some in favor of a more "realistic" definition of the work of the Holy Spirit in a believer's life. Keswick's Pentecostalism entailed a somewhat more reformed or Calvinistic emphasis in which sin's power, though personally defined, was counteracted (though not eradicated), and the individual believer filled for service. Many "fillings" of the Spirit were needed.[89]

The emphasis upon "witnessing," or telling others of the personal effects of God's grace, was matched by Keswick's emphasis upon social service. D. L. Moody's service was an example of a Keswick-inspired ministry. He emphasized renewed "consecration" and a "yielded heart filled with the Holy Ghost." Moody's work with such agencies as the Y.M.C.A. in Chicago helped establish him as a national figure and as one who demonstrated a degree of compassion for the urban poor. Moody's associate Reuben Torrey, a Keswick enthusiast, helped found, and later became president of, the International Christian Workers Association. Although this organization placed its primary emphasis upon personal salvation, its work in the area of worker rights, better housing, and racial justice helped draw such notables as Booker T. Washington to its conventions. Furthermore, this form of Pentecostalism worked through existing social service agencies and the institutional church to help establish relief agencies, soup kitchens, employment bureaus, day nurseries and even colleges. Bethany Presbyterian Church in Philadelphia, sponsored by department store owner John Wanamaker, another Keswick enthusiast, helped found a major network of social service agencies in the city. Connected to them was the pastor Russell Conwell, the Philadelphian who helped establish Samaritan Hospital and Temple College.

The record of such Pentecostals is full of instances of their social service work. However, Pentecostalism manifested a typical Evangelical dualism when it came to relating evangelism and social service. Brooklyn pastor Cortland Myers typified this dualism in emphasizing that the *chief* job of the church was to win souls and not dispense charity.[90] Justice and benevolence were to follow from, and be secondarily related to, the goal of the salvation of souls. This dualism implied that a renewed culture would follow, as a matter of course, from a sufficient number of rejuvenated souls.[91] If one area of service is more important than another, as dualism implies, then in times of stress (such as the growing critique that Fundamentalism had to endure) it seems only natural that enthusiasts would increasingly concentrate upon evangelism rather than cultural renewal. The focus and forum for revivals was the institutional church—not, say, banks. Grace was mediated through the church or through the individual, as evident in Pentecostalism's emphasis upon the "heart," the "will," and the "soul." In either case the concept of mission was truncated, leaving little room for any serious, thoroughgoing critique of capitalism.

In short, by the turn of the century Evangelical dualists like Keswick and the adherents of his Holiness movement were forced by their dualistic truncation of religion to be concerned about internal, personal consecration. They soon lost sight, therefore, of the possibility of bringing any analytical or systematic analysis to the heart of the contemporary economic situation. R. H. Tawney says of the relationship of religion to economics: "The former takes as its province the individual soul, the latter the intercourse of man with his fellows in the activities of business . . . . Provided that each keeps to its own territory, peace is assured. They cannot collide, for they never meet."[92] While Fundamentalists did in fact intersect with economics on an unintentional cultural-developmental level, they rarely crossed swords in a principled, critical systematic, or analytical manner with capitalism. By accepting this truncated, privatized view of religion, Evangelicals helped to promote the secularization of culture.

I believe it is improper to speak of a "great reversal," as if Evangelicals were at one time integrally involved in social redirection while at another time they reversed that course. Throughout the era, many Evangelicals remained marginally socially active through various mission projects. What did change was the increasing emphasis Evangelical-Pentecostal sects gave to personal and psychological matters relating to holiness, sanctification and consecration as vehicles for social renewal. If sin, for example, was primarily a personal, internal matter, then concentrating upon its elimination would simultaneously sanctify the individual and therefore society. Through emphasizing individual personal consecration (an emphasis percolating in antebellum revivalism and now hardening in Pentecostalism), Evangelicalism increasingly privatized the Christian worldview and therefore shifted, but did not reverse, its previous stance toward culture. Furthermore, when the Dispensationalists and Pentecostals attributed the basic origin and function of government to the "fall" or the advent of sin, the implication was that government could at best restrict evil but not promote social good.[93] This ambivalence towards governmental intervention into individual lives helps explain Fundamentalism's laissez-faire tendencies after the Civil War.

Much of postbellum Evangelical Fundamentalism repudiated the earlier Calvinist emphasis upon God's sovereign law as a vehicle for his reign upon earth. For the "warm," personal, romantic heart of the Fundamentalist, the strictures of divine law, apart from the basic rudiments of the Ten Commandments, seemed unnecessarily harsh and unloving. Many Fundamentalists tended, therefore, to have a dim view of social legislation, though they did hold in high regard governmental interference in alcohol consumption. This attitude is all the more ironic when we stop to consider that many Evangelicals and Fundamentalists had legal careers or were thoroughly oriented to sociopolitical law. Given their low regard of government, Evangelical Fundamentalism wanted to narrow the proper sphere of government to certain moralistic functions like liquor restriction, sabbath observance, and the elimination of gambling and prostitution.

I believe that this contradictory attitude is a carryover from the antebellum Evangelical support for Whigs and a prolepsis of modern-day Evangelical support for Republicanism and the moralistic prohibitions of some of the Moral Majority. Wanting to restrict the function of government (and hence promoting a de facto conservative view of government), many, though not all, Evangelical Fundamentalists tended to join forces with those who fought progressivism's attempt to counteract monopolistic capitalism.[94]

Postbellum Evangelicals, especially as they turned to Fundamentalism, became antimodernists. In 1909 C. I. Scofield published his first edition of the *Scofield Reference Bible.* Scofield relyied upon Dispensational theology, and his notes are replete with attacks against the various principles of Higher Criticism. After nearly seventy-five years of worldwide acclaim and five editions of scholarly revision, this translation has become a hallmark of Fundamentalist literature. Moreover, in 1910 oil millionaire Lyman Stewart conceived of a plan to publish twelve volumes of apologetic material that, along with Scofield's work, became a standard for the Evangelical-Fundamentalist worldview. This literature was meant to defend the Evangelical Fundamentalist faith against theological liberalism in its Christian and secular forms, as well as against such cults as Mormonism and modern Spiritualism.[95] Stewart assembled such notable teachers as A. C. Dixon, Louis Meyer, and Reuben Torrey, as well as a host of British and American writers, to collate material on a variety of topics. Stewart's compendium, *The Fundamentals,* affirmed the need for revivals and holiness, but was primarily a set of theological documents attempting to defend the Scriptures against the German-based Higher Criticism. It did not take strong stands on any particular millennial or Dispensational position. Stewart et al. were trying to maintain the supernatural or miraculous element of the Bible in an age which believed that such elements contradicted the canons of science. Questions concerning the Virgin Birth, Christ's bodily resurrection, his literal coming again, the person and work of each member of the Trinity, and the necessity of repentance were discussed at length. Socioeconomic questions were either superficially treated or forgotten altogether.[96]

Evangelical Fundamentalism was broadly seen as being anti-intellectual.[97] While it cannot be denied that certain elements of Fundamentalism went in this direction, a large portion of the movement was committed to a Baconian, Newtonian form of scientific analysis. Imported to this country in the mid-eighteenth century from Scotland under the banner of Common Sense Realism, this form of scientific analysis was concerned with the taxonomic classification of any given set of empirical phenomena. Many Fundamentalists believed that modern science, and with it Protestant liberalism, took a Kantian-Hegelian speculative and idealist stance towards science.

Many evangelicals were strongly influenced by the Scottish philosopher Thomas Reid, who was markedly empiric and dualistic. According to one Evangelical common sense realist, Francis Wayland, "there is a world outside of us and a world inside of us . . . both are given to us by the principle of our constitution as ultimate facts."[98] The mind's job was to link the inner world, or the world of the rational, spiritual soul, to the natural, material, inferior body.[99] Thus, a spirit/matter dualism existed in which the mind was seen as a "spiritual," receptive, creative entity which transcended and yet shaped the external stimuli. These stimuli were to be observed, classified according to groups, correlated according to interrelationships and regularities, and then organized according to universal, natural laws.

Common Sense Realism paralleled Reid's epistemological individualism. Accordingly, one American philosopher said, "the knowledge which we acquire is always of individual entities."[100] Perception yields individual entities, called propositions, that are individisible. Especially in the "Old Princeton" way of doing theology,[101] the individualistically conceived proposition became the basic entity upon which the Scriptures were founded. Common Sense Realism's epistemological individualism was amenable to Dispensationalism's taxonomic hermeneutic and to Fundamenalist acceptance of capitalism's individualism. Perhaps it even formed the basis for them.

"Common Sense" well describes the intended character of this philosophy of science. Dating back to the Jacksonian era, Common Sense Realism stressed a democratic, anti-elitist, antispeculative approach to science. The interpreter of data was not supposed to impose *a prioris* upon the phenomena being studied. Since the power to observe, classify and correlate related phenomena with universally valid natural law was held in common, all people could rationally apprehend the basic scientific and moral truth of the universe. The common person, commonsense approach to life fortified the democratic ideals that American Industrialism needed if a relatively free market was to sustain a free people. Americans not only had to be free to choose; they had to have the confidence that their choices, if guided by reason and the Bible, would be moral and hence help sustain social stability.

As urbanization and Industrialization gained momentum, so did the felt need for order. This need was especially keen in the minds of many Victorian lower-middle-class families in the Northeast. Threatened by the managerial class, anxious about their social roles and status, the lower-middle class tended to look to Victorian Fundamentalism for a theological system and for a worldview that would give them identity and legitimization.[102] Fundamentalist converts longed for a sense of belonging, especially in the more settled Northeastern urban centers, because of socioeconomic strains, lack of social recognition and anomie.

The conflict with the modern worldview was less acute in the South, since that section existed outside the Eastern educational establishment. However, Southerners did accommodate their religion to Industrialism. Liston Pope *(Millhands and Preachers)* shows the accommodation of southern Fundamentalism to Southern textile capitalism in Gastonia, North Carolina. Industrial managers valued regularity, cooperation with superiors, and class contentment as the marks of Christian character. These virtues were especially extolled in the "mill churches" of Gastonia. Southern Fundamentalists tended to be in the upper-middle-class managers, unlike their Northern friends, while the lower classes remained ambivalent about Fundamentalism. The interpenetration of Fundamentalism and capitalism in the South tended to originate with upper-middle-class managers and then to be passed on to the workers. Speaking of this form of managerial capitalism, Pope says,

> At various times and in diverse ways the churches have been both source and product of economic development. Both indifference and irrelevance to economic practices have [also] been notable characteristics of their strategy.[103]

Although Fundamentalism was originally, circa 1880, a Northern phenomenon, the aristocratic tendency of the South furnished the Fundamentalist movement with many notable leaders.[104]

We have seen that the term "Evangelical" can be commonly applied to a rather loosely knit band of Protestant Christians who stressed the necessity of a personal, repentant encounter with Christ through the person of the Holy Spirit. All groups shared, among many differences, an unquestioning allegiance to the Scriptures as the authoritative, inerrant Word of God, a dislike of modernism in some of its secular and Protestant forms, and a commitment to social service.

3

American Industrialism

We now move to a deeper inner analysis of American Industrialism, having surveyed the contours of the Evangelical-industrial fusion and the nature of religion. The economically essential elements of land, labor, and capital will be our focus. A brief historical survey will be used to highlight the profound changes that had to occur before industrialization could take place. In this context, it will be important to show why England was one of the first nations to industrialize.

The writings of many medieval economic theorists demonstrated a synthesis of the autonomous, natural rationality of the Aristotelians with the heteronomous claims of theology and the canon law of the Catholic church. While "official," such doctrine did not exhaust the variety of economic positions, however. As in any other era, some Christians were given to an ascetic temperament, while others maintained an avaricious attitude to socioeconomic affairs. The medieval church, far more than modern sects, attempted to embody a civilization or a "Christian commonwealth," especially in regards to economic reality.[1] Through ecclesiastical canon law, God was thought to present himself through the Church to all affairs of life. In this schema, society could secure a greater measure of grace or perfection by ensuring that such natural activities as economics obeyed canon law. Society was thought to be hierarchical in nature, pointing upward through the Church to heaven.[2] This upward orientation can best be seen in the visual grandeur of many medieval cathedrals. Economic activities, like all of natural life, were suspect because such activities were more removed from divine perfections than were such supernatural activities as prayer and works of charity. Trade, labor, moneylending, and profiteering were suspect because of their proclivity to moral corruption. It is no wonder, therefore, that avarice or greed was listed as one of the seven deadly sins.

Economic life was accordingly relegated to a lower or inferior realm that had to be held in check. The economic activities of the feudal lord and the laboring peasant were supposed to be transformed into stewardly service and vocation by conforming to the demands of canon law. Like the medieval sacramental elements of bread and wine awaiting transubstantiation, medieval economic activities awaited sacerdotal transformation. The uneasy mixture of nature and grace dominated much of the official dogma that informed economic practice. Economic individuality and self-interest were supposed to be subjugated to the needs of one's church, one's society, one's village, or even one's own otherworldly salvation.

The economic system of the Middle Ages, under these restrictions, was not highly diverse. Banking and lending were not fully developed. There was little economic mobility or competition among guilds, which tended to be more provincial labor fraternities than comprehensive socioeconomic forces. Work relations tended to be highly personal, labor-intensive, and less than expansive as local manorial estates generally dominated production and consumption.

Hypocritically, the medieval church, while being the richest social institution,[3] still demanded obedience to a strict ethical code in economics. Economic activities were, ideally, to serve the whole of society, not the individual. A "Christian commonwealth" meant, among other things, wealth shared in common.

A just price was supposed to be established as were the costs of labor and production. In theory, the Church attempted to influence notions of economic supply (which should never be unnaturally restricted) and demand (which should never be too high as this would betray the presence of greed).

Rent, modest profits, and local, small-scale capital were welcomed if they produced small, localized development. However, they were condemned if they harmed widows, orphans, or small farmers, or otherwise created any social imbalances. Buying cheaply and selling dearly, one of the major presupposita of modern business, was expressly forbidden in medieval life.[4]

In this tradition-oriented, nearly cashless society of the early Middle Ages, manorial estates represented a fundamental economic reality. Yet the economic aspect did not dominate manorial life. Usually manors were owned by ecclesiastical or feudal lords. Strictly speaking, property, production, and distribution were neither private nor communal. Rather, all such activity owed its origin to the nexus of social relationships founded upon obligation and reward.[5]

This agricultural society of quid pro quo, however, managed to support a commercial merchant class that initiated urbanization. It was this merchant class that drew the greatest suspicion and contempt from the clerics, as can be seen in the medieval aphorism *Homo mercator vix aut nunquam Deo placere potest* [The merchant can scarcely or never be pleasing to God].[6]

This precarious synthesis of nature and grace, like Tawney's "parallel provinces" mentioned in chapter 1, encouraged a dualistic Christianity that artificially restricted the development and restoration of economic life. Dutch theologian Herman Bavinck describes such ontological dualism:

> That which is natural (such as economic life) is not sinful, but it is that which constitutionally does not attain the supernatural. The supernatural is a donum superadditum ... consequently Christianity and grace ... transcendently supervenes upon the natural but does not penetrate and sanctify it.[7]

Modern-day concepts like markets, economic growth, and the profit motive were all but absent from this era's economic view. Rather, each vocation or class[8] was, in theory, only to receive that which could sustain its calling or vocation. The theory however, never became fully realized. Of course, the "higher" one's calling, the more sustenance was needed. Thus, except for the rich, medieval society was supposed to be a subsistence society.

This following diagram illustrates this problematic worldview:[9]

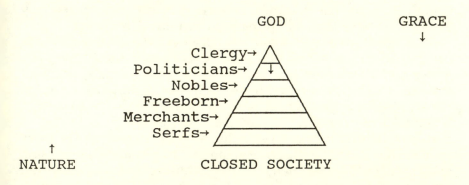

The province of heteronomous grace which, for example, forbade greed, increasingly conflicted with the growing autonomous world markets. The demands of nature and grace grew antithetical.[10] Because of advances in shipping Renaissance merchants and nobility could supply unheard-of luxuries, and proto Enlightenment-inspired theories of "free" markets arose.

Land in this feudal system was

emphatically not (autonomous) real-estate to be bought and sold as occasion warranted. Such land provided the basis of social life, status and constituted the foundation for the many aspects of society.[11]

Likewise, labor could never be rented because the notion of labor as a commodity was foreign to medieval consciousness (as was the vast network of consumers eagerly competing for labor's wares).[12] Finally capital, whether present in its liquid or developmental form, was of secondary importance to a society committed to a labor-intensive form of production. Its economy grew not from commercial, but from familial credit.[13]

The Modern Worldview and Economics

The precarious medieval synthesis of nature and grace soon fell apart. The winds of a Renaissance and Enlightenment-inspired "freedom" would soon cripple this edifice and erect a new monetary one in its place. Starting with the Renaissance, a *risorgimento* or revitalization was sweeping Europe. This Greco-Roman-inspired rebirth attempted to found a society on, among other entities, the wishes of the individual.[14]

In the Enlightenment, critical reason would no longer accept any external dictates that did not pass its scrutiny. It was this critical, literally autonomous, rationality that discovered the categorical imperative in ethics and provided the basis for natural science. The arena for the proof of humanity's freedom was nature, which in turn grew to be symbolized by a clock whose workings could be determined through the laws of cause and effect. Such laws could be controlled, manipulated, and made more amenable to human desire through rationality generally, and technology and science specifically.[15] With the discovery and manipulation of natural law, early modern thinkers attempted to establish a kind of Promethean freedom and overthrew many of the vestiges of medieval canon, natural, and biblical law.[16]

It was the philosopher-scientist Francis Bacon who said, "the purpose of science and its technique is to enlarge the boundaries of the human empire, to the effecting of all things possible."[17] However, the technological imperative demands much of people who found themselves to be a part of the "plasticity of the social milieu."[18] The advent of scientific-technological rationality placed moderns in a remarkable dilemma. Freedom meant the subjugation of nature, of which humans were a part. Could humanity and nature withstand such an onslaught?

This was not merely a speculative problem. The central notions of the manipulation of nature, the technological imperative for control, and the extensive demands of autonomous freedom proved to be necessary ingredients for modern Industrialism.[19] America's contemporary ecological problems, for example, have been in great measure caused by this secular demand for natural domination that promised material abundance as a reward for such subjugation.[20]

With the study of the autonomous LAWS of Nature[21] emerging as the mechanism by which natural harmony and social arrangements were grounded and surveyed, economics could develop as a separate discipline. The career of the moral philosopher Adam Smith helps to show how it arose. Early in Smith's career, in his *The Theory of Moral Sentiments* (1759), economics and moral philosophy remained intertwined. By the time he had published the *Wealth of Nations* (1776), he had surrendered his moralistic and theistic views of natural law and embraced deistic, empirical, mechanistic worldview. His optimistic Deism prompted his now-famous "invisible hand" theory of what guided the "laws" of market supply and demand. Smith extended his ideology to cover relations between the rich and the poor. He claimed the rich are led

> by an invisible hand to make nearly the same distributions of the necessaries of life, which would have been made, had the earth been divided into equal portions among all its inhabitants; and thus, without intending it, without knowing it, they advance the interest of the society.[22]

Smith's version of autonomous natural law and the market led to a mechanistic economic worldview in which the forces of supply, demand, self-interest, the "price of labor," and the quality and quantity of production came to an equilibrium and result in social harmony.[23]

One is amazed by early capitalism's faith in the belief that social harmony results from the aggregate pursuit of individualistic self-interest. [24] Surely, here is an example of faith as "the assurance of things hoped for, the evidence of things not seen."

The primacy of the individual, initially conceived by the Renaissance, was given a more full-bodied economic expression in the works of some Enlightenment thinkers. Whereas the *corpus Chris-*

tianum and economic restriction characterized the Middle Ages, acquisitiveness, economic expansion, and increased capitalization have marked the modern era. At the center of such a society, especially in the thought of John Locke, David Hume, and Thomas Hobbes, stood the needs and dictates of the individual. The individual and his contractual freedom were as sovereign as they were formative for society.[25] The modern economic individual—*Homo Oeconomicus,* if you will—was thought to live in a universe that was increasingly viewed in materialistic terms.[26]

Gradually throwing off the yoke of medieval restraint, the independent merchant stressed the voluntary exchange of goods and services. This mobility led to expanding trade, which in turn introduced new social traditions and created liquid capital and wider market distribution. Slowly Europe moved from an economy dominated by small, family-centered agricultural units to a more capital-intensive economy based in urban centers and stressing investment and management.[27] This resultant market-oriented society created a group of relations that revolved around cash as an easy medium of exchange. The cash nexus thus replaced tradition as one of the elements of social cohesion. "By the sixteenth century . . . cash transactions were already beginning to provide the very molecular force of social cohesion."[28] Here, then, is a good example of economic reductionism mentioned in chapter 1. To the extent that money or liquid capital was becoming the social nexus, it is proper to speak of capitalism as the exaggeration of the place and importance of money.

The notion of private property had not yet come into full bloom. The enclosure movement, by which land held in common was made into private property, was a crucial factor in defining land as an object of acquisition.

Toynbee has said that in England between 1760 and 1843 nearly seven million acres underwent enclosure.[29] By the nineteenth century one-half of the arable land in England had been enclosed by less-than-just practices.[30] This process led to the notion of, among other things, the "cash crop." The idea of a "cash crop," foreign as it was to a precommercialized society, changed the fruits of agriculture from socially useful products into the basis of private wealth. In turn, this process of enclosure and a "cash crop" created two features of proto-industrial society: the disenfranchised, landless peasant and private property. The waning of common land not only paved the way for urbanization but forced the disenfranchised into the same mold of self-interest.

We have now arrived at a crucial juncture in defining the contours of Industrialism. Manors, estates, guilds, and canon law gave way to some of the preconditions for factories, private property, a society built upon cash, and nature domination. If we add mechanical power to this era of activistic, inventive, practical spirit, we have the preconditions for the modern extensive[31] workplace.

With the invention of the steam engine by James Watt and Joseph Black, for example, growth, power, expansion, and mass production were to gain ascendancy. The only boundary was the consumer's ability to digest the fruits of mass production and thus avoid the resultant possibility of unemployment and profit loss. Mass production demands massive consumption by the masses, because of the enormous capital costs necessary for these large-scale economies.

The expanding iron works in Manchester, England demonstrates the expansive nature of the modern factory system. In 1727 the writer Daniel Defoe called Manchester "a mere village." Forty years later there were at least one hundred integrated mills and a large cluster of secondary forces and shops.[32] Likewise labor, once in theory a vocation, now had become a commodity to be "sold" by the laborer and "consumed" by the factory manager as an atomized "factor" of the production process.[33] Land, or "the free gifts of nature," because of the exercise of individual ownership and economic self-interest, could easily degenerate into an "idolatry of irresponsible ownership" as property rights, such as in rent collection (itself a form of profit), took precedence over social responsibility.[34]

The naturalistic-materialistic worldview sketched here is not simply a neutral or even a "value-added" worldview. This naturalism, which takes the pretence of autonomy as its fundamental point of departure, became the defining presuppositum of modern economic practice. Tawney says, "The faith upon which our economic civilization reposes, the faith that riches are not means but an end, implies that all economic activity is equally estimable, whether it is subordinated to a social purpose or not. . . . Such activity can lead to a reverence for economic activity, [which is] fetish worship."[35]

Our brief survey of the origins of Industrialism lacks one crucial element—its horizontal definition of happiness. Utilitarianism's calculus of pleasure, a way of viewing consumption and labor which led to mathematically calculating pain and pleasure as well as morality and human happiness, represents such an instrument. Jeremy Bentham provided the classic formulation of this worldview:

Nature has placed mankind under the governance of two sovereign masters, pain and pleasure. It is for them alone to point out what we ought to do. . . . On the one hand the standard of right and wrong, on the other hand the chain of causes and effects are fastened to their throne.[36]

Note also his autonomous view of "Nature."

In linking utility or happiness with morality, utilitarianism was attempting, in part, to unite ethics with the pleasure of consumption; it hoped at the same time to minimize the disutility of labor as a painful act. The utility of a product became determined by the amount of labor it took to make a product and the degree of happiness obtained by the consumer as measured by the sum total of goods purchased. Utilitarianism is an individualistically based worldview[37] that seeks to quantify pain and pleasure.

There are two important points pertaining to Industrialism that must be noted here. First, consumption is a must because one is governed by a desire to maximize one's utilities or happiness.[38] Secondly, an attempt is made in neoclassical economics to quantify consciousness by relating states of happiness with ordinal rank. Moreover, a consumer, who prefers ever-increasing amounts of material happiness and prosperity, always makes rational market choices based upon the ethical demand to maximize his *own* happiness. The reductionism of this calculus can be seen not only in the equation of the consumer with rational autonomous choices, but in the equation of total human happiness with material consumption.[39]

The Industrial Revolution in England gave visual expression to *Homo Oeconomicus'* faith. The commercial revolution, just outlined, depended upon the kind of strong merchant fleet which England and Spain owned. However, while Spain was clinging to the outdated view of gold as wealth, England was trading raw and finished goods to the colonies. England's more global, product-diverse view of wealth was made possible by the economic theories of Smith and Ricardo. Therefore, the English custom of "free inquiry" and the exploration of natural phenomena were requisite skills or virtues that were needed for the Industrial Revolution. These virtues grew out of England's constitutional laws of guaranteed freedom and the climate of critical thought. For example, through the Navigation Act of 1651 the English challenged the Dutch and attempted to corner world trade. England continued to prosper as her merchant trade became intertwined with nationalism.

Government-financed turnpike trusts in eighteenth-century England were financed because of the burgeoning of new markets. Such projects received help from the rediscovery of concrete by Robert Metcalf in 1790. Transportation time and costs were reduced by deepened canals and the growth of the best rail system in the world by 1830. Profits soared as a result.

Perhaps most importantly, within a period of four short years, three patents were granted that transformed the life of England forever. Sir Richard Arkwright patented the water frame in 1769, the same year James Watt patented the primary industrial machine, the steam engine. One year later, James Hargreaves invented the spinning jenny and the textile revolution was underway.[40] The remarkable quality of these inventions, coupled with England's enclosure movement and Jethro Tull and Oliver Backwell's improvement of the breeding of livestock, vaulted England into uncontested industrial supremacy after 1780.

The iron revolution in England paralleled the textile revolution. In 1740 Benjamin Huntsman found a way to separate impurities from the nearly finished steel. By 1738 Henry Cort, through the use of coal, process puddling, and rolling, discovered the reverberatory air furnace, which produced a clean steel product fifteen times faster than any previous model. Through engineering accuracy and the advent of better steel, John Wilkinson improved upon Watt's steam cylinder, thus giving industry more power.[41]

While not wanting to romanticize the Middle Ages, and while withholding the bulk of our positive views of Industrialism for the final chapter, we must note the baneful side of these developments. The Hammonds aptly describe England's economic "fruits" in terms of the legend of Midas:

> England asked for her profits and received profits. Everything turned to profit. The towns had their profitable dirt, their profitable smoke, their profitable slums, their profitable disorder, their profitable ignorance, their profitable despair. The curse of Midas was on this society. . . . For the new town was not a home where man could find beauty, happiness, leisure, learning, religion . . . [but] a bare desolate place, without color, air, or laughter, where man, woman, and child worked, ate, and slept.[42]

In short, the increasingly secular revolt of modern humanity enabled us to develop a materialistic-naturalistic worldview that horizontally defined such crucial notions as freedom, utility or happiness, the relationship of humanity to nature, the basis of social solidarity, and public and private meaning or purpose. Given the rather awesome course of events, Industrialism did indeed revolutionize modern life by providing an evangel for modern conscience and cultural expression.

The "Incorporation" of America

Let us turn our attention to the attempted "incorporation" of America. According to Alan Trachlenberg, "incorporation" involves

> the reorganization of perceptions as well as enterprise and institutions. Furthermore, it means . . . not only the expansion of an industrial capitalist system across the continent, the spread of market economy into all regions . . . but also . . . the remaking of cultural perceptions . . .[43]

In short, Industrialism becomes a "way of life." As has been noted in previous chapters, the theme of "incorporation," while having its legal side, extends far beyond a legal horizon. "Incorporation" became a religio-ethical phenomenon and people attempted to coerce much of life under its domain and dictates. Rather than the Church, Mammon (i.e., absolutized economic functions) dictated many substantive life mores in nineteenth-century America.

It is commonly held that England's industrialization formed the impetus for American industrialization. Even as goods flowed from Britain to America, so did the requisite sociopolitical, technical and scientific ideas. Changes in sources of power from natural to mechanical fueled American and English industrialization after the textile revolution. Moreover, factory systems and their extensive capitalizing plans were often copied by Americans from the British. Inventors like Samuel Slater, Francis Lowell, and James Watt frequently traveled between England and America. Robert Fulton's "Clermont" was powered by a steam engine built by the English firm of Boulton and Watt.[44] Though America lagged in steel production in the antebellum era, it was busily building 130,000 spindles for a textile revolution in 1815.[45] This was followed by the erection seven years later of the first factory system in Lowell, Massachusetts.

LAND

Above all, America possessed an abundance of land and natural resources, which are, of course, a fundamental necessity for Industrialism. These resources were untapped, untouched, and uncharted before 1820. Attempting to remedy this situation, Thomas Jefferson hired Meriwether Lewis and William Clark to "explore the vast and fertile country which [America's] sons [were] destined to fill with arts, sciences, freedom, and territorial development."[46] Jefferson had heard unofficial reports of the riches of the Missouri Valley and the Northwest, but without confirmation he could not convince Congress of the necessity of colonization. Armed with adequate scientific skills, Lewis and Clark set out to determine the exact nature of the frontier. Their mission turned into the first phase of a much larger economic process. Lewis and Clark's journey, along with the Zebulon Pike expedition and the later Stephen H. Long Yellowstone trek, marked the entry of America into the mercantile wars for the riches of the Northwest and Plains sections of Amrica.[47] Spain, Britain, France, and Canada all competed for the furs, minerals, and timber in this area.

The explorer became a de facto economic "point man" for economic incorporation. Information was gathered, fur-trading centers were established, Indian treaties were made, and scientific samples were gathered by these explorers in anticipation of much larger movements of settlers. "He is an anthropological type. He is a flexible, republican, and expectant capitalist. Moreover, he is an amateur scientist, diplomat, and soldier who was paid by the government"—so many viewed the explorer.[48]

Fur traders followed the explorers, establishing trading centers as they moved west. The Hudson Bay Company, which operated primarily in the Pacific Northwest, established their headquarters in the Willamette Valley near present-day Portland, Oregon. The Hudson Bay Company maintained in its charter that it wanted to "civilize the Indians so as to prevent the 'savages' from restricting the fur trade."[49] Hoping to "capitalize" on the good relations developed with the Indians, the Methodist and Presbyterian mission agencies established outposts which were to help Hudson Bay socialize the Indians. Such outposts were often used by this outfit as colonizing bases. They trained Indians in primitive industrial skills and enticed settlers to populate the region.

Frederick Jackson Turner reminded Americans at the 1893 Columbia Technological Exhibit that the frontier was not one solid, undifferentiated ideological unit. Rather, the fur-trading frontier was followed by the frontiers of the ranchers, miners, farmers, and finally the urbanites. In this sense, frontiers were "civilizing" stages developed to economically consolidate the American experience and to establish a line between the savage and the civilized man.[50]

As has been stated in chapter 2, Americans were prompted by both economic and missionary ideals in their movement west. They were drawn by the lure of wealth, the hope of a universal Garden of Eden or fruitful paradise, and the possibility of a continent for democracy. Clarence King of the United States Geological Society, himself a professing Christian, coined the term "natural wealth" after reflecting upon the vast natural beauty of the West. Various geological sites were immediately identified with their potential wealth-producing qualities. This labeling struck few Evangelicals, in this era, as too myopic.[51]

The Great Plains became an arena where the subjugation of nature promised freedom, opportunity, and wealth. Walter Prescott Webb shows how the Plains, being more than a mere geographic entity, radically affected American history. Arid weather, treeless plains, shallow rivers, water shortages, gusty winds, and an abundance of wild game like the buffalo sharpened the incorporating spirit. The Plains offered resistance, but also reward.

The ninety-eight meridian seemed to be especially significant as American moved inexorably toward the Civil War. The North became increasingly frustrated in its inability to stop the spread of the Southern way of life. After the Missouri Compromise, the annexation of Texas, the Kansas-Nebraska Act, and the Dred Scott decision, slavery seemed unstoppable. Ironically, however, the spread of cotton was halted not by political fiat or moral suasion, but by the ninety-eighth meridian. Because of the aridity of West Texas soil, cotton could not spread beyond this meridian. Webb suggests that the frustration caused by this natural blockade was an important contributing factor in increased Southern militancy.[52] This shows the important affect of geographic factors on wars, worldviews, and the limits to incorporation.

Northern capitalists were eager to follow the rail lines into the Great Plains. John G. McCoy, a Texas cattleman, gave them their chance. McCoy wanted to establish a place where Northeastern rail investors could meet Texas cattle barons, and in 1867, he signed a rail agreement with the St. Joe Railroad, making Hannibal, Missouri such a place. Subsequently McCoy made an agreement designating Chicago as the cattle baron's terminus and the Easterner's stockyard for meat. By 1880 however, the Eastern market was glutted with beef and the grass of the Plains was nearly gone, causing a severe market collapse in 1885. With this decline, the modern cattle industry emerged, as suppliers realized that supply and demand must be more tightly regulated.

The frontier's resources seemed boundless. People thought they could afford to deplete the prairie grass because they could always continue west. As this wave of economic expansion moved west, settlers developed increasing economic demands. Expansion meant subjugation and exploitation of natural wealth and the "savages."[53] Steam transportation, canal travel, and the rails helped make this "dominion" possible. The seemingly Edenic setting drew a variety of people. Farmers were attracted to the good prairie soil, potential landowners to the seemingly boundless expanse of open land, prospectors to the mineral deposits, and industrial workers to cheap land and the promise of independence.[54]

As "civilization" advanced, the work of the missionary, cattleman, and the speculator was not enough to secure law and order, a prerequisite for industrial growth. The West was initially perceived to be a place of "outer darkness," or a region of chaos.[55] This place of potential terror finally had to be subdued by military means. The cavalryman, military perfection of the cowboy, gave America the means of conquest. An English visitor to America, noting its cavalryman, said,

> A good rider on a good horse is as much above himself and others as the world can make him. When he bestride him soars, he is a hawk; he trots the air; the earth sings when the military rider touches it.[56]

Contrary to the beliefs of some conservative capitalists, markets never simply grow because of demand or sufficient supplies of land, labor, or capital. In spite of cheap land, abundant resources, growing markets, a sufficient (though not abundant) supply of labor, and substantial European investment, before the Civil War American enterprise in nearly all sectors required a major form of government subsidy. The federal government sent troops to protect primitive settlements and capital investments.[57]

The promise of unending land, resources, and opportunity prompted America's incorporation of the West. On a vast and grand scale, the subduing of the West became America's version of the enclosure movement.

The relatively swift possession and exploitation of "the garden" became equated with industrial progress. John Gast's 1873 painting entitled *American Progress* provides an emblem of the West's fate. The painting depicts a herd of buffalo, several bears and coyote, and "savage Indians," fleeing before Americans. The Americans are represented as hunters, settlers in covered wagons, and rail entrepreneurs. They bring with them schools, telegraphs, factories and, of course, churches. In the center of the picture stands a radiant female. She is the Star of the Empire of Progress. As all flee her presence, the message is plain: the Star overwhelms all![58]

RAILROADS

Americans had to address two practical questions before they could enjoy this cornucopia: how was the entire continent to enjoy the fruits of production, and how could goods be made even more affordable? The answer to these questions came with the universal-ization of one of the most crucial elements of Industrialism.

While the seemingly boundless West provided the basis for future wealth, the oceanic frontier proved to be an obstacle that canals, steam boats, and covered wagons could not entirely conquer. A coordinated rail system was to overcome this problem.[59]

Prior to the Civil War, local commerce dominated America, and the earliest rails primarily served its needs. The lines that led from Boston rarely went beyond Worcester, Massachusetts. In 1831, the Pontchartrain Railroad ran a four-and-a-half mile rail line from New Orleans to a local lake in order to facilitate the shipment of lumber. In the Mohawk Valley of New York local capital provided the invest-ment basis for local transportation, and Pennsylvania's earliest rails were used for shipment of anthracite coal from her mines to south-ern New York.[60]

While national markets were lagging, rail technology improved. "By 1830 Pittsburgh was producing 100 engines per year while Cin-cinnati was producing 150 per year."[61] By the 1840's, track mileage for the United States began to rapidly increase, keeping pace with advancing rail technology. Engines grew in power and were less prone to breakdowns. These and other developments enabled the several rail lines to push across the Appalachian barrier in this era.[62] Moreover, by 1850 local, state, and federal governments began to extend cash or credit to rail companies for line development.

It was not until the Civil War, however, that the rail system dem-onstrated its continentally incorporative powers. The demand for troop movements, munitions, and supplies began to suggest that a national rail system was necessary. More importantly, the forces of regionalism, division, and fragmentation threatened to split the Northern forces, a concrete means of unification was desperately needed.[63]

During the war years a train connected New York and Washington D.C. for the first time. Due to the demand for supplies and trade, by 1864 Erie was united with upper New York and central Ohio. By the end of the war, rails were carrying most of the wheat from the Plains to a needy East.[64] As fast freight lines (i.e., lines without delay or transfer points) multiplied, decay and spoilage lessened. By 1886 the final act of incorporation came about as the agrarian South was united with Northern industry via the rail lines.

It is appropriate that the technological term chosen by the rail executives to denote the unification of all rail lines was "standard gauge track." Prior to the 1880's, regionalism had plagued the rail lines. Trains trying to ship goods from place to place often were stymied by the different gauges or widths of track. The provincialism that resulted hindered the development of internal markets and promoted the sovereignty of local interests. By the late 1890s, American markets were incorporated by the four-foot, eight-and-one-half-inch track.

Postbellum articles praised the rails as a progressive vehicle of social progress and revolution. Like mass production and its fruits, rails multiplied in the Gilded Age.

Through the rail lines, America developed a powerful and practical means to incorporate markets. Rail lines, like long grasping arms, drew the burgeoning domestic markets into the bosom of the East and gave freely in turn of her manufactured goods.[65] Rails contributed to regional economic interdependence and thereby encouraged regional specialization. Pittsburgh, for example, could concentrate upon steel because it could depend upon Minnesota's wheat and ore. Moreover, as rail lines developed, colonization and settlement became more extensive because of the ease of movement.

Another important consequence of rails was the princely emergence of finance capitalism. National rails converted regional gains to profits through governmental securities that were often manipulated by entrepreneurs. Accordingly, stocks were sold at a value that grossly exceeded their real worth. Thus profits derived from rail securities went hand-in-hand with rail promotion, consolidation, and security manipulation.[66]

Perhaps the greatest benefit to the American consumer was the reduced transportation cost brought on by the rails. Such social savings[67] after 1890 saved the consumer millions of dollars. The added national income gained by such social savings amounted to approximately $214 million by 1890.[68] Of course, such savings encouraged regional specialization and further capital investment.

Although the railroad was not the sole engine of Industrialism, its existence was of fundamental importance for American industry. At least as important as the actual commodities hauled was the belief in the power of cultural progress engendered by the rails. The veins of commercial transport democratically distributed the goods of Industrialism.

Thus the railroad, the prime instrument of large-scale industrialization which re-created American nature into natural resources for commodity production, appears as a chariot winging America . . . through the new empire . . . or the new garden of the world.[69]

By the time of the Civil War, the railroad, with its enormous appetite for market goods and anxious settlers, presented an overwhelming problem for some Americans—namely, native Americans. Nomadic, animistic, tribal, territorial, and environmentally frugal, the Native Americans resented the white man and his "iron horse." Frederick Jackson Turner et al. deemed such peoples as "savages" or "primitives" in comparison with the people of civilization. While the military pursued the Native Americans with the vanguard of modernity, the railroad consummated what the fur-trappers, missionaries and calvary had begun.

> There seemed to be no place in the railroad destiny for enclaves of still-primitive peoples clinging desperately to their traditional ways. . . . Subdued by military force, dependent in large measure upon federal governments for subsistence . . . they refused to disappear into the mainstream of society.[70]

THE NATIVE AMERICANS

American desires forced a dilemma. How could citizens of the United States "protect" the Native Americans and, at the same time, secure the prerequisites for Industrialism? As the Native people moved or were forced west, rich soil, timber, coal and huge deposits of precious minerals were discovered on their lands. Various interests endeavored to determine their fate. Some extreme militarists wanted their quick elimination. In contrast, many Quakers were content to share the land and live in more-or-less mutual harmony.[71] Moderates, like Evangelicals, wanted to "civilize" them. The way Evangelicals related civilization, especially its forceful industrial components, with their Christian commitment, represents a telling feature of the nineteenth-century industrial-Evangelical worldview.

An understanding of the "Indian problem" will deepen our understanding of the industrial-Evangelical liaison. Lincoln had officially recognized the plight of the Native American during the Civil War. Federal volunteer troops, during the war, pursued the Sioux in Minnesota and the Cheyenne in Colorado. Rather than waste this kind of time and money, the government decided to put the Native American on reservations. They, faced with the dilemma of extermination or reservations, chose the reservations. After the Civil War, a dispute broke out as to which governmental agency was ultimately responsible for the Indian nations. Grant's generals wanted the Bureau of Indian Affairs to be placed under the Department of War, thus unofficially declaring them prisoners of war. Others, including the Evangelicals, wanted the reservation system to be part of the Department of the Interior and thus have Indians "managed" as resources.[72]

With tensions rising, Evangelical Alfred B. Meacham, who was regional superintendent of Indian Affairs, led a mission of peace to the troublesome Modoc Indians on the Oregon-California border. "Captain Jack," the chief, had led his tribe in battles with white settlers for years. Armed with the promise of military protection from Grant, Meacham went to sue for peace. During the peace conference, Captain Jack ordered his braves to attack the defenseless whites. A massacre ensued in which Meacham was severely wounded. Rather than become bitter, Meacham made his way back East to organize national support for the Native American cause. He launched his campaign from Park Street Church in Boston.[73]

The Modoc massacre and the ensuing war increasingly polarized the public's perceptions of the Native Americans. Settlers and politicos who favored law and order viewed the Native American as recalcitrant. Others, including many Evangelicals, viewed the Native American as "progressing" toward a more civilized stance. Those who saw the Native American as hostile wanted to incorporate them into the American cultural fabric. They hoped to do this by introducing the Native Americans to white law, schools, morality, self-constraint, Christianity and, of course, private property.

> The friends of the Indians set about with good intentions to stamp out Indian oneness altogether and to substitute for it a uniform Americanness, to destroy all remnants of corporate existence or tribalism and to replace them with an absolute rugged individualism that was foreign . . . to the hearts of the Indian people.[74]

As civilization marched inexorably on, many Evangelicals did what they could for the Native Americans. They labored to keep the "Indian problem" out of the Department of War, fought for civil rights, attempted to keep the size of reservation land large, and established Native American schools for industry and agriculture. Their hardest battle, which they partially won, was trying to keep white settlers from exploiting Native American lands.

However, the mainstream Evangelical leadership evinced some crucial elements of the industrial worldview. The commissioner of Indian Affairs, Thomas J. Morgan—an Evangelical—argued that the tribal system "should be broken up, socialism destroyed, and the family and the autonomy of the individual be substituted."[75] Such a program (or pogrom) was consistently applied, soteriologically, to the Native Americans' socioeconomic problems: "The first motto of all Indian reformers should be Indian evangelization . . . for it is only as enough individual Indians are converted that the social plight of the Indian [will] improve."[76] The priority given by Evangelicals to evangelization over that of cultural tolerance and justice shows not only the presence of the dualistic nature/grace worldview, mentioned in chapter 2, but the force of another component of Industrialism.

For the busy beehive of industrializing America, the Native Americans' acquiescence to the notion of private property became a national mania. Property meant morality, energy, and enterprise, according to some Evangelicals. Indeed, securing private property for the Native Americans became one of the preeminent Evangelical goals for the Native Americans in this era.[77]

The Dawes Act of 1886 was to signal the beginning of the end of the reservation system, as allotments were broken up into atoms of private property. Modeled on the Homestead Act of 1862, the Dawes Act provided that each Native American family be given 160 acres. The government, in taking ownership of this property for twenty-five years, allowed the Native Americans almost complete freedom as to its development. If the Native American maintained their property, they were granted citizenship. Eventually, however, Native Americans failed to cultivate the tough prairie soil and leased portions of their lands, living off of their rents. The Dawes Act attempted to remedy this "unproductive leasing" by forcing private property upon the nomadic Native American. Coerced into a strange pattern of living, the Native Americans of the West again became dependent.[78]

Like the missionaries associated with the early Hudson Bay Company, Evangelicals simultaneously helped cultivate and were used by the industrial forces that affected Native life in the nineteenth century. Rail line settlers, dumped onto Western territories, pushed to have the reservation system abandoned. Native Americans often heard from whites the cry: "Manifest destiny! The discovery of coal in McAlester, Oklahoma, spelled the end of the Cherokee, Creek, and Choctaw habitat."

Business interests had developed a group of lobbyists appropriately called the "Boomers." This group lobbied to have Oklahoma Native American land categorized as "public domain." By 1880, nearly fifteen million acres surrounding the Oklahoma Territory had been given to settlers, ranchers, rail men, and speculators.[79] Finally, on March 1, 1895, Congress created two new U.S. courts for these

"Indian territories." Sadly, tribal law came to a de facto end as helpless tribal governments accepted the final form of civil behavior.

To the extent that the Evangelicals accepted such notions as private property and made them a part of their mission strategy, they accommodated their worldview to that of Industrialism and thereby failed to minister to the deepest needs of the native Americans. Evangelicals failed to realize that the Native Americans worldview remained the complete antithesis to the worldview dedicated to productivity, profit, and private property. Tolerance and pluralism were not legally extended to the Native American way of life.

CAPITAL

Industrial capital ended up having the profoundest impact upon incorporating culture. As part of the "economic revolution" in America, the machines, credit, and sheer volume of circulating physical goods transformed American society from an agrarian pasture into a postbellum industrial complex.[80]

The managerial capitalism that spawned the modern corporation can trace its ancestry, in part, to the joint stock company of the late Middle Ages. Anxious merchants, then as now, received special legislative and juridical favor while creating (and often destroying) trade, circulating capital, and national wealth. The "corpus," or legally constituted corporate entity, survived and incorporated individual careers into its eco-legal structure in its quest for the wealth of nations.[81]

Prior to the Civil War, proprietorship, family capital, and regional economics characterized many of America's business patterns. However, after the Civil War had stimulated the need for large-scale machinery, national markets and a gradual specialization of the production process required large-scale, capital-intensive commitment. Moreover, as postbellum American business increasingly drew European capital, investors demanded more limited liability. In separating legal and financial responsibility from investment, as the concept of limited liability does, the American judicial system not only defined a crucial component of the modern corporation but allowed it to fix its gaze almost exclusively upon profits and private property.[82] Antebellum canal, road and rail construction, while extensive, did not demand the sophisticated legal structure or volume of capital that postbellum Industrialism needed.[83]

Financier Jay Cooke, who grew to be a millionaire through his financing of the Civil War for the North, is an example of the early incorporating Evangelical capitalists. To raise some $500,000,000 on a 5 percent twenty-year bond, Cooke employed nearly 2,500 agents to nationally advertise the need for financing the War. His commission was one-half of one percent on the first million raised and three-eighths of one percent on the remainder of the $499 million. Thus, a successful private career was launched because of the Civil War.[84]

On the eve of the Civil War, three important phases of industrial incorporation had strategically become intertwined: expansive capital, territorial acquisition, and rail transportation. Moral, financial, religious, and territorial forms of progress were now becoming tightly intertwined.

Though growing, the modern corporation had not yet taken on its corpulent, circa-1880 form. Standard Oil, for example, was not incorporated until 1868, and did not begin to grow rapidly until the 1870s. From 1850 to 1870, industrialization was characterized by a rather rapid growth of many smaller firms competing for a relatively small market share. However, after the Civil War, competition began to shift from price and quality to marketing, technological innovation, and packaging, as many firms rushed into burgeoning markets.[85] Supply could no longer be limited by regional competition, as it had been in the antebellum era. As markets grew, so did competition.

Accordingly, Industrialism was faced with an irreconcilable tension. On the one hand, murderous competition forced economic rivals to tortuous ends. Management and labor suffered as wages and investment capital were trimmed to the bone to meet competitive requirements. On the other hand, industrialization of almost any variety required efficiency, large amounts of fixed capital, considerable risk, sufficient profit for technological innovation, capital upkeep, and national market integration. The solution to this dilemma came as larger firms destroyed competition through combinations, pools and "agreements." In short, businesses were forced to incorporate their competitors.

Combinations were formed by private entrepreneurs in order to

> increase or protect profit, not for lowering costs. . . . They [the entrepreneurs] accomplished this by reducing costs, raising prices, controlling competition, excluding competitors from markets and new technologies, as well as by availing themselves of new sales promotions.[86]

This straightforward statement indicates the spirit of industrial incorporation. If another company was thought to be too competitive, various strategies were developed to incorporate it. Rail rebates, restriction of trade, price fixing, and watering stock[87] were among the practices used to absorb competitors. A successful takeover left a company defenseless; personnel, services, resources, and capital were all incorporated.

If unchecked, this process, called horizontal monopolization, would spread throughout a given market until a few businesses controlled most of the activity. In the steel industry, Andrew Carnegie incorporated the J. Edgar Thomson Works, the Homestead and Duquesne Works, and the Lake Superior Iron Company, as well as the Pittsburgh-based Oliver Mining Company. The resulting corporation, worth by this time over $100,000,000, was in turn absorbed by J. P. Morgan's United States Steel Company. The new megacorporation was worth $1,400,000,000 and controlled sixty percent of the national steel output.[88]

The hunger for incorporation was not yet sated. To insure the greatest possible rate of growth and profit, a vertical integration had to be secured for the steel industry. Accordingly, blast furnaces, steel converters, rolling operations and labor had to be housed and controled by a single firm. This form of incorporation evolved because of the demands of large-scale technology, competitive non-related overhead costs, and the desire for product uniformity. This form of monopoly proved so successful for Morgan that "by 1900 all operations from blast furnace to rolling mills were integrated."[89]

The result of such incorporation can hardly be overestimated. The factory, as a highly rationalized and capitalized arena where machines were assembled for the consecutive production process, became a symbol for the incorporating spirit that equated industrial size and output with progress. People and machines were concentrated and their assembled operations were manipulated for even greater yields. To become so massively productive, the "dark Satanic mills" of antebellum America had to be transformed by lighting, electric power, glass windows, cement, and steel frames. Postbellum materials permitted factory design to extend outward rather than merely upward. Factories eventually sprawled out of the inner cities to the suburbs.[90]

The factory's interior design centered around the machines, which were, in turn, driven by a central power shaft. Labor and management also revolved around machines. Therefore, men had to adapt to the needs of the machine and not vice versa. Care for human safety was often lax. The safety record of the steel industry was particularly bad. The Pittsburgh-based firm of Jones and Laugh-lin, for example, manifested a "considerable indifference to accident prevention."[91]

These vast industrial plants (note the organic metaphor) required technologies of scale which in turn depended upon large capital outlays. Ironically, formative capital requires the use of older capi-tal, and the incorporation of older capital by expanding capital must exceed the structure of older wealth if a profit is to be realized. If this profit is used for further industrial expansion, as it often is, a capital-intensive economy begins to develop. Arguably, modern Industrialism centers more upon industrial growth than it does on profit.[92]

The myth that developed to support this form of Industrialism itself incorporated components of the nineteenth-century world-view. Simple minerals could be converted into a complex compound like steel; independent workers and machines could be molded into a complex ensemble of interdependent means of production; and technological rationality could coordinate this ensemble to ensure an optimistic "progressive" outcome. In short, evolutionary eco-nomic progress became a gospel. Carroll D. Wright claimed: "Eco-nomic progress drives out poverty, superstition and ignorance; machines are human benefactors alleviating drudgery, hard-work and want. It is a civilizing force . . . for better morals, better sanitary conditions, better wages."[93]

American land, identity, and fate were being incorporated by Industrialism. For example, ores had to pass through an improved Bessemer converter that processed compounds of iron, carbon, and manganese so they would have greater uniformity and toughness. This process, called Spiegeleisen metallurgy, was in turn improved upon by the French Siemens-Marting steel-making process, later known as the "open hearth" process in America. This process en-abled Americans to shift to local ores and produce a more durable, malleable product.[94] Of course, this process hastened the incorpo-ration of vast amounts of ore-bearing lands in various ranges. More-over, modern metallurgy emerged from the technologies that developed around the Bessemer converter. For years, American en-gineers had tried to use American bituminous coal in the Bessemer furnace, only to be continually frustrated because of the high sulfur content of the coal. This failure led the United States to pioneer the factory use of the open-hearth process, and the new process was aided by the discovery of more suitable anthracite coal in Connells-ville, Pennsylvania.

This focus upon the manufacturing process is not meant to indicate that traditional sources of power like horse and water were forgotten. But, the industrial system moved relatively rapidly beyond these sources of power. The basic tenets of capital substitution, force, and mass production were increasingly gaining acceptance in agriculture, textiles, and the transportation industries. Increasingly, nature's power was encapsulated in capital instruments.

The rationalization and incorporation of the work place was deepened by the advent of scientific management, which came about through the crusading efforts of Frederick Taylor of Philadelphia. After growing up in a professional family, Taylor left in late adolescence and became a foreman in a local steel company. Shortly after the Civil War, Midvale Steel Company was organized. As in many other plants of its size, the production process at Midvale, itself not highly rationalized, revolved around the foreman. Foremen were front-line supervisors whose duties involved doing cost-analysis, maintaining discipline, and providing patriarchal care of machines and people. Taylor became concerned during these years with the inefficiency of the foreman, labor work operations, and productivity. He concluded that *the* basic problem of the production process was the inefficiency caused by the failure to adapt people's movements to those of the machines.[95] From this primary failure came such secondary failures as loss of production potential, low wages, and economic depressions.

Through a complex series of production line changes, Taylor sought to radically adapt the workplace to fit the values of efficiency, standardized movements, and predictability. Time-study analysis was initiated whereby human actions were studied to determine redundant movements. Wanting to improve human efficiency, Taylor demanded that the movements of the workers be automated and made repeatable like those of the machine.[96] Accordingly, individual worker motions *and* worker groups were atomized, dispersed, and made to fit a manager's schedule and stopwatch. Taylor believed that this industrial schema would help the overworked foreman, compensate the weary worker with more wages, and produce greater yields for hungry investors.[97] In other words, human creativity was exchanged for higher wages. Taylor was very successful. He "proved that . . . it was possible to manipulate human activity and to control it by logical procedures in much the same way that physical objects can be measured and controlled."[98]

Initially, Taylor's movement met with great worker resistance as workers complained of boredom and discontent. The discontent, surprisingly, spread to the managers who had sought to revolutionize the workplace with "Taylorism." It seems that Taylor's rather inflexible personality didn't allow him to adapt his principles to meet different circumstances. He was often called a "prophet," and Taylor used to punish wayward followers who "apostatized" from the truth.[99]

Taylorism was probably the first and most thorough attempt to rationalize human labor.[100] This incorporating rationality did not have to worry about human beings made in God's image because it welded, perhaps unknowingly, its engineers and workers to the dictates of the machine. The idea of responsible work communities, meaningfully oriented as equals to managers in the production process, had to give way to a system that demanded rational, atomized order, capital substitution of labor, and maximized investment return. Such were the demands of Mammon.

ROCKEFELLER AND THE MODERN CORPORATION

At the bottom of this mighty industrial edifice stood the keystone of the capitalist industrial schema: the much maligned "robber baron" or entrepreneur. He can best be symbolized by John D. Rockefeller. The interrelationship of Rockefeller's Baptist Christianity and his oil kingdom is worth noting.

Rockefeller was baptized as a young man in 1854 at the Erie Street Baptist Church in Cleveland, Ohio. Rockefeller's early piety was immediately noticeable; he shunned theaters, gambling, and alcoholic beverages. During his youth, he regularly read his Bible at nights while he worked hard during the days. He drew great comfort from the Bible, which he needed while living away from home, mourning the absence of his nomadic father. During these years he secured his first job as a shipping chark.

During this early period, he taught himself bookkeeping. Rockefeller was fond of recalling, though not necessarily boastfully, that the first entry in his first ledger was of a yearly contribution of $1.82 made during his sixteenth year, a year that saw him earn *no* pay.[101] He kept this ledger his entire life. Three years later, while a Baptist trustee, he helped his church face a dreadful financial crunch. Rockefeller organized a "stewardship"[102] campaign, personally asking each of the church members to contribute a tithe (ten percent of their income) to the church fund. Within three months the bill had been paid.

As he passed into manhood at age twenty-one, two important events portended Rockefeller's future: he preached his first layman's sermon and he turned his attention to Drake's Titusville oil.

Preaching on Romans 12:11, he chided his listeners to "be not sloth-ful in business, [but] . . . fervent in spirit, serving the Lord."[103] In this sermon two crucial equations were made. First, he equated the Greek word *spoudē* with the word "business" rather than with the more general term "diligence" or "vigilance." Secondly, and more importantly, he equated his business and its profits with God's gra-cious provisions.[104] This bending of the Biblical text to suit the purposes of American business became one of the crucial trade-marks of Rockefeller's generation of entrepreneurs.

As Rockefeller turned his attention to oil, God was about to take on a new partner. Capital formation, wholesale distribution, credit and rational accounting became the chief concerns of the man who bought Standard Oil before the Civil War for $72,500. As Standard Oil grew, its profits were used to swallow up competitors and im-prove capital stock and technologies of scale. Such profits enabled him to secure managerial and distributive scope which this industry had previously lacked.[105]

If Rockefeller, as an entrepreneur, started out legitimately accu-mulating capital, the incorporating spirit pushed him beyond the rather loosely defined forms of corporate legitimacy stated by the Sherman antitrust laws. Before the Civil War began, Rockefeller knew that an oversupply of oil hurt the profit margins of all oil producers. After failing in his initial attempt at market coercion through the South Improvement Company in Titusville, Pennsylva-nia, Rockefeller initiated the "Pittsburgh Plan." Through the use of rail rebates, Rockefeller tried to bolster his profit margin and simultaneously undercut competitors. Securing, over the years, re-bates of fifty cents per barrel, he was able to buy out his competi-tors by undercutting their profit margins. At times, this undercutting was merciless.[106]

Incorporation, in its vertical and horizontal monopolistic forms, permitted him to establish his own shipping quotas, which could be used to eliminate designated regional wholesalers. As these wholesalers were terminated, Rockefeller often manned the now-defunct corporations with his trustees and told them to buy up enough stock to give Standard an edge in determining the old companies' future. The holding companies were monuments to Rockefeller's avoidance of the notion of competition as the fundamental norm of economic life. By 1881 he controlled forty companies and eighty percent of the oil market.

Having amassed over $900 million in profits and capital, Rocke-feller turned his attention to philanthropy, giving away over $500 million through the Rockefeller Foundation.[107] During the 1890's, when the Standard Oil trust was being publicly rebuked, *The National Baptist*, an unoffocial Baptist periodical, took Rockefeller to task for the unchristian way that he secured his trust. *The Examiner*, an official Baptist newspaper, sided with Rockefeller and his fellow Baptists who helped run Standard Oil. *The Examiner*'s apology says something about the spirit of the age as well as about American views towards philanthropy, charity, tithing, and the interrelationship of God and Mammon:

> These men of trusts are Christian men. The four most prominent men of oil trusts are eminent Baptists, who honor their religious obligations and contribute without stint to the noblest Christian and philanthropic objects. The oil trust was begun and carried on by Christian men. They are Baptists and the objects and methods of the oil trusts are praiseworthy.[108]

In 1891, Rockefeller initiated his greatest philanthropic project, the University of Chicago. Through Reverend Frederick T. Gates, Rockefeller gave an initial sum of $600,000 to start the University. This gift was followed by another of one million dollars to help start the Baptist Union Theological Seminary, adjacent to the University. The following year, in 1892, the national denomination met in Chicago for its convention. When the Educational Society, a committee responsible for the educational stewardship of the denomination, announced Rockefeller's gift, the audience roared with delight. Immediately the audience broke into applause and began to sing the doxology, after which they shouted, "God has given us Chicago!"[109] All of this occurred just one and one-half years after the Sherman antitrust laws, aimed in part at Standard Oil, were enacted.

Surely, no one mistook Rockefeller for God. However, they did mistake Rockefeller's generosity for God's grace. Perhaps this was understandable, for Rockefeller made the same mistake. He once said,

> I believe the power to make money is a gift of God . . . to be developed and used to the best of our ability for the good of mankind. . . . I believe it is my duty to make money and still more money, and to use the money I make for the good of my fellow-man according to the dictates of my own conscience.[110]

Here is the autonomous philanthropic conscience stripped of many of its Biblical moorings.

There can be no doubt that charity is often needed and socially beneficial. Voluntary generosity is to be preferred over mandatory welfare. However, voluntarism masks great problems: deep wrongs created by capital formation do not always disappear with Band-Aid solutions. Moreover, God could be worshipped by being charitable, while Gold could be worshipped in the capital formation process through adhering to the dictates of massive incorporation. More to the point was the *Chicago Chronicle's* prophetic response to one Rockefeller statement:

> John D. Rockefeller has fallen in line with Ben Harrison and Mark Hanna [two politicos who used the name of God to justify their activities], and modestly announced that Divine Providence is keeping special watch over him and his monetary affairs. . . . The Lord gave me my money! Let the ruined refiners, the impoverished producers, the corrupted legislators of the oil stand as answer to this blasphemy.[111]

Because the Christian religion was restricted to a limited compartment of life, the superrich could support Evangelicalism without open conflict between the dictates of God and Mammon. J. P. Morgan tithed to Grace Episcopal Church in New York; the Vanderbilts regularly worshipped at St. Bartholomew's Episcopal Church in New York; Andrew Mellon built East Liberty United Presbyterian Church in Pittsburgh; and John J. Astor befriended the Dutch Reformed Church. Moreover, these contacts were not tangential. Rockefeller taught Sunday school and tithed for all of his adult life. Jacob Vandergrift fought "demon rum" and regularly prayed to protect National City Bank of New York. Department store magnate and Y.M.C.A. secretary John Wanamaker joined with the pastor Russell Conwell and regularly gave, in the name of Christ, to such noteworthy charities as Temple University and Samaritan Hospital in Philadelphia. Finally, J. P. Morgan virtually financed the ecclesiastical meetings of the Episcopal Church in New York. A noted economist of this period, John A. Hobson, speaks of how the Christian religion had come to be interpreted by capitalism: "God and Mammon have developed a partnership. Mammon presides over the accumulating and gathering department; God over the giving department. Mammon makes the money and God spends it."[112] While "God" presided over the giving, it was a God seen through capitalistic glasses. Thus, "Christianity" did sustain all of Rockefeller's activities, but it was a Christianity used to support material success.

That industrialists united God and gold should not surprise us. Much was at stake. Calling to mind Mandeville's metaphor for capitalist society, Carnegie once said, "The millionaires are the bees that make the most honey and contribute most to the hive even after they have gorged themselves full."[113] While Carnegie was not a theist, his beliefs about society and the industrialist's role in society reflected a common consensus among industrialists as to their role and status in life.[114]

LABOR

Finally, we turn our attention to the American nineteenth-century labor movement and the Protestant work ethic. Whatever may have been the validity of Weber's thesis as it pertained to Puritanism, by the advent of the nineteenth century the work ethic had become thoroughly secularized. By mid-century the material and industrial demands secularized the notions of calling, vocation, and reward to fit the duties of mass production. Accordingly, the newer secularized virtues were self-reliance, self-control, and perseverance, while idleness (i.e., play and recreation) was considered to be one of the chief sins. [115] The worldview of Industrialism had by this time gathered enough momentum that it left in tatters the network of Christian and secular values that had given it birth in the sixteenth and seventeenth centuries.

The Scottish essayist and historian Thomas Carlyle captured the spirit of the nineteenth-century work ethic when he said of this new autonomous mandate,

> Whatsoever of morality and intelligence, what of patience, perseverance, faithfulness, of method, insight, ingenuity, energy; in a word, whatsoever of strength, the man is judged by the work he does. . . . Produce! Produce! In God's name produce it.[116]

Work became, according to this gospel, the mandate for the property-owning middle class as well as for the merchants, ministers, and nonsalaried professionals and workers who labored for rewards and legitimatization.

Small, labor-intensive shops had dotted the preindustrial countryside. Between 1815 and 1850, Northerners were busy enough to promote the notion of work to a value that afforded identity and legitimization. However, mass production had not yet incorporated many American laborers. In 1832, for example, one half of Boston workingmen labored in shops with ten or fewer workers, and eighty percent of shops employed fewer than twenty employees. One hundred employees constituted a major enterprise.[117]

Nevertheless, American antebellum labor, in its white- and blue-collar forms, shared some nascent industrialist values. Expansion, upward mobility, independent action, and mass consumption became the shared virtues of embryonic Industrialism.[118] The industrial worker, like his middle-class counterpart, welcomed the advent of mass production and higher wages, for the system of mass production was thought to alleviate humanity's most global and timie-honored problem: need.

During this era, the work ethic provided engineers with the impetus for the language of calculation, the motive for diligence, and the norms for a rationalized, machine-centered plant. In turn, the secularized ethic, stressing as it did the reduction of labor into a sellable commodity, helped impel restless workers into dangerous factories. Having just left the bleak but familiar confines of rural America, or having tired of wandering through a stagnate Europe, immigrants flooded the "land of opportunity."

During the Civil War, confronted by the horrors of the workplace, American labor began its long struggle for a sphere in the American Dream. With the advent of rail prosperity and rationalized production and consumption, labor organized into rudimentary trade assemblies in response to "wage slavery" and management intimidation.[119] However, while initially successful, the amateurism of these trade assemblies and the 1857 depression all but destroyed the earliest unions. Before disbanding, however, the unions convinced a portion of the public that Northern wage-slavery was analogous in certain ways to Southern cotton slavery.

Early postbellum wage-slavery, or destitute living coupled with agonizingly long work days, effectively made the Northern laborer dependent upon Industrialism for almost all of life's necessities.[120] Some Northerners began to recognize their own brand of slavery. A *New York Times* editorial in 1869 said, "Slavery as absolute if not as degrading as that which pervades the South, grips the Northern manufacturers."[121]

Ironically, the incorporation of the American culture gave birth to coordinated trade unions. The Stove Moulders' Union was one of the first regional unions to give way to a national union, even as local labor-intensve means gave way to national mechanized production. In order to protect jobs and workers, from 1864–1873 over twenty-six national trade unions were organized following the industrial explosion caused by the war.[122]

During this period of labor solidarity, the National Labor Union attempted to develop worker consciousness. The Labor Union was the first to use the strike as a national weapon. It was also the first to organize a national labor congress (it was composed of seventy-seven delegates from thirteen states). From this congress Ira Steward emerged as a national labor leader, and shocked the nation with what was considered in that day to be an outrageous demand for an eight-hour day. The labor union broadened its horizons in the 1870s by unionizing many machinists and blacksmiths.

Management and entrepreneurs reacted unfavorably to such co-operative competition. While a significant portion of the union movement was busy trying to recapture the Jeffersonian ideal of democratic industrial freedom for the newly incorporated factory worker, many companies like Standard Oil were rapidly moving towards monopolistic capitalism. The democratic faith in individual freedom, as interpreted by the burgeoning union movement in the 1870s, became the vehicle for such laissez-faire liberals as E. L. Godkin to fight monopolistic capitalism.

Sensing the inevitability of worker cooperation, many corporations tried to implement Frederick Taylor's profit-sharing plan. Loathing industrial violence, management offered labor some industrial fruits. Accordingly, profit-sharing, from the company's view, was "a bonus and a stake in the business; to society it was a promise of industrial peace; to the employers it meant more profits and autocracy."[123] United States Steel, for example, allowed employees to buy capital stock in installments in return for a loyalty pledge. In theory, this would guarantee a full mutuality between capital and labor and hence to ensure greater interest by labor in the business.

However, labor did not miss the subtlety of management's attempt at unilateral incorporation. No seats of power for labor came with management's offer; no rank and file members sat on U.S. Steel's board of directors. In short, management simply wanted to return on its investment dollar. Companies offered stock without surrendering any of their autonomy and power, while asking that unions stop their strikes.[124] Workers concluded that profit-sharing was a bribe for their docility and substandard wages.

Between 1873 and 1877, some of the most violent years of American labor history, the national labor movement began to disintegrate. The Labor Union fell apart because it lost its economic focus trying to secure its ends primarily through political means. As cyclical economic disturbances drained union funds, the rank and file lost confidence in their union. Moreover, by the end of this period of depression, wages were lowered forty-five percent in some regions. Violence ensued as companied attempted to "bust" the unions by hiring strikebreakers (i.e., nonunion labor).

The National Federation of Labor replaced the National Labor Union as America's primary labor union. Learning from the previous mistakes, the Federation concentrated almost exclusively upon economic goals. Primarily a wage-conscious organization, the Federation attempted to organize a variety of trades in the late 1870s so as to demand the freer circulation of aggregate wealth. Repudiating strikes, violence, and forced collective bargaining, this union optimistically thought that voluntary arbitration could settle the differences between capital and labor.

Strikes and violence reached a fever pitch in 1877. For example, when the economic panic and depression of 1873 hit the rail industry, Pennsylvania Railroad cut wages by ten percent. Then, in 1877, it cut wages another ten percent. Violence ensued as sympathetic strikes and economic depression rippled throughout the economy. The management of Pennsylvania Railroad hired Pinkerton guards and nonunion workers to replace the union workers of the Brotherhood of Railway Conductors. Violence became so acute that two hundred federal troops were spread throughout Pittsburgh, Philadelphia, Baltimore, and portions of the state of West Virginia to quell the riots. Millions of dollars of damage was done. Such violence caused the federal courts to begin to reconsider the necessity of union and capital parity. Labor solidarity, the necessity for a just wage, and public shock over federal troops supporting management were vehicles that brought some much-needed respect and judicial sympathy for the unions after 1880.

The mainline American union movement—that is, the movement that consciously rejected the various socialist, communist, and anarchistic alternatives—was still, however, searching for a stable worldview around which to rally in the 1880s. There were several unique aspects of the American labor movement that evolved. The American middle class, out of which the unions were spawned, resisted being dominated in the trade union movement by the intellectual class. Rather, labor developed its identity through the hope of sharing in American prosperity.

In supporting the notion of private property through the Free Homestead Policy of the 1840's, "greenbackism" (inflated currency for the masses), and support of the workshops, the American labor movement mimicked a Jeffersonian capitalism. As such, the mainline American labor movement, such as the American Federation of Labor, fought the excesses of capitalism and not the roots of its worldview.[125] Moreover, unlike many of the European labor unions, the A.F.L. was a "wage- and job-conscious" union rather than a class-conscious union. Higher wages, a reduction in working hours, and a safe working environment became some of the primary objectives.

In 1883 the unions gained official court recognition. Accordingly, the unions' private property was protected, as was their right to collective bargaining and binding arbitration. Sadly, by 1885 an unusually large number of union officials were indicted for misusing union funds. Moreover, as they became noticeably prosperous, American unions became increasingly apathetic about addressing any cultural issues or in altering their own rationalized, centralized, bureaucratic management.[126]

During the 1880s American labor had to confront the influx of over six million emigrants who eagerly competed for their jobs. The press of immigration, along with expanding industrial production, caused industrial America to demand the incorporation of more public lands. As more and more fertile land was incorporated by Industrialism, the supply of many commodities rose sharply relative to the marginally increasing demand for laborers. The result of this confluence of supply and demand is that laborers' wages fell in the 1880s.[127]

The history of emigrant labor represents another striking example of Industrialism's incorporating ability. The European Enclosure Movement started to force poor landed farmers off of their tenant plots, and as this consolidation increased, famine, disease, social rootlessness, and economic dependency also soared. In short, they became peasants rather than self-sufficient but beleaguered farmers. By the mid-nineteenth century many European peasants became desperate owing to political injustice, famine, and a lack of economic opportunities. Lacking alternatives and tired of wandering throughout Europe, they came to America, often leaving their families behind.[128]

This geographic relocation brought about a radical change in the way the emigrant viewed the world. By the 1880s, American society was becoming much more urbanized, industrialized, and secular. This was marked contrast from an eastern European society that was often agrarian, rural, and socially and environmentally more interdependent. Before the European enclosure movements, life revolved around the village where the church, communal identity and acceptance lent a stability of life. Therefore, the relative anomie of industrializing America produced considerable confusion for the emigrant. Evangelical mores, class conflict, a predominantly Protestant ethos, and environmental damage were among the American ways that demanded a radically different way of life from the emigrant.[129]

Looking for stability and relief from such stress, emigrants increasingly took a conservative socioeconomic stance in America. By stressing clear-cut lines of familial and ecclesiastical authority, the maintenance of the economic system, and the centrality of the church in life, conservatism found eager emigrant adherents, and Protestant Fundamentalism often drew upon this class for their supporters. As they confronted secularizing American society from the beleaguered confines of the church, many emigrants became cultural pessimists, which in turn led them to a decidedly other-worldly eschatology. Many Protestant emigrants believed that sin held sway over the creation, while redemption meant an eternity in heaven.

Given such conservatism, cultural rigidity and their desire to be "melted" into the American pot of civil-capitalist religion, Protestant emigrants increasingly accepted the secularized American vision in which "religion" was relegated to being a private, sectarian, culturally conservative affair. In short, they lived a kind of split life which enabled them to be Christians in their church life and worldly people in their economic life.

Given the nature of incorporation, union capitulation to the demands of mechanization seemed inevitable. That the machine had gained such importance in the eyes of union and management alike testifies to a commonly held faith in scientific and technological thought and its ability to ensure cultural progress. "To watch a complex, automatic machine," cried Carroll D. Wright, the first commissioner of the United States Bureau of Labor in 1885,

> was to intuitively absorb lessons in science, harmony and beauty. The Brain is king and machinery is the king's Prime Minister.[130]

If one looks, for example, at the A.F.L.'s list of demands from 1890 onward, it appears rather shortsighted. Giving up on political, cultural or social change, the A.F.L. pursued the more narrow economic goals of fair wages, an eight-hour day, and various group benefits. Unions like the A.F.L. seemed to struggle for a rationalized union that made workers more efficient while at the same time richer and more secure in their jobs. By the advent of World War I, unions had become "incorporated" into the mill of domestic tranquility and mass production. As union and capital amalgamation progressed, competitive individualism began to anticipate what

J. K. Galbraith has called "countervailing powers." Concomitantly, "collective bargaining" meant not only winning increasingly great industrial rewards but exclusion for other communities like the Knights of Labor who, within the capitalistic framework, did not share the same narrow, economic ends of the A.F.L.[131] Thus, industrial violence, strikes and boycotts did not mean that unions wanted to torpedo Industrialism's luxury liner; rather, unions simply wanted to ensure its existence and to book passage.

A survey of the life of Terrance Powderly and the Knights of Labor will show how narrowly preoccupied with economic matters the A.F.L. was during this era.[132] Powderly saw economic struggles of the union within the full matrix of social relationships being affected by Industrialism. Before he became the Knights' Grand Master Workingman in 1879, he was mayor of Scranton, Pennsylvania for eight years. He fought for free public education for the worker, community centers for the elderly, cheap credit for the farmer, and a restriction of land given to the cattle, mineral and rail industries.[133] Moreover, as head of the Knight's, he fought monopolies by striking for labor and management's joint responsibility for wages, capital investment strategies, and price structure. Because of his stance against the autonomous use of private property, Powderly was often branded a Communist. In reality, Powderly's worldview was Biblically attuned, prompting him to affirm a cooperative, sensitive, stewardly use of natural resources: "Air, light, heat and food . . . are the property of all and should be husbanded, guarded and utilized for all. . . . Property is a trust from God and should be used for all."[134]

Powderly's Evangelical-like confession became the focus of a great deal of criticism from the Roman Catholic Church, to which he belonged.[135] He had argued that the institutional church had no right to assume any special place of importance in a culture that is institutionally diverse. He cried, "The great power that has come to Christianity through the teachings of Jesus Christ has largely been frittered away through the practice of Churchianity."[136] Faced by capitalism's economic demands, one can understand why the membership of the Knights dwindled to less than 100,000 by the turn of the century. But the strength of Powderly's ideals has not died, as we will see in our final chapter.

Homo Oeconomicus became the defining type for one union after another, as one can see in the works of the labor activist, theorist, and writer George Gunton. Gunton was a disciple of Ira Steward, the leading New England labor leader and one of the first public figures to argue for an eight-hour working day. Equating wealth, cultural progress, and the eight-hour day, Gunton argued in one of the most widely read labor books of its day that

> the progress of mental and moral development and of social, religious and political freedom are the consequences of . . . the permanent increase in the consumption of wealth per capita, which in turn depends upon a shorter work day and more leisure time, by the laboring population.[137]

I have attempted to trace the ascendancy of the modern spirit of Mammon by contrasting the "official" view of the Middle Ages on economic life with that of modern Industrialism. Perhaps the story can be summed up best by the noted American economist Thomas Nixon Carver. He attributed religious ultimacy, during the years surrounding World War One, to the functions of economics when he said, "The best religion is that which acts most powerfully as a spur to energy and directs that energy to the most productive economic means."[138] A secularized era thought it had created its most energetic religion in this synthesis. But was there mold growing within this gilded, caramel-coated age?

4

Classical Christian Theorists

Accommodation seems inevitable; but is it desirable?

"Accommodation," means the admixture of at least two fundamentally conflicting worldviews such that the resultant synthesis retains some properties of the original views. In this chapter we will discuss how the synthetic character of American Evangelicalism-capitalism relates to the socioeconomic views of Augustine, Aquinas, Luther and Calvin.

That accommodation would occur seems almost inevitable. Such forces as personal and cultural atomization, fragmentation and specialization, mechanization, and avarice were enormous. To counteract these forces would have required a herculean commitment to certain values that would not have played well in this era: interdependence, the sovereignty of God versus popular sovereignty, a critique of modern notions of science and technology without lapsing into either an anti-intellectualism or a cultural reclusiveness, and, finally, a rigorously developed socioeconomic alternative. When alternatives were attempted, they seemed shortsighted and reactionary rather than thetic and progressive.

Augustine, Aquinas, Luther, and Calvin were not economists; they were theologians and philosophers of religion. However, they were forced by the events of their respective times to relate the Christian faith to economic activity. Their notions were never fully elaborated into systematic economic doctrine, but when set opposite capitalism's nineteenth-century presupposita, a decided clash of principles is apparent.

Augustine

Our main intent in looking at Augustine is to see how he related the biblical themes of creation, fall, and redemption in Christ to his basic ethic and how this in turn determined his conception of meaning and limits of economic activity.

Creation, for Augustine, was the providentially ordered potentiality of meaningful relationships. However integrally Augustine might have wanted to portray his view of creation, it nevertheless contained certain Greek dualistic notions.[1] In his thinking, creation's motor was not autonomous natural law but providence qua harmony. This essentially good harmony, he thought, could be misdirected and distorted. God's creational-providential law formed the basis of human affairs, and its order was the foundation of peace and equity. According to Augustine, "The peace of all things is the tranquillity of order." Furthermore, "order is the distribution which allots things equal and unequal each to its own place."[2] This order was not meant to be inhibiting or restrictive but to function as a boundary and incentive for human action. Augustine used the term *finis* to describe the way in which each area or aspect of creation is bounded but at the same time interrelated to other aspects of creation.[3] The *finis* formed the context for human action and purpose.

Such limits and meaningfulness were established by a righteous law, an *iustitia* or law-order. The cosmic scope of this law-order was given to humanity so we could dwell in right relationship to creation, God, and our fellow man.[4] While flexible, these laws could not be broken without basic human disruptions occurring in social and personal intercourse. For example, Rome could not continually violate the notion of justice, through its imperialism, and hope to long remain a civilization. Thus, the *iustitia* or just order became both a positive command and limit as well as negative judgment upon all human action.

Augustine was no abstract philosopher. In his major work, *The City of God,* Augustine was writing to defend Christianity against the charge that it was responsible for the fall of Rome. He maintained that all earthly life was divided between the commitments and ultimacies of the *civitas Dei* and *civitas terrena,* or the city of God as focused in the Christian church and the City of Man as seen in Rome and Babylon. Both cities are characterized by love—the one by the love of self, power, and status *(cupiditas),* and the other by the love of God and service of neighbor *(caritas).* Furthermore, it is in the collective heart of humanity or religious center of life that these two cities are differentiated and initiated.[5] Rome was failing basically because in its love for itself and its own wealth and power, Rome had fallen into a cancerous corruption. In short, self-interest could not serve as an adequate social glue.

And so the two cities have been fashioned by two loves, the earthly city by the love of self to the contempt of God, the heavenly city by the love of God to the contempt of self. Lust for dominion dominates the one . . . [but] in the other rulers and ruled alike serve one another in love.[6]

The ubiquity of love, service, commitment, and faithfulness cuts across the two cities and becomes their basis and incentive for cohesion. Accordingly, Augustine characterizes the worldly city as built upon the concept of self-love which culminates in, among other things, private property. Private property and its concomitant lust for gain obscures a healthy love for neighbor and for God, according to Augustine.

Such self-love is prompted by hubris and pretension of autonomy; it forces a portion of creation to assume an affectation of divinity. Thus, Mammon can be "trusted in," "hoped for," and "depended upon" for personal and cultural meaning. As a result, an aspect of creation becomes an end in itself and hence is idolatrous.[7] Such idolatry is concretely seen in the sin of avarice or lust for objects of pleasure. "Self-pleasers" serve only their own lusts and cannot be counted upon to serve society. Augustine reasoned that this self-love, if unchecked, eventuates (because of the interconnectedness of life) in economic and political imperialism because the regard for self becomes absolute.

Two crucial points should be noted at this juncture. First, if Augustine is correct, the motor for religious incorporation, as defined in chapters 2 and 3, has been discovered. Under capitalism's definition of self-love, America has attempted to radically remake a variety of cultural relationships under the guise of self-interest. While enormously successful, the power of incorporation is limited by the *iustitia* of creation. For example, the growing chorus of protest over environmental destruction seems here and there to be limiting industrialism's waste and mismanagement. This point will be more fully developed in the last chapter.

Augustine argued that idolatry and its effects, while deep and pervasive, are not the last and most forceful power in the creation. Accordingly, sin is not sovereign. Again, "peace is tranquility bestowed by order, order is the arrangement of equal and unequals which assigns each its proper place."[8] Thus, salvation is, in part, a call to return to the creational harmony stripped away by sin; it becomes, in effect, a re-creation. Avarice, greed, and wealth-seeking for its owns sake is, after Christ, a violation of God's re-created order.[9] Any worldview, such as ancient Epicureanism, that attempts to ensure order by the principle of avaricious passions only succeeds in securing a temporary narcotic of possessions and pleasure.

Though being oriented to "the City which comes from above," Christians, Augustine argues, cannot escape cultural responsibility. The *City of God* discusses principles of commerce, art, literature, worship, government, and family life at length. The reader is struck, however, by how sharply Augustine's principles differ from those of nineteenth-century secularism and Evangelical Protestantism. In resisting idolatry while calling the creation good, Augustine would have limited the dominion of Industrialism for the sake of various sociocultural needs. For example, if family life is being eroded by the industrial process, as Thomas Bell portrays in *Out of the Furnace,* Industrialism must be restructured to avoid this. As we shall see, his emphasis upon the completely distinctive character of God's kingdom and the breadth of its scope stand in sharp contrast to Evangelical theological accommodation and myopia.[10]

The *Corpus Christianum*

The later Augustine and medieval Catholicism emphasized the institutional church and concomitant ecclesiastical relationship as the focus and goal of Christ's kingdom.[11] As we have already seen, medieval society was to be, in theory, a *corpus Christianum.* Human and natural life were situated in a hierarchical society which was undergirded by a belief in the supernatural; grace was added to life to perfect nature. The Church was to complete the state and business. The sacred was to complement the secular. The social organism was supposed to be made up of at least three distinct parts or classes: priests, monks, and laymen. The general social division was clergy and laity. Service, duty, profit, initiative, and self-interest were operative but were to be mitigated by a view of the good of the whole. A rationally based natural law was thought to guarantee one's "calling" *(officium)* within a rather rigid traditionalism compatible enough with medieval feudalism. Peasants and laborers were paternalistically protected, but forced to live in a stagnated, stratified society, headed by the instiutional church. This situation resulted in ecclesiasticism[12]—the attempted orientation of life around the dictates of ecclesiastical structures and in the institutional Church.

The church of the early Middle Ages became the central agency for social administration. A unified sacerdotal church hoped to encourage a thoroughgoing liaison between church, state, and society, and thereby to secure social harmony. Thus, the Carolingian monarchy settled theological disputes, while the Church gave the state administrative order, science, and basic agricultural development. Proving successful renters and small tenant farmers, churches were granted more land, charter privileges, tax immunities and land grants. Thus, a rural agricultural economy developed with the Church at the center of much of land and wealth acquisition.[13]

By A.D. 1000 weak administration, internal disputes, and deficits caused many proto-European nations to fragment, and their power passed to feudal lords and the Church. Augustine's proto-ecclesiasticism now became a reality as churches inherited this cultural dislocation. Concomitantly, Pope Gregory VII extended the "domain of salvation" to cover both spiritual and temporal matters. This consolidation of socioeconomic life and papal authority, completed by the time of the Gregorian rulers in the twelfth century, was justified by canon law on the grounds that social righteousness should extend to secular activities.

The new order stressed external obedience to authority and was therefore antithetical in spirit to modern capitalism's view of freedom. The fabric of society, woven as it was by canon law and duty, needed no "cash nexus" or social contracts for social reciprocity. Moreover, nature was not yet rationalized by technology (though it was by Aristotelian reason). Human labor was not calculable or something to be bought and sold. Relatively primitive forms of communication and transportation, coupled with dogmatic rigidity, seemed to ensure a caste-like societal structure antithetical to capitalism's social fluidity. Laborers who worked on common property could find release in the early towns, the existence of which was due to commercial functions. However, such commerce was predicated upon a fellowship of labor (literally, a "common-wealth").

The paternalistic mutuality of such a stratified system stands in marked contrast to modern individualism. It provided an ethic that attempted to relate all parts to the welfare of the whole. In theory, prices were set, profits ordered, and exchange managed so that no one person or group fared better than another. Accordingly, economic justice was not the product of impersonal market forces or the aftermath of charity; rather it was supposed to be guaranteed by the all-powerful church and social obligations of quid pro quo. Guilds existed so long as their existence was not based on economic egoism. Ultimately all economic interests were to be subject to grace or salvation as interpreted by canon law. Medieval theory taught that all such acquisitive appetites owed their origin to sin and were therefore made the brunt of severe legislation.[14]

In spite of its hypocrisies and abuses, the medieval church militated against the danger of unrestricted economic activity by using the state to help regulate the economy. The state could, for example, fix prices, if this was necessary to maintain social harmony.[15] While perpetuating its own form of incorporation and institutional chauvinism, the medieval church, nevertheless, attempted to create a social harmony among cultural institutions—as long as they served the Church.

Within this general framework, Thomistic economics sought to place exchange in the service of the Church. Economic value was to be based upon agriculture and local commercial exchange. The interdependent nature of society was to be reproduced in smaller communities, like guilds, engaged in similar work. Such loose-knit associations restricted entry, and hence became de facto monopolies. Whenever adverse market fluctuations occurred, these protected the social welfare of their members.

Laborers of many kinds were to earn only subsistence wages. Classes were not divided according to places taken within the commercial system but by their nearness to the spheres of grace. Physical, intellectual, political and ecclesiastical vocations were to receive "minimum" but ascending salaries fitted to their social rank. Thus, an attempt was made to limit avarice and differentiate society according to ability and worth.

Given the medieval suspicion of money, it is not surprising that avarice was deemed one of the seven deadly sins. When Florence was becoming the first successful financial capital in Europe, its bankers and merchants were often penalized by the church of Rome for charging excess usury rates. In these conflicts we not only see some of the forces of proto-capitalism at work, but a clash of worldviews. Selling dear and buying cheap, usury, and market manipulation were strictly forbidden.[16]

The full weight of Aristotle's pen, medieval exegesis and canon law fell upon the money lender. "To take usury is contrary to Scripture; it is contrary to Aristotle; it is contrary to nature, for it is to live without labor. Moreover, it is to sell time, which only belongs to God."[17] To this injunction was added the prohbitions of many church councils—those of Elvira (305), Arles (314), Nicea (325), Carthage (345), Aix (789), Fourth Lantern (1215), and Vienna (1311). But more and more exceptions had to be allowed as time passed. One such exception was the *damaum emergens*.

A lender may, without sin, enter an agreement with a borrower for compensation for the loss he incurs of something he ought to have, for this is not to sell the use of money but to avoid loss.[18]

All these policies could be maintained because the medieval system did not need large-scale commercial credits, as most loans were drawn from family or friends. But emergent capitalism, with its practices of insurance, world trade, and land speculation, strained the abilities of even the most brilliant medieval casuists. Eventually, avarice, a sign in the Middle Ages of sin, became a capitalistic virtue. While the medieval church attempted to harness economic forces, its principle economic values could not be called ascetic. A tension existed between the natural forces of economic life and those of our spiritual life, but no attempt was made to entirely purge medieval life of economic desires.[19]

The Schoolmen's notion of a just price represented yet another attempt to limit avarice or greed. Aquinas maintained that the price of goods or services should not exceed the labor and overhead of the producers. The needs of the community, or the *communis estimatio,* were to represent *the* factor in determining the price. In case a Florentine merchant in the thirteenth century decided, by reason of cupidity, to raise the price of Far Eastern silk, the Church would press strongly, through local government, for price ceilings. Local governments, however, were not sufficiently able to control prices. As trade routes yielded treasures hitherto unknown, supplies soared and pulled demand and prices along.

Moderation and traditionalism also marked medieval economic theory and practice. Market dynamism was unheard of in medieval society. Order, rank, "calling," paternalistic protection, and price regulation were the hallmarks of a society that knew and feared the potential power of unrestricted economic activity. To counteract the threat of unrestricted economic activity, rationalistic natural law, Aristotelian scientific rationality, and, above all, grace or the *donum superadditum* were applied to economic activity in an attempt to keep it "in its place"—that is, subservient to the interests of the people and the "needs" of the Church.

Ironically, after capitalism had burst these fetters of provicialism, and religion was often cloistered away in nearly irrelevant cultic institutions, the modern capitalistic state and economic agents emerged to act as the force of social glue. With all of its abuses, contradictions, and dualisms, the spirit of medieval law would speak loudly against an "incorporated" society. It would maintain that commercial and material affair can never become ends in themselves, because economic gain makes poor cultural glue. Thus, an "acquisitive society," whose primary needs are thought to be economic, would be considered destructive. Sadly, the modern era has seemingly substituted, de facto, one institutional chauvinism for another: business for the institutional church.

Martin Luther

Luther carried on, at certain key points, the medieval traditionalism of Aquinas; therefore, this section is brief. My interest in Luther stems primarily from the fact that he, as a theologian, found himself in the midst of a German cultural revolt and proto-German capitalism. Confronted with the commercialism of sixteenth-century Germany, Luther romantically longed for the day of precommercial life. But with the return to such days impossible, Luther supported a rudimentary form of physiocratic economics. Accordingly, he maintained early in 1520 "that it would be much more pleasing to God if we increased in agriculture and diminished in commerce because of its abuses."[20]

Luther's stress on agricultural economy led him early in his career to glorify the economics of peasant life. Simple labor-intensive farmers and craftsmen were the focus of Luther's labor theories, such as they were. Sellers and traders, and their profits and supplies, were considered evils, but necessary because they furnished the mandatory tools for labor. Many other forms of trade were considered excessively luxurious and therefore were condemned.[21]

Luther's primary program was theological; that is, he was trying to define the theological heart of the Christian message vis-à-vis Catholic theology. Accordingly, he maintained that one is justified, or made right with God, solely by faith in Jesus Christ and not by works. Good works, including economic ethics, became a gracious by-product of Christ's righteousness given to us through repentance and trust. Therefore, he set himself against the spirit of German commercialism, which maintained that salaries could be "earned" as *necessary* results of human labor. The exploitation of the peasant and laborer by the papacy, monopolistic craftsmen and merchants represented a departure from justification by faith alone, according to Luther, because the sale of salvation through indulgences and the restriction of labor and goods from free exchange seemed to deny the fact that life was a gift.

The exploitation of the Church by the Papacy and the exploitation of the peasant and the craftsmen by the Capitalist are thus two horns of the beast which sits on the seven hills. They are both pagan.[22]

Indeed, it was one of Luther's cardinal theses that in grace we are born and unto grace we die; so, no activity of life can be earned, only shared graciously.

Because life was a gift, the economic order was to be characterized by frugality and sustenance; it would be presumptuous to demand more. Private property was to be accorded to one's rank and shared with others, especially those of lower rank. In an agricultural economy, Luther naturally stressed a labor theory of value whereby wealth owed its origin to the amount of labor used to produce a good. Labor *(Beruf)* was both a calling to a vocation and stratification into a class. Breaking with the medieval notion of the hierarchy of rank and worth, Luther stressed that all vocations were calling of equal importance. All estates and works were to be valued, therefore, if done to the glory of God and in service to one's neighbor. Unlike the Schoolmen, Luther at times raised the status of the worker and allowed him to attain an equality with the priest and monk.[23] Such an elevation of everyday life stood in sharp contrast to the medieval vocational chauvinism of the priesthood.

Luther believed that the fruits of one's labor should never be hoarded. Personal property and wealth were collective in the sense that economic relations grew out of and had to serve society's needs. He believed, therefore, in a *gebundene Geldwirtschaft* or group ideal. Accordingly, the very fabric and structure of economic activity needed to demonstrate the mutual interconnectedness of community life. Such as ideal should be protected by both church and state, according to Luther.

After the German princes and state refused to send cash payments to Rome, Germany was faced with enormous amounts of cash begging to be invested. Hungry borrowers flooded various markets, pushing interest rates upward. As borrowing soared, so did debt and default. This situation did not initially trouble Luther, for he thought such instances gave one the chance to practice economic forgiveness.[24] He soon realized, however, the impracticality of such advice, and came to support a state-imposed limit of four percent on any loan, thus encouraging more careful borrowing.[25]

German commercial monopolies came under special attack from Luther. His words about the monopolists of his time were prophetic of nineteenth-century monopolists.

They have brought things to pass that everybody has to do business with them at the risk of loss . . . while they only win, making up their losses by increased profits. It is no wonder that they quickly appropriate the wealth of the *whole world.*[26]

Accordingly, Luther was no advocate of the unfettered expression of the laws of supply and demand. He rightly saw that unrestrained competition tears at the fabric of society. He even went so far as to reject the autonomous market view of the interplay of supply and demand, fearing that it would lead to monopoly. He favored state intervention into the economy.[27]

Commanded as he was by the ethic of love, and in spite of his traditionalism, Luther called medieval Christians away from the forces of excessive profit-seeking and easy religious accommodation. This fact is especially apparent in Luther's conflict with the medieval monopolist Jakob Fugger.[28]

During the sixteenth century a variety of conditions led to the German Peasants' Revolt to which Luther reacted. As commercial and financial capitalism grew, it spawned an international policy of trade and government-sponsored monopolies. The Antwerp monopoly took agricultural capital and turned it into venture capital for merchants hungry for Oriental goods. In turn, these monopolies controlled the market supplies, thus causing prices to rise in all economic sectors. Jakob Fugger tried to corner the copper and silver markets in Germany by buying up all the mines and introducing such proto-Industrial measures as hydraulic power and a crude form of mass production. Paralleling this movement was Germany's version of the enclosure movement, or land consolidation, and the growth of private property. The resultant mixture of capital concentration, loss of communal land, inflation, the weakened guild system, and social powerlessness forced the peasants into increasingly extreme measures.

Before 1524, Luther had tried to steer a middle course between the German autocracy, who favored the forces of protocapitalism, and the peasants, who were content to live off the land (as the Physiocrats later would be). The breaking point came in 1524 when the peasants rose up and looted monasteries, pillaged castles, and refused to tend fields. Incensed, Luther wrote *Against the Murderous and Robbing Bands of Peasants,* in which he concluded, "An ass must be beaten and rabble governed by force."[29] Luther was suggesting that the state use its powers to smash the uprising, which of course it did.

As he became more deeply involved in the plight of the peasant, Luther experienced the tension between the demands of the peasants, knights, and small landlords for justice, and the power of the rising merchant class. After 1522 Luther restricted *Beruf* or "calling" to one's station or "stand" in life. Simultaneously, he equated office or function *(Amt)* with duty or *Befehl.*[30] The effect of equating God's calling with *a particular* social function, as the linking of "calling" with office does, was to lead Luther into increasingly conservative and reactionary lines.

With the crushing of the Peasants' Revolt the strengths and weaknesses of Luther's economic ethic become clear, as does that ethic's remarkable parallel to the ethic of postbellum progressive Evangelicalism. Increasingly, Luther trusted the government for the fulfillment of the needs of his "group ideal." German businessmen could give charity for the relief of peasants, but no economic solution was found, as capitalism continued to displace the lower classes, who became the wards of a protowelfare state.[31] Such secular affairs as social welfare fell to the provincial government, while the Church increasingly concerned itself with the salvation of the soul and the "inwardness" of personal spirituality. Ironically, such personalism ended up supporting, de facto, an incipient mercantilism and proto-industrialization, as we have noted in the Evangelical context.

Luther's increasing emphasis on inwardness subsequently evolved into a form of German pietism which emphasized personal piety and salvation over effective economic equity. The stress on inner peace tended to a social quietism that placed a premium on unquestioning obedience to civil authorities. Furthermore, Luther's bifurcation of the Christian life into dualities of law and gospel, spiritual and temporal, individual and social, and grace and nature contributed to the gradual erosion of the possibility of deep social renewal, as his worldview could not penetrate to the roots of cultural development.[32]

In short, political and economic decisions were increasingly left to the secular realm of state and business while many German Christians retreated to an increasingly theologically oriented Christianity.

John Calvin

Unlike Luther's, Calvin's economic sympathies lay not with agriculture but with the urban bourgeoisie. His teaching reflects a much more progressive acceptance of capital, profits, commerce, banking, wages and rent as good gifts from God. Moreover, his version of the Christian faith as it pertains to a Christian economic ethic is much more radical and integral. He saw the force of Christ's person and work as transforming the depth or root of the human situation as well as its breadth. Moreover, he eschewed Luther's more drastic dualisms in favor of seeing God's grace mediated through a variety of social institutions. Speaking of Christ's initiated kingdom or reign in heaven *and upon earth* and its effect upon politics and economics, Calvin said, "For spiritual government, indeed, is already initiating in us upon earth certain beginnings of the Heavenly Kingdom. . . . Yet civil government has its [divinely] appointed end so long as we live among men."[33]

The civil government was to ensure smooth economic exchange and a feeling of solidarity and equity among the affairs of men.[34] Calvin's economic ethic revolved around one fundamental dictum. In his sermon on 2 Corinthians 8:13–14 he said.

> God wills that there be proportion and equity among us; each man is to provide for the needy according to his means so that no man has too much and no man has too little.[35]

This notion presupposed, as we have said, an economic solidarity that best can be demonstrated in the affairs of international trade. Calvin favored international trade so long as such trade manifested a spirit of interdependence and resulted in mutual social benefit.[36]

Calvin believed that one concrete way of fulfilling such solidarity was through one's calling. The primary calling came in salvation, but salvation resulted in a second calling, or a vocation. Unlike Luther, Calvin did not associate calling with a particular social position or rank or worth, though he did equate it with the lawful fulfillment of one's created purpose.[37] Unlike the Schoolmen, Calvin accepted one's created purpose as essentially pleasing to God and therefore allowed no ranks of vocational worth of dignity.[38]

Humanity's fundamental economic calling was to be a steward of God's earth. Accordingly, all that we possess was considered a divine deposit entrusted to us for sharing with our neighbor.[39] This concept diametrically opposes any notion of self-interest as social glue. Strikingly, Calvin says, "Thus it will come about that we shall not only join zeal for another's benefit with care for our own advantage, but shall subordinate the latter to the former."[40]

It was in the city, and not merely the church of Geneva, that Calvin practiced his concept of stewardship. Calvin helped set up a common purse for public relief, developed a low-cost hospital which cared for the widows and orphans, and helped establish a low-cost, common granary where seed and food could be bought.

Moreover, Geneva became a city of refuge for oppressed Protestants who were fleeing Catholic persecution throughout Europe.[41]

Because Calvin saw the functions of money as an essentially good gift—albeit, one often corrupted by human greed—he did not see money, as the medievalists did, as a natural means to a supernatural end. Rather, money became a natural symbol of God's grace to be used for the glory of God by fulfilling one's neighbors' needs. Calvin helped establish a bank in Geneva in 1544, and he persuaded the municipality to limit the interest rate to 5% so that the poor and working class could afford loans. Calvin arrived at the rather arbitrary figure of 5% because he wanted to prevent the bankers' unscrupulous usury. However, this excessively low rate soon caused a drain on capital reserves, whereupon he settled for a yearly rate of 6.6%.[42]

Although against excessive lending rates, Calvin could affirm the worth of circulating capital and the justice of being repaid for the use of one's money: "Usury is not unlawful except insofar as it contravenes equity and brotherly union."[43] In these last words, "equity" and "brotherly love" we see the key to Calvin's economic ethic. Equity was violated when the poor had to borrow at high rates, or when the lender took undue advantage of the borrower by making that person pay both principal and interest when his investments failed. Loans were only approved of by Calvin insofar as they promoted the public good.

Calvin always had compassion for the poor, especially when their industry could not secure their basic needs. In a famous passage, Calvin calls the poor the "vicars" and the "receivers" of God. "God sends us the poor as receivers. To give to the poor is to give to God."[44] As economic incorporation began to affect the poor, Calvin thundered against rich monopolists:

> If they were able they would have a sun all to themselves in order to say that the others had nothing in common with them. If they were able, it is certain that they would change the whole order of God and nature so they could swallow everything.[45]

Because Calvin viewed labor as a good gift from God, he could condemn idleness and indiscriminate living. The poor, he thought, should be able to support themselves by work. However, if they could not work, the fault lay not with the poor, for poverty was not the sign of God's disfavor, just as riches were not always to be taken as a sign of God's pleasure.[46] The "pious" were to be charitable to the poor. Charity started with the *manner* and *mode* of business and governmental policy, and was therefore not a by-product of a system that made autonomous profits and shared the excess with those who had been left behind by the production process.

Calvin's deep concern for rewarding the labor of the poor, his views of equity and solidarity, and his hatred of greed separated him from any economic view that values profit and expansion above all. His principle of equity, a principle not based singly on the free play of market forces, afforded no precise mathematical expression because justice was not primarily a quantifiable entity. Such principles were embedded in an integrally woven worldview that would have considered a rationalized society to be an oxymoron. Thus, I submit that Calvin's ethic would give no credence to economic individualism.[47]

Calvin's notion of salary is an extension of his view of the importance of grace in the life of the Christian. "Man has no right to remuneration from God. Anything we receive is from the free goodness of God. Out of the free goodness of God we receive a salary."[48] Obviously Calvin was not against getting paid fairly. He was speaking out against wage demands which demonstrated no sensitivity to others, such as would be the case with inflationary wage demands. Moreover, he maintained that wages do not ultimately belong to the capitalists to dispose of as they see fit; rather, they are a stewardly gift to be shared equitably and in proportion to one's need.

Calvin also had to contend with economic monopolies. Responding in Geneva to the artificial restriction of food supplies in the market, Calvin helped institute price controls to protect the poor. He spoke against the rich when he said,

> Today when everything has such a high price, we see men who keep their granaries artificially closed; this is as if they cut the throat of the poor.[49]

Likewise, Calvin attacked those who would artificially reduce the laborer's wage in the time of an abundance of labor. He would also disparage the concept of self-regulating market, because it tended to objectify labor, causing, too many class hostilities, while putting the worker in a dependent position.[50]

Thus, we may conclude that Calvin was no capitalist! Economic rationalization and autonomy, individualism, avarice, and autonomous private property were not part of his worldview (as they are in capitalism's). While not disparaging economic production and consumption per se, he did speak against their abuses. Accordingly, he established sumptuary laws limiting extravagance and waste.[51]

Though upholding the cause of the poor, Calvin did not chide the rich; he simply wanted reconciliation and harmony. In 1539 a particularly ugly fight erupted between several unions and their employers in Geneva. He argued that the local council should intervene through a crude form of binding arbitration and, thereby, bring a peaceful solution to this dispute. The agreements that were reached stressed four points. First, no managerial wage collusion minimizing labor's wage would be permitted. Secondly, journeymen laborers would have guaranteed jobs for an agreed-upon period. Thirdly, the daily hours worked would be reduced to ten. And finally, labor unions would not be permitted unless workers could receive justice no other way.[52]

It can not be denied that compared with contemporary standards, Geneva seems like a harsh place to live—but then again, so does every other place in the sixteenth century. The charge that Geneva was a theocracy—that is, a church-ruled society—is at least highly debatable. Calvin never sought or occupied a political office, and, he attempted to separate church and state much more than did many of his peers. Like other ethically sensitive thinkers, he did seek to relate his faith to life through a balance of economic and political interests.

One essential way Calvin sought to relate his faith to life was to see the sovereignty of God as joined to various spheres or aspects of life. Accordingly, areas such as the Church, state, and business were to have their own respective spheres of influence and integrity while not unduly impinging upon other spheres. Tawney says of this notion, "[Calvinism] sought to renew society by penetrating every department of life, public as well as private . . ."[53]

In one form or another, abused or not, this notion of the various spheres of life has been constantly attested to by the authors cited. The mutual integrity and interconnectedness of spheres formed the basis for a view of social responsibility in which each of the various social spheres had tasks to perform. Had such a notion existed for nineteenth-century Evangelicals, both incorporation and religious synthesis might have been lessened.

Though their economic views were somewhat different, the four authors cited are in agreement on several fronts. All condemned individualism and economic greed, as well as excessive usury. All attempted some degree of social and institutional harmony. Calvin and Luther condemned ecclesiasticism and a Roman version of natural law. In so doing, they wrestled their ethic from the jaws of an impersonal market mechanism. Finally, with the exceptions of the Thomistic view of the relationship of reason to natural law and

Luther's medievalism, the thinkers in question were *not* a conservative lot. Christian theory cannot be used as a support for capitalism's worldview.

In saying this, I am not trying urge society to return to preindustrial, precapitalistic days, days in which the great principles of Christianity supposedly held more societal sway. Even assuming there once was a "Christian civilization" and that we could turn back the hands of time (at best, dubious assumptions), we would find ourselves missing much that is good in capitalism. Circulating capital, a production rate that can significantly address human need, incentive, technological competence, and the integrity of economic activities are, in my opinion, undeniable blessings. But it does seem prudent to try to look forward and (pardon the pun) to "re-form" current economic realities.

Calvin's ethics in particular, manifests many sound economic principles. He attempted to mediate labor/management disputes and hence anticipated the modern notions of reconciliation and codetermination. While he fought greed, he could affirm the necessity and the goodness of circulating wealth, and a just interest rate when money was used to make more money. His celebration of our created goodness led him to support all forms of human labor, as long as it was nurtured in a soil of solidarity and equity. In these senses, Calvin helped usher us into modern life, though he did not support capitalism.

5

A Transatlantic Intermezzo

This chapter will focus on some crucial ties between the people of Britain and the United States. Just as Britain and America interfaced on industrial matters, so also did they blend their talents on some faith concerns. A survey of this relationship between two countries whose values are in several respects similar should deepen the hues and tones of this work.

British Industrialism and British Evangelicalism

British Industrialism began to emerge as a major social force during the Victorian era (1832–1900). The effects of Industrialism upon British society can hardly be overstated. There was, as one might expect, a "constant, rapid, enormous increase in wealth and manufacturing power."[1] This increase, as in America, was especially due to the advent of the steam engine and the widely used railroad. In fact, early British rail development greatly exceeded that of America.[2]

Victorian and industrial culture shared the values of discipline, free choice, feverishness in business relations, individualism and a hunger for "religious" experience.[3] As a result of monumental industrial changes, the British mentality, like the American, was marked by such presupposita as laissez-faire economics, free competition, individualism, and the necessity of revival.[4]

Like the classical economists, many British thinkers equated autonomous self-interest and harmonious market activity with natural law. Economic liberty was promoted to a normative social principle whose workings were allegedly guaranteed by Divine Providence. In short, self-interest and a free market were considered "gospel" for much of English society. It was thought this "gospel" would ensure universal public benefits and would naturally override excessive forms of self-interest.[5] Individualistic self-help as well as

116

social and personal optimism seemed to flourish in a British society being converted to industrial values.

Like their American antebellum counterparts, the British rode a wave of social optimism during the first half of the nineteenth century. Revivals created a confidence and hope that paralleled hopes for economic progress.[6] Like their American colleagues, many British Evangelicals increasingly confused economic and spiritual progress.

At the same time, British Evangelicals did have to respond to the problem of the growing gap between the rich and the poor during this era. This gap, in fact, became a problem of the first order in that day.[7] The Industrial Revolution was so complete and devastating that poverty "evolved" into pauperism for many in England. In Manchester, for example, shareholding took effect whereby the rich and moderately wealthy could invest venture capital in the burgeoning industrial cities. This procedure widened the gap between the rich and poor as investment was segregated from social responsibility. The quality of housing and sanitation declined and alcoholism increased. In fact, alcohol prices in Manchester were artificially lowered by the merchants so as to encourage consumption.[8]

During the British revival of 1858 (which had considerable echoes across the Atlantic), middle-class British Evangelicals began to attempt to remedy such situations through the revival mechanism. Although this revival touched all classes, the middle class molded the revivals around the virtues of frugality, diligence, and respectability,[9] as well as economic and social mobility.[10] Methodism provided a particularly striking example of upwardly mobile middle-class Evangelical revivalism.[11] Attempting to counter alcoholism, Methodist revivalists significantly sobered many an industrial mind bent on a prosperity. Religious enthusiasm inflated depressed industrial spirits, giving the revived enough hope to quicken the industrial pace.

Middle-class industrial values, although embraced by some dissenting churches, tended to divide congregations and produce hostility. During this mid-century revival, lower middle-class laborers were the class most estranged from Evangelical churches.[12] As classes solidified and divided over industrial questions, churches tended to represent one or the other of the class viewpoints. Thus, class reconciliation was difficult to establish. The division of ecclesiastical bodies according to class sympathies was especially true of English Baptists and Methodists.[13]

The reasons for this class estrangement are noteworthy. A gradual geographic separation had occurred between investors, managers and the middle class, on one hand, and workers, on the other. While the former group moved beyond the factories to avoid the increasingly destructive effects of industry, the latter group was found in the cramped row houses in or near industrial cities. This physical separation evolved into alienation. Moreover—and this was especially true in the Anglican church—as clergy became better educated, their sermons seemed too esoteric and too insensitive to working-class values. Sermons on strict Sabbath observance, the superfluousness of amusements, belief in hard work and deferred gratification, and intolerance of failure only seemed to inflame class hostilities. Perhaps the most destructive spirit that filled the churches, however, was the commercial spirit, for what spirit better breeds class jealousies?[14]

There is no clear-cut line between Evangelical and non-Evangelical social action in Britain during this period, due to the commonality of industrial problems. However, Evangelicals tended to focus their activities in three areas that were pertinent to industry. First and foremost, they built churches. In 1818, Parliament passed a "New Churches Bill" authorizing one million pounds for church construction. Sharing Anglican church sentiment, Evangelicals believed construction would help counteract social destruction. Ironically, Evangelicals favored this kind of government support of church life while rejecting governmental interference in the economic market place.[15]

Paralleling this drive was an Evangelical commitment to "mission halls." Afraid that formal worship settings would discourage the lower classes from attending revivals, monied Evangelicals rented or built auditoriums in poorer sections of urban centers. Some theaters were rented for "protracted" or week-long services that generated mountains of local publicity. By 1909 the Wesleyan Methodists alone controlled forty-one such halls around the nation.[16]

Thirdly, Evangelicals establishes settlement houses to counteract slums and to help those who were recently revived. Concerned middle-class Evangelicals moved to impoverished urban areas, bought small homes, and converted them into centers for specific problems. Many volunteers were academics who were trying to provide concrete help. Out of this movement came the Salvation Army.[17]

Much of this Evangelical social ministry to the economically and socially disenfranchised grew out of an older and more foundational movement within Protestant Christendom. Pietism, as it has been called, owes its origins to a reaction in Germany and England against the Protestant intellectual orthodoxy of the seventeenth century. Rather than being overly concerned with the rigors of theological reflection, Pietism chose to emphasize personal piety and the ascetic temperament. Stressing small group sharing, personal encounters with Christ, and testimonials, Pietism tended to shun deep ecclesiastical and social involvement. While pietists were involved in social reform, social perform per se usually was considered of secondary importance to the mission of saving individual souls.[18]

The list of more mainline Evangelical social accomplishments is considerable. In addition to helping overturn the Atlantic slave trade, they fought for Christian schools, vagrant homes, soup kitchens, factory health reforms and child labor laws, libraries and infirmaries.[19] Several Evangelical social activists, such as William Wilberforce, T. F. Buxton and Lord Shaftesbury, drew national attention to their causes because of their exceptional reputations. Although Evangelical social ministry was too often unsystematic, poorly organized and in competition with other groups working in similar areas, its revivals perhaps saved England from a social disaster through their earnest social ministries.[20]

There is, however, a more precise question that must be asked. What was the relationship between the Evangelical definition of salvation, humanitarianism, and the market structure? In rejecting the Calvinist emphasis on the sovereignty of God, nineteenth-century Evangelicals, on both sides of the Atlantic, believed that humanity could secure its own salvation through an autonomous choice of the human will.[21] This religious self-sufficiency was carried over into a second basic religious experience called "perfectionism" or "entire sanctification." According to this doctrine, Christians could become "pure from the spot of *all* sin" before they died.[22] Realizing this new, exalted state, the Christian would want to share the fruits of their religious experience and their wealth with the unconverted and the less fortunate, or so many believed. However, in spite of their notable philanthropy and humanitarian efforts, Evangelicals did not disturb the market structure. The symptoms of poverty could be fought, while the root cause—the way business was structured—was largely untouched. That is, Evangelicals did apply their faith to *social* witness but not to economic restructuring.[23] A free, unhindered market complements a free autonomous will capable of choosing salvation. And so the notion of the market succeeded in both Britain and America.

We might proceed one step further and suggest that in Britain the moral fervor of much of this era was characterized by Evangelical activism. "Activism" placed a premium upon the belief that moral and ethical busyness was a concrete sign that one's will had in fact attained "entire sanctification," or at least sufficient moral goodness. This fervent belief, however, lacked philosophical depth and encouraged an acceptance of the day-to-day workings of the economy. Many believed, erroneously, that economic maladies could be corrected relatively quickly. There was a striking lack of vision as to the structural or systemic nature of social forces.

British Evangelical-Victorian values were also informed by the transatlantic friendships with American Evangelicals. Perhaps the first major connection occurred in the First Great Awakening (1735–50) between British Methodism and New England Calvinists; Jonathan Edwards' hosting of George Whitefield is an appropriate example. Over the next century, some divergences appeared as Calvinism's emphasis upon the sovereignty of God and the inability of human methods to achieve salvation gave way to the "New Measures Revivalism" espoused by Charles Finney. Such measures stressed, as has been noted, the autonomy of the will and the sufficiency of human action for salvation. Finney had become by 1850 so well known that his *Lectures on Revivals* had sold over 80,000 copies in England alone.[24]

Both sides of the Atlantic, however, continued to share other theological points of view. Evangelicals of both countries considered the primary goal of Christian ministry to be the conversion of the individual soul, with increasing emphasis being given to ecclesiastical and para-church activities as a means to this end. Both sides tried to resist the "demonic" concepts of the "infidel." Economically, this meant resistance to utopian socialists—Robert Owen communalists in America,[25] and "radicals" and Chartists in Britain.[26] British Evangelicals, like their American counterparts, also tended to equate Christianity with the values of positivistic scientific management, benevolent capitalism, Whiggish politics,[27] and resistance to the growth of unions.[28] Moreover, revivals in the one country often initiated revivals in the other.[29]

Many British Evangelicals attempted to copy the "New Measures Revivalism" and the Second Great Awakening (1800 and following) in America because of its numerical triumphs. During the Second Great Awakening itinerant evangelists had traveled through large portions of eastern America searching for converts. Wanting to move beyond ecclesiastical bodies, evangelists such as Finney stressed a more decentralized, para-church mentality. Arminianism, which advocated a striden doctrine of free will, was promoted by many Americans, who cherished "popular sovereignty," and by many British, who longed to break free of a state-run church.

How did "New Measures Revivalism" respond to growing urbanization? Such organizations as the American Tract Society, an ad hoc organization that specialized in prerevival tract distribution, thought it had one way to meet the growing core of problems manifest in the city. However, the revival remained the chief instrument used by leaders on both sides of the Atlantic to deal with the blight of the city.[30] Many Evangelicals of this period thought that if sobriety, Sabbath observance, and shunning of profanities prevailed, then crime, vagrancy, and poverty would disappear or at least lessen.[31] When poverty did not disappear, charities attempted to correct what the market had helped to cause. A conservative, voluntaristic emphasis, especially as formulated by the London Charity Organization, became paradigmatic of capitalism's and Evangelicalism's attempt to deal with the results of industrialization.[32] In short, economic justice was thought to flow from the market. When poverty did arise, British Evangelicals, like their American counterparts, organized "scientific" philanthropic projects to meet the worsening plight of the industrial cities.[33] It is important to note that this charity originates after and in response to the effects of the market.

While America contributed to British Evangelical identity, the British also contributed to American Evangelical identity. Generally, Britain encouraged antebellum optimism with frequent millennial tracts sent over the Atlantic. This optimism was founded upon a common identity and the presumption of a common divine calling: "England and America must love each other, for they are nations by whom God will work."[34] The link between British and American Methodists was especially pronounced. To a great extent, American Methodism sprang from Britain. Before the constitutional convention, all but one Methodist minister was British.[35] Methodist leader John Wesley commissioned Francis Asbury and Thomas Coke to supervise American Methodist development and in so doing erected a deep link between Britain and America at the dawn of the nineteenth century.

America's Evangelicals were dependent upon British Methodists for many years. Between 1820–50, ten percent of American Methodist clergy were British-born.[36] Many Methodists came to America hoping to escape European poverty and to partake of American abundance. The more sophisticated British theological style soon came to define American Methodism. An increasingly educated clergy were helped by Thomas Coke's first Methodist college, named after his friend Francis Asbury. British Methodists funded a variety of colleges and seminaries, and a more refined British pulpit style began to be adopted by ebullient American revivalists.[37]

Conversely, there were American revivalists who, while establishing themselves in the United States, drew English attention. Edward Norris Kirk was such a man. Kirk was a prominent "New School" or New Measures preacher who was part of the Presbyterian schism of 1837–38.[38] Perhaps his most famous convert in America was Dwight L. Moody, who would bring the transatlantic connection to its peak. Before coming to England, Kirk had managed to alienate his respectable Presbyterian congregation in Albany, New York, whereupon he set up an independent congregation in Albany's slums and won many converts from among the poor. Traveling in Britain in 1837, he won a great deal of middle-class support with his balance of Presbyterian polish and New Measures fervor. While in Birmingham and London, Kirk won some support from prominent British pastors. Daily meetings evolved into week-long sessions designed to fix the entire mind of London "eternal truth." On one occasion, Kirk had eight hundred souls crying for mercy in a crowded London chapel. The effects of these revivals soon spread to the Baptists, Congregationalists, and reluctant Anglicans.

Such revivals rarely, if ever, immediately affected the socioeconomic mores or market structure of London. They were too removed from the inner workings of the market. Revivals were, nevertheless, used to address the issues surrounding industrializing culture. Like their American counterparts, British revivalists found themselves in a culture where class hostilities, anomie and social solidarity were issues drawing attention.

However concerned revivalists were about the cultural malaise, tensions arose within the Evangelical worldview that hindered a more consistent attempt at "witness." Revivalists preached a gospel of otherworldly relief that was at odds with cultural realities. Kirk, for example, held his greatest session during an agricultural slump in the early 1830's that affected all of England. There is no rigid connection between economic cycles and religious enthusiasm, but economic cycles *tended* to have an inverse relationship to revival cycles in this era.[39] That is, as the economy slumped, the felt need for revivals increased; and when the economy returned to normal, especially in working areas, church attendance fell.[40] The net effect of these revivals was that a "supernatural" optimism was encouraged that tended to counteract the market cycle. After the economic downturn ended, this theological optimism was no longer needed, as socioeconomic notions of progress replaced it.

Let us conclude this analysis of the interrelationship of British and American Evangelical revivalism by a brief sketch of the visits of two major American revivalists to England. Both James Caughey and Charles Finney toured England before the Civil War and found

English audiences less receptive than their American counterparts. However, both itineraries promoted lasting bonds.

James Caughey, an Irish-American, was born to a staunchly Calvinist family. The family grew disappointed when eighteen-year-old James repudiated his family's Calvinism for a brand of Wesleyan Methodism and "entire sanctification." As he grew up, his Methodism was strengthened, especially while touring England. While there, he developed a friendship with William Booth, the founder of the Salvation Army, and persuaded him to concentrate upon the primary task of soul salvation.[41]

While preaching in England between 1841 and 1847, Caughey found British Industrialism overwhelming. However, the plight of Mammon could not dampen Caughey's spirit; he could claim 20,000 converts and 9,000 people who said they had experienced "entire sanctification" or spiritual perfection.[42] These statistics, if true, show how much he overcame the initial British attitude, which had tended to dismiss his preaching.

Perhaps Caughey's most numerically successful but socially ambiguous revival occurred in Sheffield, located in Yorkshire in northern England. Sheffield was an industrial city of one hundred thousand people that specialized in iron and steel fabrication. One year before Caughey arrived in Sheffield, the area was torn apart by labor/management conflicts born of an economic depression. The workers were inclined to support Chartist agitation. The Chartists were a force for labor democracy that, while respecting Evangelicalism, tried to organize workers into a union movement and forced Parliament to support collective bargaining. While in England, part of Caughey's preaching inveighed against the "Chartist conspiracy." However, even while preaching against the Chartists, he confessed an ignorance of all the "secret combinations" of the workingmen. In attempting to address Chartist concerns, he hoped that his revivals would put an end to the class hostilities and restore prosperity to England. It was said of him, "His mind looked at things through Evangelical eyes that saw secular prosperity as dependent upon a community's religious well-being."[43]

Caughey's gospel consisted of standard Wesleyan holiness fare with the exception that the doctrine of eternal perdition or Hell took precedence over the "love of God" as the impetus for repentance. The chief sins listed were swearing or profantiy, Sabbath-breaking, whoremongering, adultery, and "mental rebellion."[44] For the Christian, Caughey offered his version of entire sanctification or "perfect love," "holiness of the heart," or "blessing of purification," all of which terms were used more or less interchangeably.

He claimed that such blessings freed Christians from guilt, giving them mental equilibrium and an acceptance of death.

Caughey's individualistic, somewhat theatrical, style drew converts from a variety of social strata.[45] Perhaps this can be explained by his noncontroversial message, which was suited to the internal, psychological, and personal moral needs of a society caught in the malaise of Industrialism. I have called this version of the gospel "personalism." The resultant reduction of the scope and influence of God's kingdom, human sin, and alienation meant that Caughey lacked the ability to penetrate to the depths of socioeconomic life. Note, for instance, Caughey's inability to substantively address the texts on riches in Jesus' parables.[46]

A more momentous case, because of the man's enduring importance, is that of Charles Grandison Finney. Finney personified the Second Great Awakening, being both the chief innovator and theoretician of the "New Measures" and a representative of the revival's link with social reform. Finney's college, Oberlin—founded in 1833 with the help of the Tappan brothers—became viable when a mass of students left Lane Theological Seminary over the refusal of its president to confront the slavery issue. At the same time, Asa Mahan, who would become the chief theoretician of "perfectionism," left Lane Seminary to assume the presidency of Oberlin. Like Finney, Mahan traveled as an evangelist to England. Although Finney joined the faculty at Oberlin in opposing slavery, his burning passion was not slavery but the training of revivalist ministers.

Before considering Finney's work in America, let us examine his British experiences. Finney toured Britain between 1845 and 1851. He met with moderate numerical success in Birmingham and Worchester, despite the stiff opposition of the established church. However, it was in London that Finney realized his greatest success and it was due to the support of Baptists and Congregationalists. Finney preached in London for eighteen weeks, often twice a day and for two hours per sermon. Like Caughey, Finney preached entire sanctification, though he did admit that (personal) sin lay close to every man's door. He attracted some of the best minds of London, but his main supporters seemed to come from the middle class. Finney always insisted, however, that he regarded class distinction as less important than one's relationship to Christ.

Finney's London sermons were significantly influenced by his legal training. His training taught him to stress the cognitive and deductive aspects of apologetic preaching. Legal maneuvers were featured, as were mechanical techniques, so as not only to convert but to purify entirely the would-be penitent. Unlike British and

American Calvinists, Finney stressed an immediate and somewhat spectacular conversion, though with less emotion than Caughey. As with Caughey and many other revivalists, the individual's purity was the primary focus. Social reform was to come primarily through the sum of the wills of individuals.

Finney's lack of ecclesiastical and socioeconomic impact in London was due to several complex factors. By the time he had arrived in 1845, London, and England in general, had been "burnt-over" by several American revivalists, and the British showed growing indifference to the once unconventional methods of the revivalists. Moreover, the current middle class, whom Finney initially appealed to, did not suffer from the anomie usually mined by the preacher. When he chided British audiences for "worshipping commercial, material, and worldly success," the middle class began to turn away. Finney blamed this indifference on "hyper-Calvinism," which wasn't true. Calvinism was not at this time the dominant social or theological force in Britain. The established Anglican church, while dominating British ecclesiastical life, believed conversion to be a more gradual affair and not an "all-at-once experience." It believed infants could be regenerated through baptism by the same clergy who could forgive sins, and that church membership did not come about by public profession of faith, but by a kind of civil right guaranteed to all citizens of voting age. Thus, no significant Calvinism was present in the established Protestant church.

Much of what constituted the revivalist socioeconomic milieu in America paralleled that in Britain. Industrial society tended to cause problems in such important concerns as identity and legitimization. Anxious workers and the would-be successful tended to try to solve their concerns with alcohol, class stratification, and militancy. British revivalism, like the American counterpart, attempted to stabilize this latent chaos. However, Evangelicalism held too many values in common with Industrialism to be of much lasting, deep relief.

Finney's American campaigns illustrate the industrial-Evangelical ties in a very clear light. Of special note are his Rochester, New York revivals, which became prototypical of a portion of American antebellum Evangelicalism. The next chapter provides a fuller discussion of Finney. This will be followed by an overview of the Evangelical intellectual Francis Wayland, whose textbooks had virtually universal acceptance in antebellum American colleges. The chapter will then conclude with an analysis of the American pastor-philanthropist, Russell Conwell, and his ministry in Philadelphia.

6

Case Studies

The case studies in this chapter deal successively with a noted antebellum evangelist, a highly successful academic, and a postbellum pastor-philanthropist. These studies, representing perhaps the heart of the work, will attempt to concretely show how and why the industrial-Evangelical liaison occurred. These representative figures were chosen because of their lasting influence and appeal for our era, as well as for their differing institutional (or parainstitutional) impact.

Charles Grandison Finney

Charles Grandison Finney was born in 1792 to a patriotic but nonpious family. His great-grandfather had arrived on the Mayflower and his father served in the Revolutionary War. He started his studies in the legal profession at the age of twenty-six, and one year later was "touched by the grace of Christ" and became a Christian. In this conversion, Finney claimed to meet Christ personally, and simultaneously to be baptized by the Holy Spirit. He said, "Electricity flowed through me like liquid love, like the very breath of God." Thereupon, Finney claimed to be in a state in which he could not sin.[1]

Finney's conversion was to lead him to a new emphasis on Christian moral perfectionism and to the spotlight of national attention. After his 1821 conversion, a milestone in American Evangelical history, Finney began an unparalleled evangelistic career which made him, among other things, one of the foremost antebellum social forces in Connecticut, Ohio, and parts of Pennsylvania and New York.

Finney was licensed to preach in the Presbyterian church in 1823. By the following year his fame for conducting successful revivals had spread across western New York and had drawn increased opposition from the Calvinists. The opposition centered around Finney's belief in the human will and its ability to ensure first salvation, then Christian perfection. In 1829 Finney met and helped convert the wealthy Tappan brothers through a series of New York revivals. The following year he went to Rochester, New York, where one of America's most spectacular revivals occurred. (We will return to look at this revival more closely in a moment.) Finney managed during these New York campaigns to convert approximately ten thousand people from the Rochester area and one hundred thousand from the surrounding area.[2] His success drew offers to lead revivals from Union College, Buffalo, Providence and Boston.

Finney returned to New York City in 1832 during a cholera epidemic to preach in the Chatham Street Theater, purchased by the Tappan brothers. Stressing a new urban theology in which "worldliness" was considered the chief sin, he spoke for nearly seventy consecutive evenings to audiences averaging around two thousand people per sermon. While in New York he wrote his *Lectures on Revivals,* which was to sell over eighty thousand copies; translated into French and German, it became the most sought-after book on revival methods of its day. At the invitation of its president Asa Mahan, Finney ventured in 1835 to Oberlin Institute in Ohio to help anchor this foundering revival college. Finney agreed to teach at Oberlin only if the classroom was a center dedicated to "revival glory and the conversion of souls for Christ."[3] In 1837 the Tappan brothers suffered a severe economic loss, quickly plunging Oberlin into a $30,000 debt. Finney's family almost collapsed due to the strain. Remembering his British friends, Finney wired England for help, whereupon $30,000 appeared, eradicating all debt.[4]

In 1845 Finney and Oberlin received international recognition when the famed missionary David Livingston sent his brother to study there in preparation for mission work. Two years later Finney's first wife died, leaving him bereft. His second wife died just before the Civil War, leaving him in grief but free to become the president of Oberlin. His lifelong evangelistic motto was: "Souls under any price and under all circumstances." It expressed a zeal he maintained until his death in 1874.

To understand the life and thought of Finney more fully we must understand what he meant by revivals. A revival, he said, was "the renewal of the first love of Christians and the awakening and conversion of sinners to God."[5] These protracted public events were marked by a conviction of sin and a new beginning of moral concern for Christians. It was definitely the work of men (as opposed to divine agency) to arouse others to conversion. Revivals, moreover, were marked, though not fully determined by, emotional excitement. Shouted Finney, "Men will not be obedient until they are excited."[6] To arouse such excitement he thought proper techniques and strategies should be employed so as to induce guaranteed results.

The sins enumerated by Finney afford an indication of his worldview. There were two major categories of sin: commission and omission. Finney's list of sins, with the exception of slavery, were all personal in nature. That is, they were oriented to the immediate internal life, and hence not intertwined with cultural structures.[7] Notably absent was any definition of Mammon as something else beyond personal greed.

Good revivals, he thought, should manifest several key elements. Chief among these were faith and repentance, voluntaristically defined: "Faith is a voluntary trust in God's person and veracity. . . . When an individual actually chooses to obey God he becomes a Christian."[8] Further, Finney's revivals, like those of his postbellum descendants, spawned a list of theological funadmentals or faith-essentials which included the divinity of Christ, the moral corruption of the entire human race, justification by faith, and the justice of eternal punishment for those denying Christ's atonement.[9]

Finney's worldview fit securely into that of the America of his time. His blending of popular sovereignty with voluntary individualism helped soothe and found support in the troubled moral order of an adolescent nation. Moreover, the implicit message communicated through a Finneyesque personalistic definition of sin was that the American experience and its unfolding incorporating expression were fundamentally right. Problems could be significantly addressed and the millennium brought in through the salvation of enough individual souls. Indeed, Finney said, "The great end of *all* ministry is the salvation of souls."[10]

Finney's revival sermons were not so abstract as to be totally oblivious to culture. However, they were vague enough to leave the structure of Gold untouched. It is crucial to note how and why Finney scorned the vanity of the world: "Men are so struck by the objects of sense . . . that they are very apt to shut out eternity from their minds."[11] This emphasis upon eternity as otherworldliness became a standard mark of Finney's sermons. He maintained, "The joys of religion and communion with God [should] keep us ABOVE the world . . . [because] this world is not our home."[12] Thus, religion or revivalism should, at best, exist alongside politics and economic practice rather than at their core. Perhaps Finney's juxtaposition of "religion" and cultural activity was due to his reduction of the depth and scope of religion to the affairs that surround the revival.

Finney's revival sermons were not without any economic references, however. His primary positive economic norm, in keeping with his personalism, was honesty. Coupling this virtue to the market system, Finney once said to an audience full of businessmen, "If we are honest we will control the market," for "the ungodly will conform to your standard."[13]

Linked with this honesty should be compassion, hope, and charity. Benevolence or charity, in turn, finds its chief end in the support of revivals. The market would exist untouched. Excess profit would, in turn, be channeled into support of revivals. Revivals are what the Tappens meant by a "moral enterprise." Said Lewis Tappan, "I have enough property to support my family and I am tired of laboring at the oar to acquire more money when so much can be done in moral enterprises."[14]

Thus, we can see that a significant portion of Tappan's business existed to support revivals and thereby weakened its inner integrity. This vision was unable to provide any deep economic transformation in Tappan's day-to-day business ventures, though it did have an indirect influence on the morals of the day. At best, the market mechanism was to be accepted as it was, with its fruits being used for the salvation of souls. By reducing the goal of business life to revivals, the closest Tappan could come to a true integration of faith and economics was his moralistic proclamation,

> In business, a backslider will take advantage and play off of business tricks and . . . will practice deception and misrepresentation, in making bargains will demand exorbitant interest and take advantage of the necessities of his fellow men.[15]

No deep transformation of the capital formation process, no penetrating concern about economic incorporation, and no rejoinder to market-oriented values can be found in the Tappan writings.

The core of sinful action, according to Finney, was human selfishness. He saw selfishness in terms of self-interest, self-gratification, and self-indulgence, all merely personal vices. Thus, he spoke of "selfishness in the subjugation of the will to the gratification of desires."[16] This state occurs when reason is dethroned and "self" becomes the focus of life. He states that "the happiness of an individual, although great, ought not be regarded as supreme."[17]

Selfishness defiles true religion, while self-denial becomes one of the chief Christian virtues.

Finney could have made a critique of capitalism on this basis. However, his personalism, or the process of abstracting persons from the cultural matrix, prevented any noticeable structural critique of the prevailing economic mores. (Moreover, notably absent is any mention of the relationship of selfishness to the kingdom of God and creation.) His lack of a cultural matrix is reflected by the methodology of his *Systematic Theology*. There is no mention made of any classical Christian thinkers, prior to Jonathan Edwards, as to their thoughts on selfishness or any other related doctrine. Like the American experience, it seems as if Finney attempted to reconstruct the study of theology and ethics out of the wilderness of totally new beginnings.

Finney was aware of the economic mores of the businessmen that he met. He correctly saw that most businessmen leave their Christianity "at the morning breakfast table only to leave to serve other gods." They engage in business for themselves and not for God, and thus their Christianity costs them little. They make it "their object to accumulate so much property that they can retire from business, living at ease, and serving their own gods."[18] He correctly maintained that such a stance leads to a "worldly spirit," and said, "These maxims and the rules by which business is done in the world are directly opposite to the gospel of Jesus Christ."[19] Thus, Finney's stated intention was to see a more integral relationship between faith and business practice. We must understand why this integration, and its full expression, never become a reality.

Surprisingly, among his repertoire of sermons on biblical themes were several on the notion of stewardship. "A steward is one who is employed to transact the business of another, as his agent or representative in the business which he is employed." Thus, "we are merely His agents and not the owners of His property."[20] Accordingly, one's time, talents, powers, possessions, and property are to be used for "the glory of God." Cried Finney,

> The world is full of poverty, desolation and death. . . . God calls on you as his steward . . . to use all the property in your possession so as to promote the greatest amount of happiness among your fellow creatures.[21]

Charity is one of the chief avenues to do this, but by no means the only one. Any resistance by the believer, such as holding money in perpetuity or charging interest to one's family, is blasphemy in

Finney's eyes. In the highest sense, charity is the glorification of God through the conversion of sinners. Said Finney to a congregation of business people:

> The only way in which money can be used for the glory of God and the good of men is to promote the spirituality and holiness of men. . . . If you prefer business to prayer, busy yourselves in your business affairs and neglect your closets, the love of God is not in you. . . . The only possible use of making money for the glory of God is to use it for the conversion and sanctification of sinners.[22]

What can be said of Finney's view of the relationship of God and Mammon? Is it fair to conclude that he "lulled the upper classes into an economic self-complacency and gave respectability to their activities"?[23] I think not. But why were Finney's views so eagerly accepted, for example, by many Whig businessmen, although they appear so stern? Moreover, was the Finney-Tappan surrender of business's integrity to salvation's domain in fact a feasible alternative to incorporating culture? And more importantly, how could Finney see so clearly the evils of greed, selfishness, and the service of one's own goods, and yet fail to provide guidelines for the inner transformation of economic action? The answer to these and other questions will come as we look at Finney's fundamental dualism and the nature of his Rochester revivals.

It seems that Finney's dualism overturned his express intentions to renew the inner principles of economic activity. He believed that the universe is evidence of God's moral government as manifested through moral and physical law. Physical law is the law of necessity, force, and that which governs the material universe. This kind of law is inferior as it restricts the voluntary free will of individuals. Moral law is, conversely, "the rule of the government of free intelligent action as opposed to necessary unintelligent action."[24] Physical law originates from common law or natural law. This law is not legislated by God; rather, He enforces the already extant common or natural law. Moral law is founded at same time in heaven upon Divine Reason.[25] This law is unalterable, supernatural, eternally self-existent and even obligatory upon God. One becomes properly moral when the moral law, mandated by Divine Reason, becomes a rule or subjective duty implanted in the mind by voluntary moral choice.[26] However, and this is the key, one's duty must be voluntarily carried out. One cannot be compelled to be moral as that compulsion would contradict morality. Thus, there is an antithetical tension between moral and physical law and their concomitant actions and virtues.

Finney's dualism is even more poignant because he was a voluntarist who believed in the freedom of moral actions; he therefore repudiated the Calvinist concept of the bondage of the will and viewed any action of the will, such as moral rationality, as *inherently* superior to physical law and actions of physical necessity. This superiority is evidenced in the autonomy afforded the "Free Will".[27] Our Free Will can choose the moral good because of the *intrinsic* power of both the will and the moral law. This intrinsic power not only rivets the moral imperatives to rational moral law, but resists God's governorship of the universe. "The fact that God is the Owner and Sole Proprietor of the universe is no reason why he should govern it."[28]

Physical necessity, of which economic needs are a part, binds us to the dictates of natural law, while the moral law, or that law that governs economic will, is voluntaristically based. Freedom is to be preferred over, but is in conflict with, the inferior virtue of necessity. This tension between necessity and freedom is amenable to no inner resolution. It is not at all clear, however, that voluntary economic exchanges and free will can ensure sufficient economic prosperity and a compatible moral order, so that a free people will be freer from economic necessity. Were it so, this "solution" would simply end up supporting capitalistic presupposita.

Finney gives clearer evidence of this dualistic tendency in his pastoral admonitions. Criticizing Calvinistic orthodoxy (and contradicting his own form of rationalism), he says of seminaries, "they instruct the intellect but they do not meet the wants of the heart. They preach an intellectual rather than a spiritual Gospel. [True] Religion is a heart's devotion to God."[29] Once Finney takes this position, no deep point of contact can be found to link the "heart" with intellect and this in turn with cultural concerns. Using such dualistic anthropological phrases as "spiritual versus intellectual," he has no deep point of inner unity between the heart and head, and is unable to intertwine his moral principles with economic affairs.[30] At best, moral matters can only exist alongside of economic concerns.

Finney never consistently supported, however, an immoral free-market orientation. Charity was to be juxtaposed to voluntary capital formation, and his moral world differed at least to some degree from that of the capitalist. There developed a deep conflict, however, between the dictates of spiritual, moral law for charity and the natural law for profit, *both* of which were to function in the business enterprise. The acquisitiveness of the profit motive was held in tension with that of charity, with the former gaining ascendancy.

This tension, strangely enough, helps explain Finney's success. Businessmen, anxious about their social and moral status and eager for legitimization, found this tension acceptable, for it allowed them to promote profit maximization while being charitable. The burgeoning middle class of merchants, large-scale farmers, and proto-industrialists could without surrendering the incorporating spirit, back Finney's revivals and support charities because the profit structure was left intact.

Finney's fundamental dualism and links to capitalism are manifested most strikingly when he seeks to apply moral law to natural law. Moral law or absolute good seeks to realize itself in natural or common good. À la Plato, Finney says that our minds behold certain archetypes, and as we contemplate these entities we experience mental satisfaction. He identifies these archetypes with Divine Reason or the Divine Mind which, of its own nature, seeks to realize itself in our minds.[31]

Now we are at another crucial juncture in Finney's thought. Trying to merge the world of ideals with the world of reality, Finney fused a crude Platonism with a subjective utilitarianism. Of course, he did not make utility or mental satisfaction the sole end of life. Rather, utility or mental satisfaction was to be the happiness obtained in obedience to the moral law.[32]

Unlike the consistent utilitarians, Finney maintained that mental satisfaction does not lead one to hedonism but to benevolence. Benevolence was not only a glue for moral and physical law, but involved the moral denial of particular gains in life. The financial sacrifices provided for necessary moral campaigns like revivals and various additional socially progressive causes.

As with Luther's, Finney's dualism could not withstand the social tension created by various dichotomies. Either he had to endorse the basic structure of business and use excess wealth for benevolence—which in practice meant sanctifying market operations—or he had to turn businesses into charities, which in effect meant eradicating natural business life for "supernatural" ends. The practical resolution of this tension never came.

Finney needed enormous amounts of wealth to conduct his revivals. In the Rochester revivals, the wealthy were initially the ones attracted to Finney and the ones who supported him. It is not an exaggeration to say that much of his success "rested on the wealthy and their monetary support and the system of their trading."[33] But although the wealthy supported Finney, it would not be right to suggest that labor control was the primary motive behind Finney's Rochester revivals. What then did happen in this crucial series of revivals?

Let us turn to a close examination of Finney's Rochester, New York revivals. There were three—in 1830, 1842, and 1855—but we will concentrate on his 1830 campaign, because it coincided with Rochester's incipient industrialization.

Finney was asked to come to Rochester in 1830 by three feuding Presbyterian churches and the merchants who guided them. Crowded rooms and sweltering nights did not stop him from preaching every night and three times on Sunday. It was here that Finney first designated an "anxious seat," a separate set of pews where inquirers could come after the service and settle their fears by surrendering their lives to Christ. Winning massive support, especially among the merchant class, Finney left Rochester having reached predominantly, in his own words, the successful classes.[34]

Finney was passing through Rochester in 1842, hoping to rest after having preached throughout New England. This time, a judge and several members of the Episcopal church asked him to stay and preach. In this revival Finney emphasized a few new themes. Preaching to lawyers, he argued for the cogency of belief in Christ which, if denied, would result in eternal damnation. When he preached in the Episcopal church, he pleaded for an "entire consecration" to God whereby one's heart, body, soul, mind and spirit would be surrendered to Christ. Finney stressed the voluntary surrender of the will. This revival was so successful that the judge who asked Finney to stop himself became a believer.

Finney returned for one last series of revivals in 1855. This time the local Congregational and Methodist churches sponsored him. Again it was the more successful classes that responded favorably to his message. By 1855, busy Rochester worked seven days a week, provoking Finney to give a series of sermons about strict Sabbath observance. Rail engineers and workers left their jobs on Sundays as a consequence, proving that his campaigns had some impact. Finney's greatest success in this revival, as it had been in his earlier revivals in Rochester, was acceptance by the wealthy. "What was quite remarkable in these revivals that I witnessed in Rochester," said Finney, "was that they all commenced and made their first progress among the 'higher' classes of society."[35]

One can discern a pattern in these three episodes. There was a wave-like ebb and flow quality which betrayed a waxing and waning of Christian fervor and zeal. There was a push for temperance,

Sabbatarianism, and class reconciliation, but no mention of a change in basic economic doctrines. When the class hostilities ceased, it was because workers were incorporated into the entrepreneurial worldview.

In the 1820's Rochester was experiencing a rapid population increase. The increase was made possible by such advances as the Erie Canal, which helped promote the commercialization of agriculture, especialy wheat. Rochester became one of the milling centers of the United States. The resultant influx of wealth brought a flood of luxury items to once economically simple people. Simultaneously, Rochester's capitalists, like many capitalists of this era, needed rails and were planning for the completion of the Auburn Railroad when Finney came to Rochester in 1830. By this time the Rochester millers

> commanded an immediate agricultural area larger and wealthier than did any other canal town. . . . By 1835 the burgeoning merchants produced goods worth more than two and a half times those of Buffalo or Syracuse.[36]

Thus, Rochester was becoming an industrial center.

During the 1830's Rochester's capitalists were at the center of changing cultural mores. Families were still clannish and suspicious of outsiders, yet modern enough to know that pooled capital was a necessity. Caution, cooperation, and a muted ambition marked the dealings of Rochester's merchants in this era. It was the consortium of families that controlled Rochester which invited Finney for his first visit.[37] The mores and myths that preceded Finney's arrival virtually ensured his success. Rochester was filled with "self-made" people whose poverty was eradicated by the flurry of white flour and representation in Congress. Mobility and the myth of the self-made people were the sociological counterparts to Finney's free-will, optimistic voluntarism. Moreover, the rugged individualism of a frontier town was beginning to evolve into a community of consensus among ruling elites; it was a two-tiered society marked by social stability in the managerial community and dislocation in the laboring community.

The social dislocation experienced in this era was a key factor in Finney's success in Rochester. This economic revolution, like those before and after it, "produced unregulated greed, family collapse, social trauma, status anxiety, cultural confusion and loneliness."[38] The cultural atomization and fragmentation, and the technological reconstruction of society created immense cultural disorientation. Industrial masters, who had previously enjoyed a face-to-face, paternalistic relationship with their laborers, became more concerned with the objectification and purchase of labor and raw materials than with the more human view of production. Entrepreneurs became the economic equivalent of absentee landlords, and discipline faded with this structural impersonality. Could class antagonisms be far away?

As a result of this fundamental reorientation of society, violence and alienation spread. Such divisions as Anti-Masons versus Masons, Democrats opposed to Whigs, temperance factions warring against laborers wanting alcohol, and Sabbatarians against profit-hungry owners provided fissures in Rochester society. Attempting to reconcile these rifts, Rochester elites tried a variety of methods. Heavy-handed personal discipline failed to control the work force, as did edicts passed by the town council. Voluntary restraint and free-will cooperation also failed to unite the fractured society. Industrialism's atomizing work and worldview demanded a magic elixir.

Paul Johnson, whose history of the Rochester revival we have so far followed, is only half correct in maintaining that revivals are society's antidote to individualism.[39] The other half of the truth is that Evangelical revivalism shares an individualistic a priori with Industrialism. It is the individual, supposedly outside any cultural or creational matrix, who is to make his de novo commitment and then reform his life, with God as a partner. It is the individual who, through his associated autonomous roots, is to form various collective societal institutions and then carry out their missions. And finally, it is the individual, like Bunyan's lonely pilgrim in *Pilgrim's Progress,* who makes his solitary way to the beauty of heaven's shore. Evangelicalism does not deny all forms of collectivity; rather, it subsumes collectivity under individuality.

Finney's 1830 Rochester revival was one of the most impressive of his or any day. As the revival spread to the Rochester countryside, literally tens of thousands of people accepted Christ by faith and prayer. In addition to the initial anxious entrepreneurs, real-estate magnates, commercial tycoons, and laborers responded positively to Finney's sermons. The moral fervor of Finney's revivals led to a desire for temperance, blue laws, antislavery campaigns, and tract-distribution societies. But the converts' moral fervor was decidedly more ambiguous when it came to the patterns of Rochester's economic growth.

Some of Finney's success can be explained by his "new measures." Prior to meetings, lay Evangelicals, usually women, would form small prayer groups that canvassed local residents, urging revival attendance. Generally, male household heads were the targets. Once an anxious sinner had taken his seat on the bench, confessed, and trusted Christ for his salvation, he joined other Christians in small prayer groups and waited for others to follow.[40] The cumulative effect was a wave of human fervor that could not help but direct culture into certain predetermined paths. How strong was this wave? "Finney's revival created a community of militant Evangelicals who would remake society and politics in Rochester."[41]

That those most anxious for, and initially responsive to, Finney's revivals were the wealthy, is not surprising, given Rochester's burgeoning capitalism, alienated class structure, and cultural dislocation. As Finney himself said, the wealthy led this millennial charge. "With few exceptions, Finney's revival was the strongest among entrepreneurs."[42] It was the wage masters, who preferred personal privacy and profit to the older face-to-face paternalistic relations, who responded most favorably to Finney. His revivals helped these entrepreneurs maintain their personal and economic autonomy while securing a measure of cultural cohesion. The revival also temporarily broke down Protestant sectarian boundaries, and mobilized the Protestant community while radically curtailing drinking and labor amusements. Such working-class amusements as theatergoing came under open attack in the 1830 revival. These activities were deemed evil because they were believed to waste time, cloud people's minds, and block the anticipated millennium.

Around 1830, belief in the millennium firmly wedded the concepts of God and economic progress. In both their public and private morality the world of Rochester seemed to await the dawn of the Savior's quick return. Rich merchants organized charities for the poor; pew rentals or contracted worship seats were abolished, as were burgeoning class tensions. The Rochester Savings Bank was opened to encourage working-class thrift and make reasonable loans to struggling homeowners. More importantly, the worker and his manager worshipped together, the latter promising all the while to give interest-free loans and provide free legal service. Workers were guaranteed greater job security and increased pay. Thus, the revival harmony led to hopes for social peace and economic prosperity.

But the Evangelical millennium was interpreted through decidedly Whiggish glasses. In 1834, just four years after Finney's revival, Rochester Whigs were among the first to denounce Andrew Jackson for the removal of federal funds from the banks of the United States;

it was the same business elite who had sponsored Finney's revivals who signed a local petition decrying this act.[43] After day laborers joined revival churches, they supported the Whiggish worldview of the wealthy entrepreneurs, thus creating an unbeatable conservative coalition. As long as this tenuous harmony lasted, conservative laissez-faire culture dominated the region. Thus, it seems that the free will-free market millennial vision captured both the disenchanted Jacksonian and Whig, both of whom longed for peace and prosperity. "Evangelism solved the problems," for the moment, "of class hostilities, legitimacy and order, social control and discipline."[44]

Francis Wayland

We now turn from Evangelicalism's great mobilizer to its preeminent intellectual. Francis Wayland demonstrated excellence in the pastorate, in scholarship, education, and social benevolence; but it was as a leading economic thinker of his day that Wayland has enduring significance. His most influential work, *The Elements of Political Economy* (1837), went through twenty-three American editions, three English, and one Hawaiian, selling over 14,000 copies.[45] It was the standard text in most colleges before the Civil War. We can see in Wayland's work a representative and highly influential statement of antebellum Evangelical socioeconomic theory.

Wayland's economic doctrine drew heavily on the utilitarian and classic schools of capitalism, but fundamentally his economic views were dependent upon his ethical and moral theory. This, in turn, was founded upon his version of Common Sense Realism and its conservative view of natural law. Wayland also shared a crucial notion of American identity: that a special divine providence governed the affairs of America and its economic and spiritual progress. Wayland gave intellectual strength to Finney's contemporaneous demands for charity and acquisitiveness—a conjunction that we shall call, in the rest of this chapter, the "gain-give principle." I will argue that Wayland, while trying to transform culture according to the dictates of Christianity, almost necessarily become intertwined with the spirit of industrial incorporation.

Wayland's parents, naturalized English Baptists, gave birth to Francis just twenty years after the Revolutionary War. Wayland's father was a businessman and a pastor who agonized between the two careers—a "secular business" career with its values of industry, thrift, hard work, and frugality, and a "religious" pastorate which stressed the values of piety, compassion and tenderness. Ultimately, Wayland's father could not reconcile the two sets of values, though he left his business for the pastorate in 1807.[46] The tension between economic and "religious" values would become a major theme in his son's academic work.

Wayland's unusual academic ability became apparent early in his life. At the age of eleven he was reading Greek and Latin (including Virgil and the Westminster Confession).[47] By 1811, Wayland had enrolled in Union College as a sophomore, skipping his freshman year. By age seventeen he had graduated from college and entered medical school. While there, he complained of an inability to integrate his faith with his studies. "Much of his medical education was spent in reading 'religious' books, praying and seeking Christ, yet without transformation . . . conviction and gospel rest for his soul."[48] In 1816 Wayland tried to resolve this tension by leaving school and traveling to a Baptist-sponsored medical mission in Colorado. Like his father, he could find no point of internal contact between religion and vocation.

Wayland returned to enter Andover Seminary in 1816. During his first year he met the Evangelical scholar Moses Stuart, who helped him become "more engaged for souls" and more able to put off the "worldly spirit" in preparation for heavenly contemplation.[49] Three years later Wayland met the famed Calvinist evangelist, Ashahel Nettleton, and took part in his first revival, seeing nearly 800 students saved at Union College through Nettleton's preaching. Unlike Finney, Wayland took a strong stand on the human will's inability to secure salvation through free choice. Wayland believed that man and God could not enter into an equal partnership either for justification or for sanctification.[50]

Wayland had entered his first pastorate by 1821. During his pastorate, he often became depressed. Feeling inferior, he often shied away from people. "His ideals were high and his inabilities to attain them overwhelmed him. . . . As a result, he often became nervous, felt depressed, pained and embarrassed."[51] Perhaps these were symptoms of the stringent demands placed upon him during his youth.

Interestingly, this psychosocial complex can be connected with economic systems. Capitalism depends upon production as a measure of self-worth. Suffering from impossible ideals would keep one productive but also unhappy, since basic ego satisfaction can never fully be reached due to the incessant demands. Wayland knew this despair, and felt it was contrary to the grace of conversion. He believed and taught that self-worth, like grace, is a free-gift and therefore cannot be earned. This drove Wayland out of the pastorate. As he intimated in his first sermon: "I was not sufficiently religious . . . nor was I pious or dependent upon God to any sufficient degree."[52]

In 1823, while still a pastor, Wayland had become chief editor for this denomination's major periodical, the *American Baptist Magazine.* This Boston-based publication gave Wayland a national readership, and he was considered for the presidency of Baptist-related Brown University. The *American Baptist* was dedicated to the "moral duties" of citizenship and the missionary glories of American citizenship. It featured articles on the Revolutionary War and touted the stability of American government in contrast to the political chaos of France's recently overthrown monarchy. We first see Wayland's glowing Americanism in these editorials.

Because of Wayland's academic renown and Baptist commitment, many New England Baptist pastors joined the chorus that pleaded with him to become the president of troubled Brown University. In 1827, he took the post. The college was in a poor spiritual and academic condition. Wayland quickly asserted himself by demanding of himself and others the virtues of exactness, discipline, piety, intellectual rigor, and "the love of labor." Within his first year, he helped pave the way for Brown's first revival by initiating prayer meetings, Bible studies, visitation of unbelievers, and benevolent acts.

During his first years as president of Brown, Wayland developed his more mature thoughts on the relationship of Christ and culture. In keeping with the nineteenth-century habit of seeing America in a special millennial light, Wayland said,

> it has been reserved for us in the providence of God, to be the first people upon earth who should commence the fulfillment of the prophecy "men shall beat their swords into ploughshares and their spears into pruning hooks."[53]

Wayland's optimism in the early 1840s changed into a dire pessimism when the pruning hooks and ploughshares were converted into spears and swords in 1861.

Wayland left Brown in 1840 for a much-needed rest. After returning from Europe he was aglow with Americanism. In comparing American virtues with those of Europe he said, "Our country, bad as it may be, is simple, virtuous, moral and religious in comparison with other countries."[54] During this period, he came to reaffirm his faith in the individual and the individual's ability to shoulder the

responsibilities of a free society.[55] One of his first social crusades—
for prison reform—was predicated on this individualistic assump-
tion. Appalled at Rhode Island prison conditions, Wayland argued
for the absolute moral dignity of every individual prisoner and won
better lighting, libraries, improved medical care, a new chapel, and
better food.

His energetic individualism met its greatest test in confronting
the slavery issue. Wayland opposed the Kansas-Nebraska Bill (1854)
because it would allow slavery to invade the Western territories.
Consistent with his individualism, he declared: "I protest this bill
. . . because it promises to violate the great elementary law . . . of
society, the principle that every individual has a right to himself."[56]
But Wayland faced a profound dilemma as the war drew near. What
should the Union's response be if the South continued in its refusal
to give up slavery? If the individual's rights are supreme, only a
voluntary surrender, and not governmental force, could be demanded. Like many Evangelicals of his day, Wayland turned to
moral suasion in an attempt to halt slavery. His optimistic tone
began to fade, however, as "religion" turned from being a cultural
force to being an otherworldly contemplation.

> To abolish slavery is a good thing, but it is not religion. The Christian
> must look to God and [then] arouse Christian feeling of compassion in
> men. . . . I have no faith in any other means for curing the evils of this
> present situation. . . . What is needed is a general revival of religion . . .
> nothing else will save us.[57]

This pattern of individualism, the compartmentalization of religion, and the cultural pessimism which led some Evangelicals to
social irresponsibility seemed to increase as the horrors of the
century multiplied. Eventually the individualism and special millennial optimism for America had to give way before the apocalypse.
Speaking of God's judgment upon America and the coming eradication of the South's individual rights as a result of the Civil War,
Wayland said: "His truth and justice, his hatred of sin, of oppression,
of treachery, are all involved in the termination of this struggle."[58]

Wayland died, aptly enough, in 1865. He left as his legacy a solid
antebellum connection between capitalism and Evangelicalism. In
order to understand this connection more fully, let us turn our
attention to his major academic doctrines and works.

Wayland's worldview contained three basic elements. First and
foremost was his view of rationality as crystalized in Common Sense
Realism. Like many Evangelical intellectuals of the nineteenth cen-

tury, Wayland explicitly founded his positions upon this school. Secondly, his views of morality contain, as do Finney's, a fundamental dualism or tension between the natural laws of God and reason and the grace-filled laws of revelation. Thirdly, Wayland propounded a version of laissez-faire capitalism that was consistent with his views on rationality and morality. Characteristic of his academic works and his preaching are the emphasis on the supremacy of the individual, the overestimation of the value of labor, and the simultaneous need to maximize both charity and capital.

We can see the basic postulate of Common Sense Realism in the statement: "There is a world outside of us and a world inside of us ... both are given to us by the principle of our constitution as ultimate facts."[59] According to this Scottish-based philosophy, the mind links the inner world with the outer world. Wayland maintained that the proper job of philosophy was to observe various phenomena and their interrelationships and then to integrate this material with the universal, natural laws, to which they are subjugated. This philosophy's alleged objective origins were to mitigate any speculative or subjective effects.

There are at least two dualisms that characterize Wayland's version of Common Sense Realism. There is the mind/body dualism whereby the mind, as a Lockean sheet of blank paper, was believed to be rational, "spiritual," and bound to the soul and hence superior, while the body was thought to be natural, material and hence inferior.[60] An object is presented to our brain by our senses, whereupon the mental act of "knowing" occurs. Furthermore, there is a spirit/matter dualism whereby the mind, as "spiritual," receptive, and creative transcends (yet shapes) external stimuli.[61] If one is deceived in correlating mind and matter, it is not because of the power of different presuppositions but because of an improperly drawn inference.

In accepting Thomas Reid's version of realism, Wayland rejected speculative idealism and attempted to provide an operative method to prove God's existence. But Wayland's version of realism forced him into a kind of epistemological individualism. He maintained that "the knowledge which we acquire by perception is always of individual entities."[62] In theology, these entities were called propositions and were unique and indivisible. Such absolute individualism became the basis for Wayland's views of economic justice.

Reason was for Wayland universally held, commonly practiced, morally binding and necessary. His view of rationality forced him to maintain that common sense rationality could be nonspeculative, democratic, self-evident, and thus suited to a American culture.

This arbitrary elevation of one human aspect to an authoritative position led Wayland to equate reason's function with the laws of God for creation.[63] His acceptance of this form of rationality ultimately led Wayland to support the views of the Scottish economist Adam Smith, himself a secular natural law theorist. Thus, Wayland came to share the same view of natural reason's commonality, universality, and necessity as did the secular theorists who attempted to found the laws of supply and demand upon a rationally constructed universe. At this point, he surrendered his Calvinism, with its emphasis on a fallen reason, for a quasi-deistic formulation that sought to demonstrate capitalism's alleged universal necessity.[64]

In Wayland's view there was a connection between rationality and morality. Wayland divided the study of moral science between the study of natural or moral law and the practical application of ethical principles. The former included the laws of nature, mathematics and jurisprudence, while the latter included piety and benevolence.

Universal moral law impinged upon human consciousness because it was established as part of the universe by Divine Will. Divine Will worked through natural law to impress upon human reason the necessity of the dictates of moral or natural law. Natural law led to a natural religion in which "the light of nature" was established by the "Universal First Cause."[65] The First Cause so designed the universe that the study of Virgil, Horace, Homer, and Plato could sufficiently elevate the mind to a natural morality.[66]

Yet the Calvinistic part of Wayland had to condemn pagan ethics to some degree, due to his belief in the radical nature of sin. Because he believed that sin hindered but did not destroy natural morality, he had to demonstrate the insufficiency of human morality while "making room" for grace. Basically, Wayland resolved this tension by positing two realms of authority. In the "natural" realm the "worldly" sway of human reason pertained. In the "supernatural" realm, revealed religion and grace were sovereign. Revealed religion was to perfect and complement natural religion. Speaking of the pagan anticipations of truth, Wayland said: "Each one of these anticipations furnishes a distinct a priori presumption in favor of the truth of revealed religion."[67] Thus, a basic dualism is established whereby the light of natural reason, sufficient unto itself for natural morality, is perfected by supernatural grace. Grace crowns (autonomous) nature.

What was Wayland to do if the skeptic would not believe in the revealed religion of the Bible as the final source of authority for morality? How could one be sure that the scriptures were true? His reply was that it is by the general laws of evidence that proofs of the authenticity for the Scriptures as a capstone to natural religion can be demonstrated.[68] Universal yet common reason could establish the need for the Scriptures and could vindicate and validate the Bible's authenticity. Ironically, though their methods produced vastly different results, Wayland shared the same allegiance to the authority of human reason as did the postbellum biblical critics. Both believed in the inherent superiority of human reason over revelation: the one to defend, the other to detract.

Wayland's reliance upon a kind of Aristotelian First Cause and the morality that resulted from it met with acceptance for more than one reason. Wayland's views were part of a more or less commonly held moral, rational consensus in nineteenth-century America. This universal yet syncretistic moral consensus was the glue that held an unwieldy but promising union of states together. To jeopardize the consensus was to jeopardize the union of states. Understanding this fact helps one understand Fundamentalism's reaction to secularization.

In his attempt to unite nature and grace, Wayland wanted to address the fundamental gap between the sacred and the secular that had haunted his father. He thought the "lower" or natural areas of life and their concomitant virtues could be coupled with, and perfected by, the "higher" areas of life revealed by religion. This basic dualism enabled Wayland to be both a vigorous supporter of public education (where common sense reigned) and an enthusiastic supporter of revivalism (where grace perfected the world). Yet this was an artificial restriction of grace and a compartmentalizing of religion. Ironically, this stance undercut the power of revivals.

In his practical ethics and morality, Wayland was a consistent individualist. He felt that morality could not be legislated by society for the individual, for society is itself "composed of individuals and hence society can have no other rights than individual rights."[69] As one might expect, this notion led him to be an enthusiastic proponent of private property. It was a social absolute and its use had to be guaranteed by the social contract. Private property was secured through labor and the multiplication of capital. Through the interaction of capital, labor, and private property, Wayland hoped that domestic tranquility would be ensured. Private property demands the "exclusive enjoyment of the benefits of my labor," said Wayland. "The more rigidly contracts are observed, the more capital will multiply, the greater will be the inducements to industry and the stronger will be the barriers against extravagance, vice, and barbarism."[70] Wayland here accepts the myth of private property. Civility and social cohesion were thought to flow from private property.

Wayland's theory of society was divided between simple and civil society. The former was rooted in a social contract, which in turn was based upon rational conscience, while the latter was supernaturally instituted by God and expressed through the agencies of the local, state, and federal government. Simple society was based upon voluntary associations that civil society could never coerce or form. Both simple and civil society (the distinction shows yet another dualism) drew their earthly authority from the individual. Society's job was to protect private property, redress individual wrongs, and guard the sanctity of the contract.[71]

Wayland's view of natural law entailed a profound dilemma. As a Calvinist he wanted to affirm God's sovereignty over all of life. This he did through the agency of civil society. However, by accepting a Lockean version of the social contract theory, he unwittingly accepted popular sovereignty as the basis of authority for simple society. This tension was allegedy resolved by exalting the individual over society; he hoped thereby to find a common ground between Christianity and the Enlightenment. Society thus became the constituted body of sovereign individuals.[72] With capitalism's views of the social contract in place, Wayland forged, however, a crucial tie between God and Gold.

Having looked at the link between Wayland's ideas of rationality and morality, let us now turn our attention to his specific economic theories. Wayland's most noteworthy economic treatise was *The Elements of Political Economy,* published in its final edition by his sons seven years after his death. A compilation of classroom lectures, lengthy research, and excellent scholarship, this book became a classic economic textbook in the decades surrounding the Civil War.

Political economy is, according to Wayland, the systematic study of God's universal laws that govern wealth. Wealth is defined as any object or service capable of gratifying a desire. One's possessions or the lack thereof define the degree of one's wealth or poverty.[73] Wealth is, however, not merely defined by the amassing of goods and services. Following such classical economists as Adam Smith and David Ricardo, Wayland defined wealth according to its value or utility. The utility of a good is the pleasure, satisfaction, or need-fulfillment derived from production and consumption. "The DEGREE of intrinsic value of any substance depends on the NATURE and the NUMBER of the desires which it can gratify."[74] In addition to its implied subjectivism, one should note the psychological and quantitative aspects of value. Classical theorists, and Wayland with them, placed the origin of value in the labor it takes to produce goods, as validated by choices in the market.

Further, he borrowed the classical school's labor theory of value. According to this, the degree of value of a product depends upon the amount of labor that went into producing it. Wayland said of this theory:

> it ALONE enters into computation in fixing exchangeable value. Thus, the exchangeable value of iron and of gold depends upon the . . . labor which must be employed in preparing them to gratify desire.[75]

But acceptance of the classical theory of value posed a problem. How could one account for creation's intrinsic potential and its relationship to value? Does not air, for example, have some intrinsic value before it reaches the market? Therefore, has not God imputed value into the creation before human labor transforms the raw materials?

In confronting this question, Wayland was forced to contradict himself. He believed that God placed intrinsic value in raw material. However, this value could only be realized in consumption. He talked of the raw material's value but could not measure it, because his view of full value was tied to consumption and to the market. In short, Wayland was never clear as to how the mixture of the consumer, the laborer's efforts, and nature's intrinsic worth contributed to value.[76]

Wayland also reduced the worker's value to the labor imparted to a product, a reduction typical of capitalism.[77] The classic Christian theorists we have studied would reject such a narrow, incorporated definition of man; they would choose rather a definition that honored the many sides of human value and worth. This reduction of the worker's value to the production activity comes dangerously close to idolatry and to the diminishment of human worth, both of which Wayland, as an Evangelical, of course abhorred.

Wayland's economic theories were predicated upon utilitarian principles and laissez-faire doctrines. In order to understand his utilitarianism more fully, we must look briefly at some of utilitarianism's fundamental notions. Like the classical theorists, utilitarians believed that value or utility was to be equated with happiness or pleasure. Happiness or pleasure and the avoidance of pain were the only universal human laws governing life. Jeremy Bentham said:

> Nature has placed mankind under the governance of two sovereign

masters: pain and pleasure. It is for them alone to point out what we ought to do, as well as to determine what we shall do. On the one hand the standard of right and wrong, on the other hand the chain of causes and effects are fastened to their throne.[78]

Utilitarianism not only had moral absolutes, but it also evolved into a view that attempted to calculate the relationship between morality and happiness. Utilities, or individual bits of desired happiness, could and should be numbered so as to ascertain individual and collective utility or happiness. In effect, by numbering preferences, utilitarianism attempted to calibrate consciousness. Bentham said,

> Sum up all the values of all the pleasures on one side, and all those of pain on the other. The balance, if it be on the side of pleasure, will be the GOOD tendency of the act upon the whole, with respect to the interests of that INDIVIDUAL person. . . . Sum up the numbers expressive of the degree of GOOD tendency with respect to each individual . . . and you will ascertain the GOOD upon the whole.[79]

Morality and pleasure so defined became readily amenable to calculations of consumption and production, as we shall shortly see.

Bentham's statement just quoted betrays the presence of what has been called the felicific calculus. Felicity (happiness or pleasure) could be calculated for an entire society by calculating the sum of individual consumption. Indeed, Bentham believed that groups are composed of individuals.[80] Consumption was said to bring pleasure exactly in proportion to the number of goods and services consumed; and this state could be calculated. Thus, the more one increased possession and consumption, the more utility or pleasure would arise. But increasing utility was not only a matter of multiplying pleasure; it was, it must be remembered, a universal moral obligation.

> Thus, it becomes evident how the relationship between prosperity and morality has come full circle. The only valid moral principle in life is equated with the acquisition of the greatest number of utilities. In addition, goods are positive factors of utility, and labor is a negative factor of utility.[81]

In sum, utilitarianism was a deeply religio-moral movement that would shape a considerable part of classical economic theory and would, in turn, influence nineteenth-century Evangelicalism.

Wayland assented to and consistently applied utilitarianism in his formulas. Happiness and pleasure were equated with the increase in consumption and production of capital-related goods.[82] The same equation was held to be true for one's labor. Wayland said, "If a man increases his labor ten times, there will be ten times more value created and thus ten times more enjoyment or happiness."[83]

Like many of the utilitarians, Wayland was, however, no crass hedonist.[84] He fought for frugality, fair wages, and justice for laborers while warning against all extravagances. He hoped thereby to personalize sumptuary laws. Nevertheless, because of his need to maximize utility, his mandates to be both benevolent and "happy" contradict each other. Speaking of consumption, Wayland said: "Every man is permitted to enjoy in the most unlimited manner the advantages of his labor . . . gaining all that he can."[85] Nevertheless, "the habit of benevolence tends to moderate and correct the intense love of gain."[86] In modifying this lust, benevolence adds greater amounts of utility through the "joys of giving." Like Finney, Wayland was reaffirming a uniquely American project: to gain all one can so that one can give away as much as one can in charity. Justice, in part, was defined as the ability to purchase, consume, and labor while being benevolent. This notion of justice is discernible in Rockefeller as it is in Henry Ford.[87] It remains a solution to poverty in a voluntaristic, capitalistic society. This voluntarism only furthers serves to strengthen, however, the ties between God and Mammon, through the maximization of the gain-give principle.

Wayland extended his concept of utility to define the class structure. Wayland defined a class, as did the classic capitalists, by its relationship to the function that it held within the production process. Specialization, division of labor, and a rationalized workplace were the specifics that determined class position. Like the utilitarians, Wayland believed that labor was a disutility—painful, boring, and dangerous per se. Humanity was caught in an impossible dilemma: it had to work in order to maintain itself in the world, but because of its sin, labor was painfully done in "the sweat of our brow." In this schema, work was not under a curse but still redeemable; it was evil because of an inherent malady.[88]

More frighteningly, Wayland related his theories of utility to the *consumption* of labor. He viewed the laborer as a means to the end of production. If a laborer was injured, the primary harm was done to the workplace and not to the worker.[89] In this schema, labor became objectified under the norm of efficiency; it aimed at the realization of maximum utility and, hence, profit.[90] Nevertheless, Wayland's theories of utility, along with a rather automatic view of circulating capital, were preached as a *working-class* doctrine.

Wayland argued that the greater the ratio of capital to labor, the greater would be the stimulus to work as greater profits could be realized. According to Wayland, "the laboring classes are really more interested in the increase of capital than are the wealthy class."[91] He hoped that the laborer would bank his surplus wealth, thus creating future investment capital. He took it for granted that the wealthy would never spend any capital on unproductive luxuries.

The relationship of utility and production to the work of the institutional church did not escape Wayland's notice. Science, the Scriptures, and productivity became his watchwords while at Brown. "The circulation of the Scriptures, the increase of Sabbath schools and the preaching of the gospel are of the very greatest importance to the productive energies of the country."[92] Here in Wayland's theory is the correlate of Finney's Rochester revival. The work of the institutional church was to provide the motive force necessary to sustain the grinding factory process and to restrict the social decay caused by the industrial machine.

Nationalistic chauvinism seemed also to be tied to theories of utility and capital formation. In keeping with the incorporating spirit of the times, Wayland argued that civilization advances through the gratification of the greatest number of human desires that can be accommodated within God's framework. Western superiority over "savage" nations could be determined, in part, by a calculation of final capital.

> We see that the advantages which we enjoy over savage nations result ... from a greater possession of fixed capital or pre-exerted industry. ... Hence savages can only barter inferior goods. ... An Indian who exchanges pelts ... for a rifle, powder and bullets has improved his condition.[93]

This statement first appeared in print in 1837, and we can see why Wayland's work was almost universally accepted by a young republic moving toward a manifest destiny.

There is a *reductio ad absurdum* in his theory of the military use of gunpowder which parallels the *reductio ad absurdum* in currently held doctrines of nuclear "realism." Wayland argued that gunpowder had a moral advantage over other methods of warfare; since its introduction, wars had been conducted on a more humane principle. He argued that the more energetic the means of destruction, the more the enemy would pause. One wonders if Wayland, had he remained intellectually vital after the Civil War, would have reversed his position.

In summary, we have seen how a mid-century Evangelical intellectual succeeded in establishing a socioeconomic theory based upon the classical doctrines of capitalism. We can see in Wayland's masterfully constructed edifice that he gave credence to proto-industrialization. Acceptance of Wayland's views was due to the consensus surrounding Protestant hegemony and liberal-democratic values. Common Sense Realism provided a foundation for a consensual worldview that acted as an apology for a disrupted industrial culture. However, as Evangelicals came to adhere to this worldview, they increasingly moved away from their reformed moorings.

Russell Conwell

Having completed a study of an evangelist and a scholar, we now turn our attention to one of the most prominent postbellum pastors. In the late 1880s Russell Conwell pastored Grace Baptist Temple in Philadelphia, at that time the largest single Protestant congregation in North America.[94] In addition to being a pastor, he was a philanthropist, educator and one of the most respected orators of his day. His most famous speech, "Acres of Diamonds," was given over six thousand times in the span of fifty years.[95] Above all, he was a strong defender of the democratic ideals that were so necessary for an increasingly beleaguered free enterprise system.

Conwell was born in 1843 in the Berkshire Mountains of Massachusetts, a long distance (in many respects) from Philadelphia. Conwell learned the values of patience, self-control, sacrifice, and perseverance from his farmer parents. Conwell once noted that by the time he had reached high school, these virtues had become a fixed part of his personality.[96] While in high school (which he had finished by age sixteen), he mastered Francis Wayland's basic texts, *Moral Science* and *Political Economy*. In 1860, owing to the sacrifice of his family, Conwell enrolled in Yale University. During his one year there, Conwell arose at 4:30 A.M., made his way to a part-time job, and then to a day of classes and a night of study. As a collegian, he later confessed, he had developed a desperate atheism due to the bitterness he felt over his poverty and its injustices. He had promised himself never to return to these depths.

In 1861, at the age of seventeen, he enlisted in the Army. Because of his leadership qualities, he was elevated to the rank of captain at the request of his peers. During the war, Conwell's company was once pinned down by enemy fire. Johnny Ring, one of Conwell's men, sacrificed his life to save the lives of the entire company. As Ring lay dying, he presented a sword to Conwell symbolizing this sacrifice. It carried with it a debt which Conwell spent the rest of his life repaying.

A handsomely decorated Conwell was about to emerge from the Civil War unscathed when he was seriously wounded. His life lay in the balance. While Conwell was in the hospital the chaplain repeatedly tried to speak with him about "eternal things." His atheism held. Finally, the chaplain's persistence paid off and Conwell experienced a conversion. The most remarkable thing about his conversion was that the standard Evangelical signs—repentance, surrender to Christ, and a filling of the Spirit—were lacking. In their place were (in Conwell's terms) a "change in thought," a renewed sense of sacrifice and discipline, and a vision of "eternal things."[97]

In 1865 Conwell left the Army and started the study of law in Minneapolis. There he helped establish the *Minneapolis Daily Chronicle.* and a local chapter of the Y.M.C.A. In the pattern of the 1858 Wall Street revival, noontime prayer meetings were held in his office. It was during this time that Conwell's true Evangelical roots began to bear fruit.

Tragedy struck in 1868. One wintry night, with the temperature at 35 degrees below zero, Conwell's house burned to the ground. Running without a coat from his office to his home, he damaged his health. For two years his health and family suffered immensely. With his career prospects looking bleak in Minneapolis, he moved to Boston, where his considerable journalistic skills helped him find a job for a then-prestigious newspaper, the *Boston Traveller.*

His salary as a journalist, the royalties gained from several noteworthy articles he wrote about his career in the Civil War, and the income from his new legal practice enabled Conwell to become more financially secure. As his public status and financial security grew, Conwell was able to offer free legal advice to widows, orphans, and soldiers seeking Army pensions. Such acts of kindness and sacrifice became characteristic of Conwell's career. It seems Conwell had begun to repay the debt engendered by Ring's death.

Between 1872 and 1874 two major events took place in Conwell's life. After his first wife died of heart problems in 1872, Conwell took up a self-taught program in theology. His studies in theology led him to his first pastorate in 1874 in Lexington, Massachusetts, where he dealt with the loss of his wife by taking on increasing amounts of work. His tiny, disaster-ridden congregation grew in membership and national renown. Within a few short years his fame as a journalist and lawyer was surpassed by the fame of his homiletical abilities.

A small but promising congregation in Philadelphia called him to be their pastor; he accepted in 1882.

When he arrived at Grace Baptist Temple, he found that debt, internal disputes, and a dwindling membership had put the church in a precarious position. By the end of his first year as pastor, however, Conwell had secured one thousand two hundred new members and had begun to erect one of the world's largest, most handsome edifices. Initial pledges totaled over $9,000.

In part, the secret of Conwell's success was his practice of the virtues he preached in the pulpit. He believed in sacrifice, saving, the necessity of conversion and flexibility. The resulting worldview appealed to a variety of socioeconomic groups. Conwell used a blend of fairs, dinners, promotional events, and congregational sacrifice to secure the needed monies for a blossoming mission and outreach program. His earliest budgets included a legion of charities. Indeed, the increasing ecclesiasticalization of mission and outreach became a marked characteristic of his ministry. By the zenith of Conwell's ministry he had provided important support for Temple University, the Conwell School of Theology, the Garretson, Greatheart, Samaritan hospitals, and numerous charities—all from within the institutional church.

Conwell carried on a correspondence with rail magnate Anthony Drexel, and started, while at Grace Baptist, a chapter of the "Do-It-Now" Club. Likening his ministry to a busy, growing urban center, Conwell never put off for tomorrow what he could do today. His excessively busy schedule oftentimes wearied him, but he persisted. Conwell additionally strengthened the church's mission by attracting some of the foremost business minds in the area to voluntarily help him in managing the church.

How did these businessmen affect the worldview of Grace Baptist? "What has contributed most as a means used by God to bring Grace Church to efficiency? It was inspired, sanctified common sense in enterprising, careful businessmen. These men were earnest and conservative."[98] Here is all the antebellum nervous energy and postbellum efficiency thinking anyone could want. What was called "sanctified common sense" was nothing less than popular forms of managerial efficiency voluntarily applied to the institutional church. A bicameral board, with Conwell acting as an overseer, ran the business side of the church through the board of trustees. A "practical business model" was adopted, based upon the principles of efficiency, productivity, the gain-give principle, and the institutionalization of charity. Hard work, sound investment, and discipline helped Conwell start his charitable empire. He said of his business managers, "When they needed money they knew where the money was and what securities were good in the market."[99]

Conwell's fame spread. Historians of the Republican Party asked him to write stories about several of their prominent members. Not to be outdone, journalists from the *New York Times* and the *Boston Traveller* asked him to write columns about the populist values beginning to solidify in the United States. During this era his favorite subject was his recollections of Lincoln, whom he had met during the war.

In 1886 Grace Baptist Church was to make history: Temple University was started in the basement of the church. Like Conwell, the earliest students were working-class people who studied at night after a long day of work. Temple was thus founded upon Conwell's own working-class ideals of hard work, sacrifice, discipline, and open admissions. Temple gradually helped blue-collar students assume their place within the managerial and professional classes of incorporating culture. "It is our first aim," cried Conwell during a commencement speech, "to teach people to be more useful to their employers."[100] Conwell would even say euphorically of education that "want of food or clothing, or home, or friends, or morals, or religion, seemed to stem from the lack of right instruction and proper discipline."[101] Indeed, Conwell's institutions were founded as institutions of, for, and by the people—upon working-class, not aristocratic ideals. Overall, Conwell's values were those of a Christian populist.

Conwell's fear of a monied aristocracy grew as the century came to a close. This explains, in part, why Samaritan Hospital was established for the poor patient and the financially dependent student. He feared that if monied people financed and endowed medical colleges, the middle class would eventually be excluded. Hard work and not state aid made good doctors, according to Conwell.[102] He did not mean to keep education mediocre but he did mean to prevent "approved schools" from being funded and accredited by the wealthy.

Conwell's working-class, democratic ideals are most clearly seen in his study of Abraham Lincoln. Having met him while pleading for the life of one of his men, young Captain Conwell grew to admire Lincoln. Like Conwell's family, Lincoln's had nothing by way of education, wealth or social position. Both men had to work hard, living but one step away from poverty. Both remained honest and generous throughout their lives. Conwell's compassion faltered only when he spoke of various white people who had passed up the opportunity that Lincoln took. Conwell sang the industrial melody: "Those poor whites, lazy people that lie around the grocery stores and who drink, who chew tobacco and who swear and shoot each other occasionally . . . they have lost their chance."[103] Such homilies, given on the occasion of the celebration of Lincoln's birthday, served to remind aspiring managers and Philadelphia workers that the industrial system had room for them.

Conwell took the opportunity, fifty years after Lincoln's death, to reflect more systematically on Lincoln's virtues. Lincoln was, for Conwell, a study in contrasts. On one hand he was pale, gaunt, poorly dressed and socially unpolished. On the other hand, when speaking against slavery, "wave after wave of telling eloquence rolled forth from this uncouth, gaunt figure and literally clashed itself against the hard, resisting minds of any prejudiced audience."[104] Lincoln's soft "woman-like" compassion for the South did not hide, according to Conwell, his gigantic strength and capacity for decisive action. Such delicate balances enabled Lincoln to laugh at pretentiousness while attempting to forge a Union around those virtues that Conwell both shared and admired. Incorporating culture could do no better than to adopt the virtues of the Lincoln who relativized overwhelming situations with an understanding and compassionate laugh.[105]

Conwell's apology for democratic values peaked when he preached on the virtues of free enterprise. In a sermon on Romans 13:7, "owe no man anything, but love one another" (AV), Conwell took the text as a warning against debt. "Anyone who sleeps overnight with money in his pocket which is overdue, is a thief."[106] Conwell then placed Paul's injunction in Romans on a par with the Ten Commandments, thus making it a universal moral law. To violate such an injunction, he thought, was tantamount to lapsing into slavery. "Let not the sun go down on any debt . . . and let not the new year come to an end with any bill unpaid which you can pay," was Conwell's advice for his congregation.[107]

Interestingly, few modern exegetes agree with Conwell's interpretation of this passage. A closer look at this passage will demonstrate how thoroughly Conwell was influenced by incorporating culture. He treats "debt" entirely in economic terms and thereby truncates the passage. Reformed church exegete John Murray says,

> This should not be taken as a general exhortation that we are to discharge our obligations to all men. It is to be understood of the obligations we owe those in authority in the state. . . . The "tribute" corresponds to our term tax levied on persons and property.[108]

By reading the Bible through incorporated glasses, Conwell unwittingly bolstered a credit system whose expansion rested upon dependability. Moreover, the one-sided injunction aimed at the borrower virtually ignored Calvin's warning that a lender may be "stealing" or gaining excessive interest rates through a variety of deceptive means.

Conwell's sermon on Deuteronomy 30:19–20 is also telling. The text talks about Joshua's entry into the promised land. Joshua wants Israel to make a choice as to what gods/God they will serve and thus how they will develop their culture. This "choice" is prompted by a religious reenactment of how God rescued them from the bondage of Egypt.

Conwell chose to use this text to challenge introspective graduates to find a place in industrializing culture. Said Conwell,

> The wise way to decide how to be the most successful is to learn what the world needs. . . . What does the world need in business . . . in agriculture . . . in art, music or religion? Decide what is the most-needed thing and put yourself in the place where you will be the most needed.[109]

Conwell linked Joshua's call for covenantal obedience to faithfulness to the workplace.

Finally, Conwell was not beyond using a certain measure of civil religion to secure support for the free enterprise system. Conwell used Flag Day to warn the nation of the large monopolies being formed which would hurt "the people's" chance to participate in economic gains. Speaking of the flag as a symbol of America's liberty, Conwell said, "We see it shelter great combinations that . . . by force of capital are taking your liberty from you and from your children, and raising up a monied aristocracy that would rule the land instead of the people."[110] Conwell's statement came on the heels of a populist and progressive revolt which he, in part, tended to support.

In siding with the Populists and the Progressives, Conwell tended not to disagree with many of the basic tenets of capitalism; he simply wanted to make the system more serviceable to all the people. His famous "Acres of Diamonds" speech clearly demonstrated his support for industrializing culture. Conwell earned over five million dollars in royalties and honoraria from this speech, all of which he gave to disadvantaged students. In this speech his famous "supply a need" vision help determine nearly every known vocation in America.[111]

Diamonds, so Conwell thought, existed in one's own back yard.

Riches or acres of diamonds were within the reach of almost everyone if they would but seize the opportunities that beckoned them.
"I say that you ought to get rich, and it is your duty to get rich. To
make money is to preach the gospel."[112] Not only did he believe
that making money was equivalent to the heart of the gospel, but
he also believed that a vast majority of those who made large sums
of money did so honestly. Speaking of entrepreneurs John Jacob
Astor and Cornelius Vanderbilt, Conwell said, "The men who get
rich may be the most honest men you find in the community . . .
ninety-eight out of one hundred rich men of America are honest."[113]
It is not an exaggeration to suggest that the theme of this speech
was that the practice of godliness leads to the collection of gold.
Indeed, money printed Bibles, built churches, sent missionaries,
and paid preachers. Conversely, the poor were being punished for
their sins and were not therefore godly in conduct.[114] We must note
here that Conwell directly contradicts all classic Christian reflection.

Conwell did not attribute basic economic evil to "the people," as
did the Populists of his day. He placed the blame for the economic
evils of the day on the structure of monopolies and not on the
people who built and supported them. Curiously, Conwell the Evangelical unwittingly mimicked some of the Protestant liberals of his
day by viewing evil apart from human responsibility. In both scenar-
ios, evil is externalized, responsibility diminished, and the inherent
goodness of man is not fundamentally questioned.

We have noted Conwell's decided support for the virtues of democratic capitalism. We must also note his "ecclesiasticism," or wholesale attempt to influence culture through the institutional church.
Conwell's church and its activities were the largest and most vigorously philanthropic in North America. Grace Temple was literally a
public welfare agency in its own right. Conwell did not follow, in
any sense, Dwight L. Moody's model of cultural irresponsibility. A
blanket of humanitarian agencies, originating from Grace Baptist,
covered the city as a winter comforter would a bed.

Yet it was precisely through this ecclesiasticism that Conwell
served the forces of industrial culture rather than reformed them.
One historian lists Conwell as part of the "institutionalization" of
welfare in the late nineteenth century. Under the auspices of ecclesiastical associations, voluntary mission projects like tract societies, hospitals, colleges, employment centers, nurseries, health
centers, and philanthropic organizations, an ecumenical service
network was established. These agencies, while ecumenical, never
forgot their particular ecclesiastical roots. Denominational and con-

fessional boundaries were strictly maintained, as was the power of the clergy to oversee these ministries. Often the stated purpose of such organizations involved both a "sacred" and a "secular" agenda, and as time went by the secular agenda gradually gained ascendancy. Indeed, "in a broader sense, the institutional church was the 'religious' phase of the increasing determination to implement, under urban conditions, the inherited ideals of humanitarian democracy."[115] This strategy attempted to address industrial results through para-ecclesiastical associations, defined by democratic, progressive ideals.

Like many influential people of his day, Conwell showed a decided tendency to support wholesale philanthropy and charity while downplaying social justice or treating it as a phase of market activity. Conwell did not have the resources to give away vast amounts of money like Carnegie and Rockefeller. He did believe, however, that charity was among the primary virtues. At the opening of Samaritan Hospital (named, of course, after the biblical parable of charity), Conwell said,

> Charity is composed of sympathy and self-sacrifice. To make a gift become charity the recipient must feel that it is given out of sympathy; that the donor has made a sacrifice to give it; that it was not intended as permanent help . .; and that it is not given as a right.[116]

Conwell went on to say that state charity, or any other form of mandatory charity, is not voluntarily given and, therefore, borders on fraud. Conwell honestly believed that large-scale, voluntary, institutional charity or philanthropy would adequately cover many, if not all, social needs.

Conwell's approach to wholesale charity represents a significant departure from antebellum practices. Industrial culture needed more relief than mere individuals could give. Large institutions, ecclesiastical networks, and vast amounts of money had to be coordinated, especially in an urban environment, if adequate relief was to follow. Although the individual was still the primary social unit—indeed it was this ideology of individualism that helped precipitate this crisis—large philanthropic institutions were created to counterbalance the phenomena surrounding Industrialism. In this sense Conwell and Rockefeller were alike; both believed that some form of individual associationism was necessary.

Such postbellum philanthropy had a momentous task. Large-scale charities—often run by the clergy—helped sustain entrepreneurial legitimacy[117] and were used to fight urban decay. This fact helps explain Conwell's friendship with department store king John Wanamaker. The men shared similar Evangelical and worldview commitments.[118] While some, inspired by Carnegie's "Gospel of Wealth," preached Social Darwinism for the marketplace, Wanamaker's charity manifested a considerably greater degree of compassion.

In surveying the lives of an evangelist, scholar, and pastor, we have noted how one version of Protestantism attempted to accommodate itself to secularizing culture. That such an accommodation was bound to wax and wane in influence and popularity seems evident. It remains for us to legitimize our critical analysis by suggesting alternatives to the problems at hand.

7

Exploring a Richer Life: Alternatives to the Problems at Hand

Industrialism and Evangelicalism seem to contradict each other in principle and intention. The naturalistic materialism of Industrialism seems to sharply contradict Evangelicalism's notion of a supernatural theism. Deism's explicit rationalism, replete with a self-contained mechanistic view of the world, seems to differ from the notion that God providentially governs the world. The pessimism of many postbellum Evangelicals seems to contrast with the belief in economic progress held by industrial enthusiasts. Finally, Evangelicalism's dualism seems to stand in sharp contrast to modernity's materialistic monism.

However both views, as has been argued, are united at a deeper level—perhaps a religious level. Both shared a commitment to democratic individualism and an autonomous will. Each, especially in the antebellum period, grew enthusiastic about the notion of progress, with many Evangelicals connecting economic and technological progress with the millennium. For both, happiness was significantly (but not totally) oriented toward the production and consumption process. Both endorsed current views of the workings of natural law, thus legitimizing a mechanistic view of market operations. The result was a similar social commitment to the values of republicanism, discipline, voluntarism, and personal benevolence. Most surprisingly, both believed that religion was a compartmentalized phenomenon. These deeper liaisons force us to conclude that Evangelicalism in this era became a culturally captive religion!

If we are to free Evangelicalism—and perhaps Protestantism in general—from its Babylonian captivity, we need to see if any of its core beliefs can provide us with an alternative to the present era.

Such a concern with core beliefs is also central to much contemporary work in the philosophy of science. The work of Thomas Kuhn on paradigms, Michael Polanyi's view of "commitment" and

159

Gerard Radnitzky's work on "steering fields", for example, point out the need for a less positivistic view of science and of life more generally. Let us see if something of the same can be done for Evangelicalism.

Perhaps as we discuss core alternatives we can begin to address Marx's concern with a narcotic effect of religion upon people and Weber's analysis of the inner affinity of capitalism and Calvinism (which is in the ideological family of Evangelicalism). Recent scandals within portions of Evangelicalism and the increase of the problems surrounding poverty, moreover, make such deliberations mandatory.

Core Alternatives

First and foremost, the notion of the "gospel" has always been a core concern for Evangelicals. We will try to relate this core notion to the concepts of the creation, the fall, redemption, cosmology, and the nature of evil and its remedy. As to the problem of an incorporated culture, we will use a cluster of terms related to the concept of the "simultaneity of norm realization."[1] (that is, a harmonious blend of societal demands).

CREATION

Evangelicalism and capitalism both need to consider an alternative view of creation. If we try to flee culture, as Dwight L. Moody does when he speaks of an otherworldly lifeboat, then little help can be offered to the suffering we see around us. If we accept the supernaturalistic, Aristotelian rationalism of Common Sense Realism, then we reinforce the individualism of capitalism, as we saw with Wayland's view of the cosmos. Finally, if we accept capitalism's mechanistic view of the world, then indeed "the free gifts of nature" become so much fodder for the industrial machine. Thus, an alternative cosmology seems warranted.

"Creation" here means the entire cosmos to which God "speaks"—an orderly matrix, the home for humans, animals, plants, and natural substrata. This order simultaneously provides the context for the meaningfulness of all life and the arena and means of divine revelation.[2] Although any discussion of creation must refer to nature and culture, the definition of creation is not ultimately founded upon either of these. In keeping with the central theme of this work, we shall define creation at its root as:

a "religious" ... idea, because it provides an answer to one of the fundamental religious questions of man's life, namely, the question of the ultimate meaning of life as a contingent, temporal being set in the wider context of nature and of history.[3]

The terms "contingent" and "temporal" expand upon our Augustianian assumptions. By contingency we mean dependency and by temporal we mean time and being. God has created the cosmos and is intimately related to it, while not being dependent upon it. God exists "above" it in the sense that God is superior to, and therefore sets the conditions for, life. It is proper, therefore, to call God supratemporal in that all of life is ultimately dependent upon God for its meaning and development.

This concept of dependency affirms that God, as revealed in the Scriptures, is the origin and the root of all temporal and cultural diversity.

We are raising questions of origins because we are asking about the ultimate security, the meaning, the destiny of our own experience . . . . We are talking about mysteries, not problems, something we must think about, but not something we can control, dissect, measure, test or even fully contemplate objectively and define clearly.[4]

This view of the creation suggests its goodness, inherent meaning, ultimacy and theistic governance. While not inimical to empirical investigation of natural phenomena, it does not depend upon the verifiability postulate for its raison d'etre.

To speak of creation's dependence upon God for its structure and efficacy is to affirm simultaneously creation's referential character and its lack of absolute necessity. To assign it such a humble role does not destroy creation's dignity and majesty; rather, it affirms God's awesome beauty and holiness, his essential otherness from creation. To set creation in this framework is to place it in flux, partiality, finitude and incompleteness. "It therefore follows from this that in all creation there is nothing worthy of our ultimate worship for there is nothing that is not finite, partial, and transitory. The doctrine of creation is the great bulwark against idolatry or the worship of a creature, or of one partial aspect of life in the place of God."[5] Thus we begin our address to Mammon.

This view of the creation stands in sharp contrast to those of Deism and any other dualistic worldview[s]. In Deism, the world machine is wound up like a clock and forgotten about by God. God's "otherness" here means, at the extreme, a laissex-faire attitude (an attitude mimicked, not so ironically, in the economic sector). God is therefore in Deism always to some degree finite, in that he is restricted by an antithetical principle that forbids his entry into the world. God is forbidden to enter the world because of the absolute principle of creation's autonomy: creation runs itself and may have no interference. This deistic view of creation simultaneously forces creation into a mechanistic mold and frees autonomous humanity to rule the world. In contrast to this is the concept of *bara,* the Hebrew designation for the sovereignty of God. According to it, "creation was created . . . called out of nothingness, without conflict, without contradictory effort, by the absolute, invincible decree of an omnipresent power having unlimited control over the world."[6]

Divine Providence or sustenance of the creation means maintenance and preservation as well as the unfolding of possibilities.[7] These notions can form the basis for human stewardship as a caring, developing, blessing attitude towards the creation. Moreover, divine sustenance means that as creation evolves, its evolution manifests something of the original purpose and meaningful patterns placed in the creation by the Creator. Biologists have helped us see this continuity. These patterns are kept and maintained by a covenant or a pledge of unending fidelity by God with all of the creation.[8] In the keeping of the covenant, God provides all that is necessary for the maintenance and the rich fruition of the creation.

However—and this is crucial—God's governing of the world must never finally and fully be equated with any particular human conception, any "manifest destiny," for this leads to chauvinism. God can especially bless a single nation, but the fruit of that favor is gracious and must therefore be shared; its expansion must be non-chauvinistic. God's intentions speak to all cultures and peoples, and all have something therefore to contribute to the common human fabric of life.

Thus, the domain of Providence cannot be restricted to one's personal life, as Evangelicalism tended to do in this era. Still less can it be truncated to suprabiblical categories, as in Dispensationalism, because of the cohesive ongoing organic nature of the process. Providence can never be associated merely with increased wealth, or poverty with God's wrath, as this would make Christ—the "Son of Man" who had no place to lay his head, who was economically poor—a terrible sinner. In short, "popular sovereignty" cannot be equated with divine sovereignty.

This view of creation may seem abstract and impersonal in that the description of God's relationship to the creation is couched in language that does not fully reveal who God is and therefore seems not to touch our lives. But only God can truly reveal who he is. The concept of revelation has traditionally meant the self-disclosure of God, who acts in freedom to faithfully and truly reveal who he is and what he wants.[9] Although revelation has as its context the entire creation, its origin is in God. "We can only speak of creation on the basis of revelation. . . . It is the same Word which created the world which also reveals to us the truth that the world has been created."[10] This unitary Word, which created the world, comes in three forms: as scriptural, as general or creational, and as Christ, the "Word Made Flesh." For the moment we will concentrate upon the creational Word of God, or "the book of nature" as many natural scientists have called it.

The term "general" or "creational" tells us the scope but not the significance of this form of revelation. It speaks of laws, norms or principles, and universal divine disclosures about the broadest possible intentions of God for the creation. He reveals himself to the creation and to humanity, its crown, so that the creation may enjoy the mutuality of convental love and find in him our meaning and purpose. Thus, we must stand against the predominant nineteenth-century secular view which attempted to find meaning and certainty in a deistic "rational substantial activity."[11] We also must object to the Evangelical view of an Aristotelian reason complete with semi-autonomous natural laws, whose origins were not in God's freely given covenantal faithfulness. It is a hypostatization or idolatry of the rational mode. Such a stance narrows life's possibilities. Our view of God's free activity seeks to reverse, moreover, a tradition that would force God to obey the dictates of reason. Our view in no way detracts from the culmination of God's revelation in Christ. Rather it seeks to affirm the cosmic scope of God's revelation and thus to broaden the seemingly truncated Evangelical soteriology and cosmology.[12]

Our alternative view of the creation suggests a critique of Wayland's views of natural law. We find no fund of universal, natural, value-free, objective, rational knowledge available to humans, as natural law theories tend to do. Such theories typically abstract such knowledge from the thinker's ego and the flux of history, and therefore tend toward a static, conservative worldview. (As we see it, general revelation is a driving force in the development of history and is therefore progressive.) Natural law formulations, moreover, tend to restrict the force of sin by arguing, sometimes subtly, that reason is somehow not subject to the same degree of evil influence as other human functions. This often leads to an optimistic view that expects a rational, moral order—oftentimes statically conceived—to culminate in a millennium, or at least in greater amounts of peace and prosperity. (Such a view once held by Woodrow Wilson.) The human projection and absolutization of rationality confuses the "sovereignty of reason" with the lawful structure placed on the creation by God.[13] By so confusing the issue, reason believes that it has found an order in the creation that in reality is little more than a projection of its own ultimacies.

These projections do not occur only on the conservative side. In reacting to a mechanistic-deistic form of natural law economic theories, the economist Lester Ward, was more than simply rebutting his colleague William G. Sumner. He was attempting to assert human freedom over the forces of nature and culture by stressing the human ability to manipulate and change economic reality. Because the laws of supply and demand were not believed to be immutable, it was thought the government should coordinate aspects of the economy for desired ends. Ironically, this intervention, which was supposed to promote human freedom by promoting "justice" and broadening consumption and regulating excess, became itself a form of lawful regulation. The functions of Providence became increasingly secularized in the nineteenth century as government at all levels began to manipulate markets—a fact all too clear to us today.

A truer notion of creation must suggest a natural and cultural environment that is a rich milieu of coherence and meaning for human activity. "Meaning implies, then, that our life exists within an environment of events coherent enough so that what we do can be regarded as an effective means for what we want; unless there is a coherent relation of means and ends, our life seems to be pointless."[14] In the nineteenth century the themes of expanding income, leisure, and "happiness" attempted to give meaning and purpose to life. In this respect, both the Christian and the secular economic materialistic worldviews offered patterns of coherence.

What is meant by the term "meaning"? In the Augustian tradition, it is related to time. Time, for Augustine, is not simple duration. It is the *context* of creation or the temporal modes of diversity.[15] Because meaning can never originate from the creation, but can only be given to it, time and temporality are said to be referential; we must look beyond creation for ultimate meaning. This referential character of time forces humans to look beyond flux and diverse ways of living to the true origin of meaning. If the heart, the central agency of human conviction, should vest creation with the attributes of divinity, restlessness occurs. Such restlessness includes, but goes far beyond, anxiety and mere hyperactivity; it extends to the very depths of human existence and betrays a lack of security.

This fact explains Augustine's famous aphorism about God that "our hearts are restless until they find rest in Thee." Meaning, then, can never *ultimately* be found in the creation, for God does not owe his origin to any part of the creation nor is anything in creation ultimate.

Thus, God has been called "transcendent" in theological studies. This transcendence does not refer to his isolation from the creation or lack of care for it (for he has revealed himself); rather it refers to the fact that God is not dependent upon creational forces but rather rules them. Humanity is called to place final trust in this transcendent God precisely because it is God who orders the flux and diversity of life.

> Through man's certainty in God's transcendent ordering of life, meaning, purpose and purposefulness can be salvaged from the abyss of inner futility, cultural idolatry and truncation. Only if we grasp some assurance of life's ultimate coherence and purpose and we affirm the immediate meaning of day-to-day life.[16]

In viewing God's transcendence in this manner, humanity can not only find meaning but a God who, while revealing Himself, gives purpose to life through transcendence.

In chapter 1 we referred to Dooyeweerd's idea of the various aspects of our lives and their relationship to meaning. The intent of his system is manifold. Suffice it to say at this point that questions of meaning, ultimacy, and aspects are directly relevant to our discussion. The aspects of our lives cannot sustain all of life's meaning; they must refer beyond themselves to a more ultimate origin. When the self—or some aspect of economics—becomes the referent or ultimate for life, reductionism occurs. While truncating life, such idolatry is nonetheless religious in nature.[17] Moreover, all aspects are interrelated, a fact that field theories of knowledge are beginning to recognize.

Categories of law, fundamental principles, or patterned regularity are universal in that all worldviews recognize them. The versions of the law structure or patterned regularity of the creation may vary between the static view of natural law theories or the view of positive or pragmatic law taken by those who believe natural law theories to be too rigid. It is not a question of the actuality of principles, but the functional force of presupposita that concerns us here. It remains for us to develop our theories concerning the ontic structure of law and thereby deepen our discussion of creation's meaning.

The creation manifests an order, structure or lawful arrangement, and integrality which can legitimately be linked to God's revelation of himself to the creation. This structure is not immutable, eternal, rational and fixed for all time, à la Plato. It is rather the delimiting dynamism of history. As delimiting, structures differentiate objects from other objects—plants from animals, say. Much of natural science is based upon a search for, and a dependence upon, these mechanisms of predictability for its functioning.

These structures are *not* found or manifested like Platonic ideals or ideal types and cannot be realized through the vehicle of metaphysical speculation or Gnostic emanation theories. Rather, the societal and natural structures, just like the overall governance given by God for creation, cannot be fully realized until there is a deep historical unfolding of their meaning by humans for culture and nature.

This view of law, though it forms the basis for human freedom and responsibility, lies in direct antithesis to the various secular theories. Like Luther, the various secular theories have pitted law against freedom, thus creating an artificial tension. The law is the context for our freedom, as evidenced by the nearly universal cry for justice or fairness and the ratification of positive laws to address grievances. There can be no freedom without law.

The law for creation, in addition to providing the context for responsibility and freedom, gives us the basis for a consistent theism. If indeed "God so loved the world," as Evangelicals are fond of saying, then his constant care for the world, including the chaos of Industrialism, is a manifestation of his covenantal or faithful care of creation in spite of its resultant disruptions. This view of law provides a rationale for an environmental and an economic ethic. Such an ethic can be provided because human autonomy is *not* ultimate. Lands cannot be raped forever; there are limits. Entire sectors of culture cannot be defined by their wealth-producing or consuming potential. Families, states, governments, and churches have a character and meaning that, while needing the various activities of wealth production and exchange, extend far beyond these necessities.

Creational law, moreover, overturns dualism, defined as it is by tensions, gradations, and autonomies. The creation is structured—in toto—in a manner that can only be called "very good." Accordingly, Christians should no longer consider evangelization as inherently superior to economic activity, or sexuality (properly conceived and practiced) as more suspect than prayer. All of life, being very good and referring beyond itself to God, has been given divine blessing. It is ours to enjoy! Thus, a gospel or an ethic that relegates one aspect or area of life to an inferior status contradicts the holistic goodness of life experienced every day.

Because religion is the radical, integral force of life, a "conversion" orients one deeply and thoroughly to the creation. Thus, the terms "world-flight Christianity" and "culturally irresponsible Christianity" are oxymorons.

Where did such social institutions as businesses, families, churches, and schools originate? What are their central purposes? Did they ultimately evolve out of human need, as naturalism suggests; or did they spring up because of the power of human adaptability? Were they the products of man, the master of nature? The answer to these and related questions will vary according to one's fundamental commitments and worldview. In our view, these societal structures have been adapted by persons and cultures to situations, but they originated from God and are, therefore, meant for human good and the glory of God. Their continued existence forms the basis for our resistance to reductionism.

Societal structures, resulting from God's commanding revelation, are meant to be made relevant. There is pattern for a community like a family and, carried within the pattern, a need for a response by particular families. The universal presence of family life helps explain its divine initiated pattern while its varied manifestations help explain its human subjective character. Although expressions may vary, however, "no structures arise solely out of the mere interactions of individuals in a situation";[18] they are given to us by God.

The phrase used by Kuyper and Dooyeweerd is *souvereiniteit in eigen kring* or sphere sovereignty. It means that various

> distinct spheres or structures of human authority . . . each having their own responsibility and decision-making power, which may not be usurped by those in authority another sphere, are operative in human affairs.[19]

The consequence is that while economics and the various functions of worship life, like our faith life, have their necessary places within the creation, their duties and responsibilities are in reality limited by other spheres of life. Any violation of the more or less specific boundaries of these spheres produces the kind of truncation, chauvinism, and myopia we have outlined. Without recognition of the integrity of each sphere, there arise "isms" or cultural reductionisms which seek to reduce the expression of life's rich meaning to one mode. Incorporation, economism, and revivalism are such reductionisms.

Classic liberalism has said that the reality and authority of such structures arise out of a state of "nature" and come to accommodate the needs of the free or autonomous individual. Since the actions of free autonomous individuals create and sustain these structures, people can mold these institutions to meet their perceived needs. In liberalism, to deny this freedom or autonomy is to violate a basic secular postulate of life. By accepting this functionalistic origin of business, Evangelicalism forsook its theistic roots and accepted the premises of secular individualism. This basically religious decision helped further cement Evangelicalism to Industrialism.

Because creation does manifest a basic coherence and a wholeness, as educational and scientific philosophies are recognizing, when one mode is absolutized, like the economic mode in economism, a corresponding mode or cluster of concepts is often exaggerated so as to correct the original imbalance. Thus, when industrialism with its materialistic, impersonal, manipulative, secularized worldview was promoted, Evangelicals like Finney were called upon to provide a counterbalance. Accordingly, Evangelicalism arose with a worldview that stressed a "supernatural," personalistic, "born-again," otherworldly, sacred gospel that did little more than raise one truncation against another. Evangelicals, defining themselves in reaction to secular tendencies, formed an accommodated worldview. One myopia faced off against another. But the balancing act carried within it an inherent tension that needed to be eased, and, as the century wore on and as secularization increased, it *was* eased. Evangelicalism lost its cultural power, and became somewhat more secluded and divided as reactionary Fundamentalists drifted farther away from culture and classical Christian expression. More than "balance" was needed.

An additional distinction needs to be added to our discussion about the lawfulness of creation. There is a difference between the laws for nature and laws for culture. The former laws are, for humanity, more or less ironclad. Assuming no external intervention, if one jumped off a roof one hundred times, one would suffer the consequences one hundred times. However, the laws for culture are not that immediately binding. If one were to own a business, for example, and if one were to violate the law of stewardship[20] by repeatedly dumping waste into a river, the destructive effects of such an action might take several months or years to be fully realized. Thus, "the rule of law is immediate in nature but mediated through humanity in culture."[21]

The exalted human status so implied by mediation serves to reinforce human dignity and responsibility in freedom. God's law never merely "floats" down to creation. It is fully realized through humanity for the creation. In this sense humanity is indeed the "crown of creation." Although frustrating at times, God's continual action of mediation or channeling the law through humanity serves to remind us of our value to God and for the creation, in spite of humanity's sinful abuse of the creation. Thus, whether Christian or not, humanity continues to develop businesses toward some ultimacy through their response, obedient or otherwise, to God's commands. And, to be sure, Christians with a self-conscious worldview have not been the dominant community in the development of economic thought or practice.

While my critique of Industrialism has been pointed, I do not mean to imply that the various factors of Industialism are *per se* evil. Capital, sales, credit, technological activity, mass production, etc. are not the origin of evil, nor are they the origin of today's cultural malaise (as Marxism would imply). Rather, their abuse seems to be the problem. Throughout much of Christian history there has been a temptation to refer to one aspect of the creation as inherently more evil or to remove oneself from material or economic contact. Our notion of creation forbids the equating of any one class, aspect or process as inherently any more evil than another. Entrepreneurs, capital, and management are no more or less greedy and power-hungry than are the unionized workers and state socialism that Marx so righteously heralded.[22] Thus, "the goodness of creation is the Biblical antidote to all worldviews, religions and philosophies which single out some features of the created order as the cause of the human predicament."[23]

Worldviews are informed by a more or less conscious philosophical anthropology. Langdon Gilkey has written,

All political, social and cultural development presupposes an anthropology. Behind Liberalism (or Capitalism), Totalitarianism, Communism, there is always a certain view of man, just as, on the other hand, particular social political or cultural postulates are deduced from the Christian view of man.[24]

Our anthropological designations of *Homo oeconomicus* and *Homo religiosus* refer to the central core of human identity, and, beyond this core, to some ultimacy.[25] In the former ideal type, human functions refer to, and find their culmination in, economic activity. In the latter ideal type, the heart, or central agency of religious commitment, finds its destiny in God and its context in creation.

Both designations call for human responsibility in developing the rich potentials of the creation, secularity by defining freedom as mastery over nature and Christianity by man's calling as steward caretaker over the creation.[26] The development of the creation generally means the movement of culture from the singular, undifferentiated, and less complex to the more diverse, differentiated and more complex. In the process of the Industrial Revolution, a violent change came about whereby, in a relatively short time, a rural, hierarchical, labor-intensive, relatively cashless society evolved into an urban, class-distinct, capital—intensive, cash-filled society. In spite of all the surrounding problems, the circulating capital, global trade, relative specialization and increased technology indeed helped to lessen the burdens of labor. Furthermore, Industrialism, although not fully manifesting a just distribution of wealth, represented new possibilities for initiative, creativity, individual rights and responsibilities, and contributed to greater product diversity and economic options for many.

This notion of creation provides an effective remedy for pessimism of any type. While not falling prey to a nineteenth-century style optimism, this notion of the creation enables one to maintain a certain aplomb, even in the midst of cultural destruction. Nature resists industrial effluents by throwing, as it were, the poisons back upon humanity. The environment is not capable of sustaining "nearly infinite economic growth" because of its abundant but limited resources. Human labor associations cannot be brutalized continually, like the steelworkers in nineteenth-century Pittsburgh were, without at least a measure of justice being given to them. And capitalism cannot be counted upon to continually belch out a ubiquitous flood of products and rewards without some form of maintenance of capital and the natural environment, which it denied, only causes decay and destruction. Thus, the covenantal faithfulness of God for his creation endures in spite of human abuse,[27] and thus forms the basis of our social ethic and practice.

The creation will not be destroyed at the Second Coming as some Fundamentalists love to maintain. We can look forward to a "new heavens and a new Earth,"[28] for "the humblest element of the first creation [will not be]annihilated but transformed into something nobler" at Christ's return.[29] Much of modern Protestant thought has seen the link between the Incarnation of Christ and the creation: if

Christ has been manifested and resurrected in a human body, then material life, in a consummate sense, is honored. This eschatological consummation suggests a continuity of events and intentions between our age and the one to come. The prospect of consummation or radical renewal provides both the incentive for renewal and gives noble meaning to the world, its many aspects,[30] and our labors.

This discussion of creation would be woefully inadequate if we did not include at least a brief survey of Christ's role in the creation. In texts such as Colossians 1:16f. and especially 1 Corinthians 8:6, we see Paul focus his attention, for the benefit of beleaguered first-century Christians, upon Christ's role in creation. Len Scheffezyk remarks,

> Christ's exemplary causality in the work of creation has been established by Paul in these verses. . . . For the First Born is also envisaged as actively participating in the creation, as an efficient cause, since all things were made, "through him." This same Christ is also represented as the goal of creation, as its power which still preserves and sustains the being of every creature.[31]

This view of Christ's role and significance, sustained by a legion of New Testament passages, is further developed in the first chapter of the Gospel of John. Christ, in being the Divine Mediator of the creation, becomes the "functional reference" for the continued supply of life and meaning in the creation.[32] Christ is not in competition with other members of the Trinity. Rather, his work forms one crucial link in the overall plan of creation. As such, he enjoys an equal status to the other members of the Trinity. The connection of Christ the mediator of redemption with the act of creation forms an effective antidote to some of the narrower Evangelical christologies described in chapter 2. Christ, the origin of temporal diversity, becomes, at the time of redemption, the means of an entirely renewed creation!

THE FALL

Modern humanity hardly needs to be convinced of the presence of evil. The crime against Jews at Auschwitz, rising poverty in the midst of nearly a decade of economic upturns, and the destruction of parts of our ecosystem all testify to the reality of evil.

The Augustinian tradition has always emphasized the radical (i.e., deeply rooted) and integral effects of the fall into sin by humanity.

The fall has not been seen as tangential to the creation. Rather, it has crippled the free will of humanity and plunged us and the rest of creation into alienation, despair, and addiction-like dependencies.

In the state of paradise (as in the Enlightenment paradigm of the "state of nature"), humanity possessed the ability to choose either good or evil. As humanity was created, there was no external compulsion to do evil; thus, evil is not constitutionally a part of our being. In choosing to disobey God, however, humanity fell into a state of corruption and bondage, thus losing its ability to choose God in any consistent way. Modern addictions of many types testify to our bondage to creational entities. Thus, Augustine said, "My will as an enemy has held me and thence has made a chain for me and bound me."[33] Sin was thus voluntarily committed, apart from external compulsion, and resulted in a bondage which restricted a fundamental intent to please God. The only way to choose God and win his favor is to be freed of this bondage. It seems, therefore, that the demonic forces of the twentieth century powerfully grip the human condition, a fact that Evangelicalism with its optimistic view of the freedom of the will cannot fully appreciate. Whether this claim can be substantiated without falling prey to either a pessimism or a determinism is an important question.

G. C. Berkouwer speaks of the "surprise" of many contemporary thinkers and many secular philosophers at the (re)discovery of humanity's radical evil. Kant, for example, said that radical evil affected the entire span of human actions.[34] Although they differ as to its remedy, both Berkouwer and Kant point to an original sin which perpetuates a commonly held inherited inability to secure salvation. We do violate God's commands, because we have inherited through our lineage the inability to secure salvation. Modern studies in the psychology of family systems testify to the fact that there are transgenerational behavior characteristics. Thus, traditional Christianity and some aspects of modern psychology seem to sustain our belief in the transgenerational nature of evil.

One may object to the notion of inherited guilt because such a doctrine seems to weaken human responsibility and dignity. Inherited guilt, and therefore condemnation, seems unfair. Calvin and his contemporary Reformers dealt with the objection in the context of human responsibility and human solidarity.[35] Adam, as the "federal head of the human race," brought ruin to the race, not because we "imitate" Adam every time we sin. Rather, precisely because humanity is not a series of unconnected individual atoms and because we are bound together. Guilt and responsibility can be passed from generation to generation. Transgenerational guilt rests upon a sinful disposition that is commonly held. While we inherit the propensity for sin, we do not inherit an *external* compulsion to sin. Our guilt is real because we are born with a natural, though not created, disposition to choose evil. We are responsible for *our* guilt; it is not an "alien guilt," because sinful humanity stands in solidarity before God.

The ramifications of this corporate notion of sin stand in sharp contrast to nineteenth-century revivalism's notion of sin; they show why the then-current, optimistic definitions of sin and human responsibility tended to be superficial. Finney and his followers had this concept of the corporate view of human sin as one of his primary targets of critique.[36] The machinery of revival, fit as it was to a "sovereign people," emphasized human emotionality and instrumentality as the means of solidifying God's favor, and could not affirm so realistic a view of human nature. Because humanity was believed to be less than radically corrupt, the human will was thought to possess the autonomous power to cooperate in salvation, rather than respond to salvation's offer. Thus, revivals become democratically defined, uniting God with a sovereign people's will for salvation.

More importantly, Evangelicals gradually reduced the effects of sin to a personalistic, moralistic, psychological malady. Human bondage was an interior, individual affair. Such truncation was not due to a more "realistic" view of humanity. Rather, it was born of an accommodation to an optimistic, democratic American culture in the antebellum era and to the increasing despair Evangelicals felt as they withdrew from a rapidly secularizing postbellum culture. It was simply easier to change the definition of sin than to fight the drift of American culture.[37]

But what alternative can there be to this process? We will answer this question by examining several terms from the Old and New Testaments, and showing their connection to Evangelical preaching. Then we will look at sin's relationship to the creation and its effects upon the meaning structure of the creation. Finally, we will briefly address the "problem" of the origin of sin.

The Hebrew word *hata* is the term most often used to denote sin in the Old Testament. It means to fail someone, miss the mark, forsake wisdom, choose not to listen to a word, or forsake the rule of a leader.[38] To commit *hata* is to disobey the divine sanction as attested to by cosmic wisdom. In passages like the eighth chapter of Proverbs, wisdom is personified as one present with God from the foundation of creation, and one who cries or begs for attention at the gates of the city—a place of special judicial importance in

Israel. The creational or cosmic context of this passage indicates that wisdom and obedience have a more profound dimension than personalistic moralism. That is, the very universe is constituted in wisdom, which in turn testifies to human conscience in everyday affairs. In accordance with this, a polluted stream or a brutally monopolized industry seem to "cry for" or demand restitution.[39] "Sin" therefore does violence to all of humanity and the creation of which we are an integral part.

Likewise the word *awow* means to depart from favorable ground, to harden one's heart through repeated sin. Repeatedly sinful acts produce "twisting" or "deviation."[40] The corruption so implied fits well our discussion of creation and sin. The order of creation may be twisted beyond human recognition but never totally destroyed. Nineteenth-century industrialists may have trampeled on the dignity of blue-collar labor by calling them "factors" of production, but they could not eradicate the dignity of labor. Too few labor leaders beyond Terrance Powderly thought of labor in terms of dignity. However, twisting did not stop God from securing a measure of dignity and justice for the worker as the century progressed.

Finally, *pesha* denotes a broken alliance or covenant; it signals a revolt.[41] This term points to the covental structure and to the "kingly" nature of God that undergirds humanity's relationship with God and the creation. To violate God's commands is not only to do violence to one's relationship with God, but it also is to reap alienation in the creation. When Andrew Carnegie chose to pit himself against the unions in the Homestead strike, he not only produced profound alienation and bloodshed but set up a spark of violence that ignited subsequent labor unrest throughout the nation. Because he considered "loving his neighbor" irrelevant to business practice and because he advocated an adversarial system (as did others), many families, unionists, and Pinkerton troops had to suffer. Ironically, when the nation found out that private troops were used to support Frick's decrees, public opinion began to turn in support of the union movement. However, while the Homestead strike is but a memory, the politics of confrontation still exist in the very valley that Carnegie once ruled. Does not this fact testify to the relevance of *pesha* for economic relations?

The gospel records modify this account of sin somewhat while not repudiating its Old Testament roots. In the Gospels, sin is said to produce a state of guilt. This "state of guilt" is not defined *at heart* in a moralistic but ontological manner. Our fundamental guiltiness does not arise out of a personal trespass of moral dos and donts which may or may not be related to a social order. Rather, our evil is an ontological or existential condition that fundamentally ruptures our ability to live in the world as it was constituted. Moralism distorts the nature of evil because a myopic checklist of behavioral codes is substituted for a more radical and integral, existential way of living in the world. Alcohol abuse is a locatable, personal trespass that may or may not arise out of a fundamental posture, says the moralist. My state of being that can be called acquisitive nearly always affects my personal behavior, says the Augustinian. It is this state of guiltiness which Christ addressed in many of His sermons and which signals the distinctive stance of his message. Herman Ridderbos says,

> The fundamental conception of redemption as remission of sins not only distinguishes the gospel from all non-Christian religions, but also from all humanistic and modern dualistic interpretations of the gospel. The latter holds that the starting point of Jesus' preaching lay in the infinite value of the Human Soul, or in the antithesis between nature and spirit. . . . The starting point for the gospel is not the value, but the guilt of man; and redemption is not the preservation of the soul as a higher part of man, but it is the saving of the whole existence of man in the last judgement.[42]

The infringement of God's commands disrupted the basic harmony given in creation. If a confession of sin forgets about the radical and existential effects of rebellion, the ensuing "life of belief" manifests a superficiality that will ultimately undercut a truer, more comprehensive redemptive effort. In fact, if repentance is not an all-embracing attitude of life, if it is an incidental act, then a continual repetition of the conversion act might well be necessary. That is precisely the record of nineteenth-century Evangelicalism. A better alternative might have involved *one* radical renewal and comprehensive, persistent action.

Of course, no account of the New Testament definition of sin would be complete without considering the Pauline school. Paul's use of the term "flesh" recalls that universality and depth of sin presented in the Old Testament. According to Paul we inherit, through our flesh, the attributes of weakness, dependence and perishability, as well as sin and rebellion. The former set of attributes is by no means to be despised. As Martin Heidegger reminds us (though he obviously speaks from a different starting point), they are the glory of human finitude. It was by the vehicle of "flesh," conceived of as dependent, that God chose to reveal himself to humanity in the person of Christ. As for the other sense of flesh, that of sin and rebellion, Paul said that we inherit in Adam our disposition for evil. As Ridderbos explains,

> the presupposition of all sinning in Adam points to a supraindividual situation of sin and death represented by Adam. Here again the basic structures of Pauline theology are not individualizing but redemptive—historic and corporate.[43]

The essence of this sin is the rebellion of the creature against the Creator and against his laws for life.

The universality and depths of sin holds another corrective for nineteenth-century Evangelicalism and capitalism. It contradicts *any* dualistic, nationalistic claim to a special place in Divine Providence. No "manifest destiny" can be conceived of apart from radical repentance. In fact, such pretensions only manifest the presence of sin as arrogance. Such pretensions have thrived in American history; there was even a supposed divine sanction for massacring Indians.

We have attempted to argue that sin is as wide and deep as the creation because human action affects the creation to that extent. Thus, when God cursed the creation because of our sin, as noted in Genesis 3:17, humans continued to develop creation, thus testifying to our cultural abilities. Humans continued to be culture-formers, but in a myopic and an oppressive way at times. However, while the creation was cursed because of sin, one cannot conclude, à la Marxism, that a part or aspect of creation is in itself evil. Evil is not inherent in the human condition—"there was once a completely good creation and there will be one again."[44]

Thus, while we have argued for radical corruption, we have not argued for the inherent evil of any aspect of economic reality. The origin of modern evil does not lie in any one class or function, as Marxist-inspired worldview would suggest. To argue that one class is inherently more evil than another, or more inherently responsible for corruption, is to narrowly select the field of view. This contention seems to be substantiated by our discussion of unions. Of course, in any given era one class or group of people may assume a more responsible position by virtue of its *particular* actions. One cannot, however, argue from a particular consideration—such as early Industrialism's impoverished entrepreneurial worldview—to a grand view of history in which "good" and "evil" are respectively posited in the laboring and management classes.[45]

While "sin" is included in the discussion of religion, it may not be subsumed under the category of ultimacy. The classical Christian tradition has attempted to steer a course between monism and dualism with respect to God and the problem of evil's origin. God is not a monad or an undifferentiated one from whom one can rationally deduce evil's origin. Sin was not created by God, nor is it a coeternal force that God must somehow compete with to determine the outcome of the world. The origin of evil is not the purpose of revelation; its guilt is.[46] Nevertheless, evil's origin remains a mystery and hence a difficult issue for Christians to address.

At the same time, classical thought has repudiated a primordial dualism whereby Good and Evil conflict and, out of this battle, a creation is spawned which is forever riddled with this primordial war. In attempting to protect the majesty and sovereignty of God, classical thought has not allowed evil the implied autonomy that goes with any primordial dualism. The apparent omnipotence and independence of evil cannot be established upon an ultimate paradox, for this would lessen the responsibility of humanity and the freedom of God. Humanity could then always correctly maintain that since sin is eternal, *all* of our posterity is born into evil and our continued commitment to evil is to be expected. It was against this dualistic Manicheanism that Augustine argued after his conversion.[47]

Sin is not ultimate. Sin is a parasite; it presupposes that which it perverts. The good creation and its structures are prior to, and form the substratum of, human evil. Though myopically, entrepreneurial greed builds upon the goodness of flowing capital which, if left truly free to circulate, will bring benefits to many. The labor/management adversarial system is based upon a healthy sense of task differentiation and specialization of the production process. Mass production, in spite of its gluttonous abuse, rests upon a bounteous creation and its potential to lessen human need by mass consumption. Revivalism, with all of its machine-like abuses, presupposes the universal necessity of faith to find an ultimately suitable resting place.

The classical tradition has confessed sin to be a *privatio* or privation. Sin is a concealment, a lessening of the good in creation, just as it is a loss of the original intent for the creation.[48] "At the Reformation," moreover, "*privatio* was defined as *astuosa privatio* [active privation], or as enmity, iniquity, apostasy, antipathy, and the trespassing of God's commands."[49] The very fact that it was considered active privation presupposes a good creation. This enmity is not merely directed Godward; it rips through the very fabric of life, as we see in this century's wars. Thus, even in the depths of degradation, idolatry presupposes the creation. To believe in an otherworldly gospel, as some Evangelicals did, is to live a myth.

Sin cannot be defined, however, merely as privation. "The central dynamics of the spirit of apostasy is not 'nothing'; it springs from creation, and cannot become operative beyond the limits in which it is bound to the divine order of meaning."[50] Sin is powerful and dynamic, yet it has no real power *in itself*. It is parasitical in that it draws its power from the creation. "It is nothing and has nothing and can do nothing apart from the creatures and powers which God has created; yet it organizes all of these in open rebellion against God."[51] Behind this gilded era's seemingly generous hand lay a heart bent on monopolization and economic acquisitiveness, but for the perspective viewer the masquerade of benevolence could neither obscure or diminish the evil of greed nor the goodness of business as a potentially wholesome task.

Sin's dynamic force receives its power, in part, from the pretensions to human autonomy. When the serpent asked Adam and Even whether God said they should not eat of the tree (Genesis 3:1), "the question suggests to man that he should go behind the Word of God . . . and to judge God's Word instead of simply hearing and doing it."[52] Belief in autonomy led humanity to believe that it would be "like God." No longer was humanity to obey God's given limits. Boundaries were deemed unnecessary as humanity sought wisdom in its own counsel. Humanity thus attempted to be its own lawgiver, living out of its own resources and creating its own life. In the make-believe attempt to escape the limitations set for creatures, humanity distorted its essential humanness. The prolonged borrowing binge that we as taxpayers have witnessed testifies to the reality of our inability to accept limits with the consequence that our economy is slowly eroding in power.

In this pretension, we have the origin of "incorporation." Out of the confessed unlimitedness of economic expansion, the wealth of the few became bondage for many. Indian tribal law, natural beauty, and human dignity were all trampled under the feet of eager Americans who assumed any limits were to be equated with a doleful mentality. In the boundless passion to secure our "manifest destiny," many Americans secured for themselves and their posterity a worldview that valued quantity over the more sublime and healthful norms of justice, stewardship, and mercy. The full pretension of this act became apparent from its often being attached to the name of Christ.

It is fair to ask at this point whether or not sin can eradicate the very fabric of life. If meaning is the structure of all that is created and constantly points beyond itself to the true or pretended origin of that meaning, can sin destroy the meaning of creation?

It must be admitted that the struggle between the kingdoms of light and darkness will continue until the culmination of history. Any worldview that does not acknowledge the full effects of sin does violence to reality. At the same time, while some may give full credit to the reality of evil, they err in describing its influence. A more pessimistic conclusion emerges, for example, from the work of Jacques Ellul on the "technological society." Under the influence of autonomous, "demonic" technology, Ellul argues, cultures and persons are becoming enslaved, losing their essential freedom. Would the same argument apply concerning the "incorporated system" we have described?

Persons or cultures resist incorporation to the degree to which they yearn for humanness. Though human pretension has radically affected social structures, governments still legislate measures of justice, businesses continue partially to fulfill stewardly acts, and marriages remain at least marginally based upon commitment. The growing objection to technology's tyranny, incomplete as it may be, testifies to the lack of absolute technological determinism. Thus,

> sin in its full effect does not mean the cutting through of the relation of dependence between the Creator and the depraved creation; but that the fullness of being of Divine Justice will express itself in reprobate creation . . . and in that process depraved reality cannot but reveal its creaturely mode of being as meaning.[53]

Moreover, sin is not simply restrained by the structural limits of creation; creation is preserved by grace. It was Abraham Kuyper who most helped to restore the doctrine of "common grace" in modern reformed theology. Kruyper believed that God remained active in creation, in spite of and through sin, preserving the works of his hands. In Christ, all of creation, though ravaged by sin, continued to develop for the benefit of humanity. Often this preservation and development came in spite of sin; the creation remains rooted in Christ and remains the home of humanity.[54] Notably, Kuyper developed this view at the same time (ca. 1900) that American Evangelicals were accentuating their cultural pessimism and passivity.

Thus, the unfolding of subsequent aspects of the creation—say, the aesthetic or educational—will vary in overt quality according to a person or culture's stand with respect to sin and redemption, that is to say, with respect to myopia and wholeness. To the extent that areas of life begin to lose their integrity to economics—as is the case with much of current higher education's desire for "marketability"—life will increasingly lose its zest. Such abuses are to be disdained without disparaging the basic human activity of, say, business as part of the social fabric. By treating sin in this light, evil is given full recognition without despairing of creation or locating sin's origin in one aspect of the creation.

The term "world" has a variety of usages. Sometimes refers to the creation as a whole (Colossians 1:16), sometimes to the inhabited earth (Romans 1:8). It is well said that the term describes "the totality of unredeemed life dominated by sin outside of Christ. . . . In other words 'world' designates the totality of the sin-infested creation."[55] There is no notion here of the inherent evil of the creation, but rather of universality and radicality of evil's force within the creation. Thus, when the Scriptures speak of "not loving the world" [1 John 2:15], not creation but a false principle of life, rebellion against God, is repudiated.

The world cannot be juxtaposed as a "secular" realm to a "sacred" or "spiritual" realm. To do this would be to compartmentalize religion. To truly flee the world is to run to Christ and thus find the king of creation. To falsely flee the world by shunning erected created life is to hasten the process of secularization, a process Evangelicals hated. Thus, when Dwight L. Moody asked God for a "lifeboat" for gathering souls for the next world, he contributed to cultural decay by abjuring cultural responsibility.

Humanity attempts in sin to exaggerate the activities in some aspects of the creation, and to locate self-sufficiency and divine attributes in some aspect of the creation. People say that business can be "trusted in" to bring "progress" to a culture and that money can secure utility or "happiness." As a result of such exaggeration, humanity weakens its dominion over the creation. Rather than creation serving humanity, people serve or commit themselves to their ultimate. The subordination of humans to the machine, as outlined in our discussion of Frederick W. Taylor, illustrates this phenomenon. The exaggeration of economic and technological progress under the aegis of scientific management drives man into subservience. This critique is not meant to destroy the machine but to caution against the one-sided and oppressive use of the machine inevitable in a troubled world.

How has human work fared after the fall? All labor was given by God to humanity at the creation and hence is part of the "very good" creation. That it has become dangerous, boring, and doleful needs no demonstration. The crucial question, however, concerns the origin of this malady. Our concept of sin can account for both the value and the oppressiveness of labor. In sin, humanity lost its easy domain over nature. "The productivity of nature was impaired ... due to the form in which the curse had been described: hard, fatal struggle with the soil."[56] Bread could still be cultivated, but now it had to be done by the "sweat of the brow." Thus, we must disagree with Wayland and his assertion of the curse of labor being an *inherent* part of human nature. This confusion of a fallen state with the essential nature of humanity is dangerous, as Wayland's own logic proved: if labor is inherently evil, any oppressive labor situation may be rationalized as the natural lot of humanity, rather than evil and therefore to be resisted. The success of child labor laws is testimony to the necessity and benefit of resisting injustice in labor.

We have thus far outlined our view of evil. Though attempting to give full weight to evil, we have stressed that sin can not eradicate the good meaning structure of the creation, a structure that holds and reflects God's revealed intent for the creation. We have not, however, delineated a fundamental antidote for this dire situation. This corrective will come in the following discussion of redemption.

REDEMPTION

The notion of redemption must interrelate with the notion of creation as well as provide any antidote to evil. This is not to say that the origin of redemption can be equated with the dictates of cultures, the error of classic Protestant liberalism. But salvation supremely seen in Jesus Christ is correctly said to originate with Yahweh, who though in heaven is greatly concerned to actualize his purposes upon earth. In a tradition that differs from ours but testifies to the necessity of linking creation, salvation, and economic well-being, a strong voice has arisen. Noted Liberation theologian Gustavo Gutiérrez is correct in saying that "the God who freed Israel is the Creator of the world ... then its Re-creator."[57] Indeed, whatever may be said of Christ's person and work cannot be said apart from the context of creation and its fall into sin. The act of redemption serves not only to remove the curse of sin from creation, and thus free humanity from the bondage of oppression, but also affords the motive power for new meaning for the creation. Accordingly, in classic theology the order of redemption includes the order, motive force, or new direction, for the order of creation.[58]

Applying this point to the matter of the competing universal claims of the kingdoms of light and darkness, it can be argued that the dawn of redemption means that naked self-interest no longer holds total sway over humanity. Reinhold Niebuhr correctly maintains that moral cynics, or those who have forgotten about the power of sacrifice and love, commit themselves to economic self-interest because it allegedly serves as a self-justifying socially regulative principle. This is an "evil" principle, claims Niebuhr, "because its adherents know of no law beyond the self."[59] Consequently a culture of narcissism has arisen because of the acquisitive individualism of our day, an individualism that is eroding the public well-being. The modern economies of capitalism testify, however, to the necessity of sacrifice: if all interested parties do not sacrifice some of their gain to maintain capital stock, considerable suffering and dislocation results. On the one hand, these "children of darkness" are often culturally "wise" because they know the ways of Mammon. The children of light, on the other hand, want to discipline self-interest by subjugating it to a "higher" universal law and bringing it into service to the universal good. These "children" appear to be unwise because they can become morally sentimental. Consequently their alternatives seem irrelevant and idealistic.

The term "redemption" has several cognates. Redemption can mean to "buy back" a captive or a slave by means of a ransom. The goal is a restoration of freedom once enjoyed. In this sense, the word is used to highlight the price paid by Christ *and* the effect that it has upon the believer. We can be freed from the addiction to selfish individualism.

Redemption also connotes a reconciliation or an end to hostilities. This state, though not denying personalization, is not marked by an internal disposition; rather, a convenantal cooperation and submission is called for by this reconciliation. We are reconciled to all that we are alienated from: God, each other, creation, and ourselves. Therefore, for example, we no longer need to treat nature and culture as our trash can; creation is our home.

The Greek term *anakainōsis* means renewal, or being remade after an original image. Closely associated with this usage is regeneration or a return to life after having been dead. The emphasis is on the newness of life offered to the believer by Christ. Such newness of life is needed because the net effect of sin is said to be death or loss of our essential humanity. To experience a renewal of life is to begin to rediscover something of what it means to be human. Finally, the Greek term *sōteria* means health, security or a return to an original state of harmony. Evangelicals have used the latter two concepts to speak of the "born-again" experience in Christ. It has been argued that when such terms are stripped of their creational context, a loss of potency and relevancy occurs. In the cases of both anakainōsis and sōteria, concrete, practical, earthly changes are said to occur.

In the preceding paragraph, the prefix "re" occurs frequently, and always signifies a restoration to an original state. Thus re-creation or re-demption is a restoration or a salvaging of an originally good creation. Because of his commitment to the creation, of which humanity is the crown, God refuses to abandon the works of his hands.

> Redemption does not mean the addition of a spiritual or a supernatural dimension to creaturely life that was lacking before, but it brings new life and vitality to what was there long ago. . . . At bottom, the only thing that redemption adds which is not included in creation is a remedy for sin, and that remedy is brought in solely for the purpose of recovering a sinless creation. . . . Thus, grace does not bring a donum superadditum to nature . . . but grace restores nature, making it whole once more.[60]

Redemption has manifold meaning; its scope is as great as that of the fall and creation. The whole of creation is re-claimed by Christ.[61]

There is a measure of agreement among various Protestant traditions as to the scope of redemption. Gustaf Aulén argues that the "classic" view of the atonement or Christ's salvific work at the cross represents a catacylsmic victory by Christ over the forces of oppression. The "dramatic" or dynamic view of the atonement, in Aulén's version, states that "the atonement was a divine conflict and victory; Christ—Christus Victor—fights against and triumphs over the evil powers of the world; the 'tyrants' under whom mankind is in bondage and suffering, are despoiled; and in Christ God reconciles the world to Himself."[62] The result of this cosmic drama of redemption is the establishment of a new relationship in which the forces of sin are in principle in service of Christ. This is not to say, à la nineteenth-century optimism, that the forces of evil are in retreat. Rather, the forces of evil finally serve God's purpose, as seen in the cross.

Aulén finds historical support for this position in the second-century apologist Irenaeus. Irenaeus maintained that the Word of God—or Christ, the Word made flesh, who has created the world and entered into the arena of death—has freed man. This freedom was a "recapitulation," or a restoration and a perfection of the creation.[63] Accordingly sin, organically conceived as the deep corruption of the creation, was stripped of its tyrannical power, thus affecting a restoration of divine communion with humanity.

The "devil" cannot be allowed any rights over us; he is a

robber, a rebel, a tyrant, a usurper, unjustly laying his hands on that which does not belong to him. Therefore, it is no more than justice that he should be defeated and driven out.[64]

Moreover, God is the effective agent working redemption from beginning to end. With this sovereign victory over evil and the resultant restored creation, any creational dualism is ended. Money and power, capital and faith, worship and labor are given anew to us to enjoy.

Like many modern Protestants, Aulén is repulsed by the classical description of God's wrath and its function within the atonement. When Christ suffers the punishment of God's judgment upon sin, the wrath implied in this act is *only* against the devil for oppressing humanity and not punishment for human guilt, according to Aulén. It is the "will-to-reconciliation" that prompts God to express his wrath at the devil. Going one step further, "law" and "wrath" are among the tyrants that God judges at the cross, because God's "love" and his desire to secure love are the new motor force of the universe. And while Aulén "allows" a place for wrath, this wrath is opposed to Divine Love and juxtaposed to retributive justice.

One of the net effects of such a theory is to create an antinomy between love and justice. However unintentionally, it also makes humanity the victims of devils rather than responsible for their own sin. Aulén finds the thought abhorrent that humankind, represented by Christ, would have to placate a vicious God. How could it be just, cries Aulén, to send an innocent man to suffer and die to satisfy the dictates of a tyrant? Indeed, I also find this position repulsive; but it hardly represents the traditional view.[65] Retributive justice need not be antithetical to love any more than a parent's correction of their children is antithetical to love. In fact, love requires correction.

Guilt, enmity, alienation, and despair were the conditions that were in view by Christ at the Incarnation. The birth and life of Christ is marked by an overriding set of ironies.[66] He enters in humility and exits in glory. He lives in humiliation and ends in exaltation. The ignominy of the cross leads to the glories of the resurrection; the suffering paves the way for the joy of a finished work. The implications for this theme of irony are rich for those people beset by Mammon. Can "riches" lead to poverty: can economic riches lead to an impoverishment of the richness of life's meaning?

There is a mystery to the Incarnation, a mystery that does not contradict reason, but simply exceeds rational categories. The great mystery is the reality and depth of the fullness of the Godhead dwelling bodily amid the death and despair of humanity. The Incarnation shows the lengths to which God would go so that Christ might conquer our guilt and thereby secure dominion of all that enslaves humanity, including the effects of reductionism. The seeming excesses of this view may be lessened if one contemplates the gravity of evil, especially that of greed. The black slave, the Jewish seamstress in a sweatshop, the Eastern European factory worker, and the Chinese coolie did not find themselves bearing the burden of the American dream because of an incidental defect in human character.

In the historic suffering of Christ we see the overcoming of evil. God uses the evil, injustice, and oppression of all of the events that surrounded the cross to accomplish his ends. Christ takes upon himself the curse placed upon fallen humanity and the creation by his Father.[67] The *skandalon* or offense of the cross means that such a price must be paid, and paid by the only one who was pure and free enough to secure freedom for humanity. Purity and innocence exchanged for guilt and evil—that is the scandal of the cross. But, "the reality of death and burial contains God's new beginning, and thus the humiliation eventuates into exaltation."[68] What a profound and sublime irony!

At the resurrection, death is conquered; the new future has begun. While agonizingly real, suffering, including the despair of poverty, is not the final word for history. The corporal death and resurrection overcome the last tyrant—death in all senses—that oppresses humanity. To surrender to Christ, the Resurrected One, is to have access to life, in its fullest creational sense. "While we were enemies we were reconciled to God through the death of His Son, much more being reconciled, we shall be saved by His life."[69]

The cross and resurrection present the strongest possible foundation for a resistance to Mammon. To understand the cosmic significance of Christ's victory is to understand the end of the permanent tyranny over man by Mammon. This victory and its unequivocal call to worship either God or Mammon should have been sounded—and fully understood—in all of the revivals discussed above.

The ascension—the "taking up" or return of Christ to the Father—is the final aspect we will treat of Christ's work. His exaltation after his suffering affects the presence of the Holy Spirit, the Comforter. This is not a personalistic kind of comfort, required because the pressure of a secularizing culture is too great. Rather, it is a communion, a deep bond with Christ through the work of the Holy

Spirit, whereby Christ mediates his rule upon heaven and earth. In the messianic activity following the ascension, Christ's rule is established upon earth, thus providing a more integral view of the relationship of grace to nature. Nature or the creation is restored to us as the context of divine activity. In this sense, the future of hope is already in principle present with Christ. Christians, therefore, ought not to flee into the future or hope for the past, as many Evangelicals and Fundamentalists are wont to do. We may literally rest assured in the universal, external presence of a Holy Spirit and the hope it gives to a world often gripped by revolutions, industrial or otherwise. The realities of changes in Eastern Europe and the crumbling of the Berlin Wall testify to the presence of hope and the victory over tyrants.

I am suggesting that, if properly viewed, the incarnation, suffering, death, resurrection, and ascension of Christ promote a more healthy acceptance of necessary economic activity like capital circulation as redemption and creation becomes intertwined. A fuller view of the person and work of Christ also reveals *abuses* of doctrine. Even while fully affirming the Second Coming of Christ, for instance, one might rightly ask why, after the Civil War, Evangelicals began to stress the Second Coming. Was it born of a spirit of pessimism? It has been implicitly argued that the process of secularization, of which Industrialism was but one key element, was ineptly met by Evangelicals like Moody and Conwell because of their incomplete Christology. The premature and shrill emphasis upon the Second Coming betrays a fundamental fear and loss of self-confidence which gradually paved the way for further cultural accommodation. Ironically, Fundamentalism contributed to the process of secularization by hollowing out the work of Christ and by too often fleeing cultural responsibility.

The wrath of God is yet another facet of God's love. The irony of this fact is poignant. The consequence of evil must be halted if God is to remain faithful to his troubled world and if our humanity is not forever lost. Wrath or divine anger serves to reveal the faithful, loving, protective character of God. It is not arbitrary, unbridled, or normless rage. It is rather the further revelation of his loving intent to maintain the lawful boundaries of the creation, the dignity of humanity, and his creation as a palace of integrity. Furthermore, God's displeasure is set against more than the bondage of human oppression. It is revealed because of humanity's willful, continuous lusting to be like God and thereby to remake the creation after its own distorted image. The wrath displayed by God—for example, against Egyptian oppression of Old Testament Israel—meant more than the liberation of slaves. It meant that by the anger of God against such oppression, slaves were to inherit an entire land as their fortune. That few Evangelicals saw the Civil War and the 1857 Wall Street crash in this light manifested a notable lack of understanding. The Civil War could have been a truer, more profound emancipation. Furthermore, is it offensive in any way to speak of the lives and freedom that were spared because of God's wrath that halted, say, Hitler in 1945?

The notion of justification is also of importance when we speak of redemption. The Calvinistic wing of Evangelicalism has always stressed this doctrine of the primacy of grace for the initiation and completion of salvation as being of crucial, if not primary, importance. I affirm its import. However, I believe that the *entire* New Testament witness points to a more holistic approach, an approach we have taken throughout this work. As crucial as this doctrine is for salvation, the Corinthian letters speak of the evils of hubris, the Thessalonian letters of the return and future of Christ, the Colossian epistle of the lordship of Christ, and the letter to the Hebrews of Christ as the fulfillment of the Old Testament promises.

Justification is unique in that its intent is simply to deal with humanity's standing before God as a result of the revelation of the righteousness of God in Christ. The forensic background of this doctrine is especially noteworthy for Evangelicalism given Finney's legal training and Evangelicalism's moralistic bent. By faith we receive Christ's gracious righteousness imputed to us and thus can claim to be sons and daughters of God with all of the rights and privileges thereof but cannot "earn" or demand a living.

The explicit integral connection expressed in this notion is the complement to the organic solidarity mentioned above in the discussion of Adam. In this more holistic notion of justification we find another "Americanism" in revivalist doctrine. By advocating an individualist view of redemption's course, Evangelicals tend to deny the indissoluble link between Adam's sin and the redemption of the second Adam, and thus the cohesiveness of life. In their view of salvation ontically discrete persons make volitional contact with God. This individualism weakens the forensic nature of justification, however, for sin is then viewed as an atomistic, moralistic violation of God's love and not as a collective, ontic rebellion against his purposes. Repentance was narrowed both in theoretical scope and in practice as individuals repented for fewer personal codified violations. National campaigns like the temperance movements attempted piecemeal moral reforms as opposed to fully political renewals.

The sentimental and romantic revival sermons served to attract wary sinners who were fundamentally disassociated from their past. Ironically, while D. L. Moody believed that he was being more true to the gospel by preaching "love," he was in fact weakening its impact because of the weakened view of evil. At the same time, while Charles G. Finney was preaching "holiness" and denouncing slavery, his primary means for combating slavery was for *individual* slaveholders to break with this evil through the agency of individual will.

Let us turn to the term "reconciliation." This term, as we have mentioned, is the most comprehensive in the New Testament; indeed, Colossians 1:20 uses the Greek term *ta panta,* (all things) to refer to the scope of Christ's reconciliation. His reconciliation restores a deeply bonded relationship and peace between God and all things, first through the acts of Christ, then subsequently through the acts of the Church. This reconciliation "prepares the way to receiving a share in the new creation, the new things; it affects peace as the all-embracing condition of salvation."[70]

By *hilastērion* (or expiation founded upon the blending of justice and love) we understand a sovereign love that becomes both penalty and pardon. Its image is rooted in the sacrificial system of the Old Testament. "Christ's blood as atoning blood covers the sin which until now has been passed over and by it we receive Christ's deferred righteousness."[71] The blood of the sacrifice constitutes the basis of a religious liberation that, as Gutiérrez correctly declares, must have social, political, and economic consequences.[72] I hesitate somewhat in using the word "consequences," for it may imply a secondary or nonradical effect. Following our definition of religion, I prefer to think of the relationship of "depth," religiously conceived, to "effects," economically conceived. The closest possible tie between depth and expression is here intended. It seems necessary for our existence that justice and mercy blend to form the conditions for our life. Our court system, when it functions properly, is based upon this blending of justice and mercy. Standards, laws, and norms are necessary for healthy social functioning. Their violation needs to be redressed. However, God mercifully extends to us a new beginning, a liberation, a new perspective on life. The historic Christian tradition has chosen this view of expiation because we can not only thereby "measure up" but be ensured of our continued acceptability when we overstep our boundaries. Christ, then becomes our ransom, which in turn eventuates in our liberation from the addiction to evil.

I have spoken to God's anger at sin, turned to the topics of justification and reconciliation, and ended by speaking of liberation. The net effect of such a liberation would be, I believe, the potential renewal of all of one's inner, physical and cultural associations. Members of the Gilded Age might have led a fuller, more holistic life if these notions had been productively employed.

This leaves one last and perhaps most crucial theme: the kingdom of God. This theme was the central element of Christ's preaching. It is the Christian counterpart to Industrialism's "Busy-Beehive." The term "kingdom" comes from the Greek word *basileia,* meaning kingship, kingly domain or the arena in which the king rules. This notion, then, implies both a ruler and an area to rule. One may not properly call Christ Lord, as Evangelicals do, without also visualizing a terrain in which a king should rule. When Christ "came down from heaven," he thereby extended his domain from heaven to earth—that is, the creation.

Over against the Busy-Beehive, the kingdom of God is not deistically conceived; rather its origin is theocentric in nature. "The coming of the kingdom is first of all the display of divine glory, the re-assertion and maintenance of God's rights and earth in their full sense."[73] This idea is wider and deeper than the notions of covenant and justification, while giving specificity and clarity to the term reconciliation.

The kingdom of God is not primarily a mental state, nor is it the inward filling of the Holy Spirit. It is not, moreover, submission to Christ apart from cultural reality. Rather, it is "the rending of the heavens" and the influx of God's rule upon earth, the commencement of the divine reign, which judges all human pretension while saving that which unfolds to the glory of God and benefit of humanity. The part played by the Judeo-Christian tradition in the development of hospitals, labor laws, civil rights, antislavery campaigns, and universities testifies to the reality of God working through people.

The dynamic and progressive character of this kingdom centers on the "Son of Man," so designated because through his suffering and concomitant exaltation he is given "all power" in heaven and upon earth.[74] The coming of the kingdom into history does not end or negate history and culture. Rather, the coming of the kingdom represents the consummation, fulfillment, and continuation of all aspects of the divine work in history through humanity. As such, it has a past, present, and future reality. Fulfillment is not a paralleling of grace to history; rather it is a radical impregnation of history with the salvation of God.

Perhaps the most visible manifestation of salvation is the advent of the Church or the body of Christ. The Church in this instance is not fundamentally associated with an institutional, ecclesiastical association. No, the Church consents of the "called out" ones; they are no more special or more morally upright than others. They are called, however, to testify to what they know to be true in all areas of life. To this end, it is proper and even mandatory that the Church should associate in every area of life. The worship, cultus, or ecclesiastical aspect of life is a central, though not primary, relationship to other institutions. Using the analogy of a wheel, we may say that the cultus or worship aspect of life represents the hub, while other equally necessary cultural institutions, such as business, represent the spokes.

With the coming of the kingdom all optimistic/pessimistic dilemmas are overturned. Revivalists may no longer trumpet the hopes of a fully realized eschatology as the century wears on, because the reality of sin and oppression, while stripped of its power in principle, remains forcefully present. At the same time, pessimism is foreclosed. Because Christ has won the great victory and will not give up on the works of his hands, and because he rules even now, we may legitimately hope that oppression and sin can be historically addressed and at least partially overcome. Current events around the globe and especially in Eastern Europe powerfully testify to this reality. Furthermore, while we are called to be "realistic" about the power of evil, we may not use this "realism" as an excuse to countenance evil in any form. It must be kept in mind that evil, while forceful, has no power *in itself;* it is only a parasite on the good creation.

There remains for this age, however, a consummate age of hope when all evil will be finally overturned. It is to this vision that many postbellum Evangelicals turned.[75] Against Fundamentalist exegesis, however, we maintain that when the Scriptures speak of "the end of the world" they do not mean the end of the earth and culture or even of history.[76] The *New Scofield Reference Bible* contains several interesting footnotes on eschatology or the notion of last things. In a note to 2 Peter 3:10–16, a passage about the Second Coming of Christ or the Great Day of the Lord, Scofield interprets this text to mean "the destruction of the heavens and the earth in the Day of the Lord."[77] He cross-references these verses with Revelation 21:2 and speaks of "New Jerusalem," the heavenly city (meaning that its origin and destination are heavenly).[78] The net effect is the final eradication of culture and history. Therefore, Evangelicalism, at least in its Fundamentalist variety, has no *ultimate* incentive to be involved in cultural transformation because of its eschatological stance on cultural annihilation.

We believe that these texts do not support such theories. Behind the "burning up" of 2 Peter 3:10 stands the Old Testament passage of Malachi 3:1–6 which speaks of a refiner's fire, not a destructive fire, that comes in the Great Day of the Lord. The refiner's fire is meant to purify a precious metal, not destroy it. Furthermore, in 2 Peter 3:13 the text *clearly* indicates that a "new heavens and a new earth" are the final intent of the great day of vindication and judgment, or the Day of the Lord. The purification of that which is precious—the creation—issues forth not in a heavenly city that has nothing to do with earth. Rather, an earthly city, whose origin (like the Jerusalem of the Old Testament) is from heaven, is intended by these passages. In this great day the creation will not only be cleansed from all taint of sin, but the poor in spirit, those who cry for God's justice, will be vindicated.[79]

One of the central themes of Scripture is the comfort and justice that God sends to the poor. Great controversy has surrounded two parallel beatitudes: "Blessed are the poor in Spirit" (Matt. 5:3) and "Blessed are the poor" (Luke 6:20). Depending upon one's worldview, these passages could be interpreted to support a dualism, Marxism, or an internal personalism (poverty of all kinds is of the spirit or internal inclination). Such controversy (and from our vantage point, confession) restricts the potential comfort and radical effects of these and similar passages.

Both passages have a social reference while simultaneously pointing to ultimate religious rest and trust in God. The Greek phrase *hoi ptōkhoi tōi pneumati,* or "the poor in spirit," refers to those who realize, in humility and in suffering, that they are oppressed by all that is demonic.[80] The believer, while actively resisting *all* forms of poverty, should realize that his *ultimate* source of deliverance is God. The poor person, simply put in Greek as *ptōchus,* feels a particular burden in socioeconomic poverty. These are the people, who, because of the greed of Mammon, must live in the subhuman conditions of oppression, their freedom nearly forgotten.[81] The poverty refers to socioeconomic poverty, but *not* in isolation from its ultimate religious depths. Because the poor may more fully realize their dependence upon God, even in the midst of the struggle for liberation, they are considered to be special in God's eyes.[82] If this dependence evaporates, as was the case with Soviet Marxism, one oppression is simply substituted for another.

Economic Alternatives

In the reformulation of the gospel meaning of creation, fall, and redemption, we were attempting to show how core concerns can broaden one's vision, and thus allow one to address questions of myopia and synthesis. Now we turn our attention to hopefully relevant alternatives to "incorporation" or economism. The goal is to point to a rethinking of the function of land, labor, and capital, as well as related institutions, all in a manner that does honor to the basic process of wealth creation and distribution.

Land or natural resources afford a variety of riches, not the least of which is economic potential. Circulating capital deepens opportunities for those who possess it. The advent of modern technology, spurred on as it has been by modern economic incentive, can ease the burden of physical and mental labor while reducing the threat of "nature" to man. Labor can be a joyful, meaningful calling.

However, all of these benefits can be and have been abused. Broadened consumption has been twisted into conspicuous consumption, even gluttony; creativity has been perverted into commodity inundation. Circulating capital has fallen to raw greed, technological ease and leisure have become the excuses for lethargy. It is to these phenomena that we now turn.

LABOR

It seems dehumanizing to refer to labor as a "factor of production."[83] Instead of using this secular designation, let us return to the concept of calling as one's fundamental service to what or whom one deems ultimate.[84] Following Paul Marshall, it seems wise to distinguish between vocation, job, and labor as concomitant results of one's basic religious calling in life. Vocation means the avenue of professional service; jobs are work that earns money; labor is full-life effort.[85] While the designations overlap, we will concentrate in this section on "jobs" and "labor" because of their significance for the rise of the American labor movement in the nineteenth century. Our focus upon what is commonly called "blue-collar" work should not obscure the fact that all of life, and all vocations, constitutes a "cosmos of callings."[86]

In Genesis 6:26–28, God calls humanity to develop the creation in all of its potentialities. This fundamental commandment addresses humanity at its depths: we are culture-forming beings who direct culture to some ultimate concern. The question is not if, but how, we will develop culture.[87] We must also remember that in spite of reductionism, cultural formation can be a fruitful task. For example, one can see in Genesis, chapters 4 through 11, that God graciously protects humanity despite the curse of sin, through the advent of various technological devices that facilitate cultural development.[88] Thus work, as aided by technology, retains some dignity and creativity.

In the New Testament Saint Paul uses the same term, *ergon* (work) to refer both to the act of manual labor and to his efforts as an apostle.[89] He hardly means to downgrade his apostolic authority, but rather to upgrade the usefulness and dignity of labor with one's hands. Paul's job was that of a tent-maker, while his calling was that of an apostle who labored, with all of his might, in the Lord.

Much of the Judeo-Christian tradition has affirmed the full dignity of work; however, not all Christians have been inclined to view work that way. Augustine, for example, divided the vocations of a Christian between the "active life," consisting of preaching, teaching and labor and the "contemplative life," or monasticism. Both sets of vocations were considered good, but the contemplative life was considered superior to the active life. Moreover, earthly life, however necessary, was but a "school" for eternal life. Thus, unwittingly perhaps, Augustine weakened the biblical concept of work.[90] Of course, Augustine's ideal of the supremacy of the contemplative life found its culmination in the medieval monastic system.

All of the Protestant reformers attempted to overturn the exalted estimation of the institutional church. Some, like Luther, reworked the notion of vocation only to fall (as we have seen in Chapter 4) into a social conservatism by equating calling and socioeconomic class *(Stand)*. The English reformer William Tyndale, following St. Paul, maintained that "there is no work better than another to please God; to pour water, to wash dishes, to be a souter [cobbler] or an apostle, all is one; to wash dishes and to preach is all one, as touching the deed, to please God."[91] In thus formulating the concept of vocation, Tyndale managed to escape much of Luther's implicit conservatism. Calvin went beyond both when he saw trade, division of labor, and mutual exchange as signs of the social solidarity of humanity. Thus,

> Companionship is completed in work and in the interplay of economic exchanges. Human fellowship is realized from the division of labor . . . wherein each work complements the work of others. The mutual exchange of goods and services is a concrete sign of the profound solidarity which unites humanity.[92]

This statement portends our first principle of labor: labor is productive insofar as it manifests a mutual expression of human interdependence. Far from being a tortuous "factor of production," labor, in its blue-and white-collar forms, becomes dignified and regains its created potential when the division of labor fosters interdependence, not an adversarial relationship or an isolated overspecialization.

The Protestant reformers did not escape all of the dangers of conservatism, however. Many, at times even Calvin, tended to equate "calling" with the form of work or jobs that people already had in everyday life. The effect of this equation was to identify the particular content of human labor with the commandments of God. Hence, to disobey one's vocational masters was to disobey God.[93] This is the general error of conservatism: the equation of a particular social phenomenon with a more or less fixed principle of life. When this equation is formulated, rigidity can set in. At the same time, the secularization process proceeds to strip a calling of its theistic moorings and fills it with capitalistic presupposita.

Of course, one's "calling" in Christ or in Mammon cannot be entirely separated from the various vocations, forms of labor, or jobs; one's religious starting point does define the content of one's vocation and jobs. To use Christian language, all of life's vocational efforts are part of the plan of redemption, while at the same time not identified per se with salvation. While rejecting the myopia of Mammon's identification of labor as a "factor of production," I am arguing that labor's motive force must not be equated solely or even primarily with the take-home pay received by a worker.

We have seen that classical economics defined all value by labor, thus overestimating labor's ability. For such theorists as Smith, Ricardo, and Marx, not only labor's value but all social value of a good originated in labor. Thus the origin, purpose, and meaning of society became too narrowly equated with economic activity in general and labor in particular. The emphasis upon the importance of economics in the context of other areas of life helped promote the free market and, alternatively, labor's revolt as surplus value was stripped. It was argued by Marx that because labor is basic, its rewards are primary. The similarity between the classical capitalistic and socialist/Marxist emphasis upon labor in particular and economics in general betrays their deeper unity.

The neoclassical redefinition of the origin of value hardly brought clarity; utility or "happiness" was shifted from labor to personal and aggregate consumption. Thus, to maximize consumption became equated with social good or utility as measured by aggregate individual utility. Labor took a back seat to consumption in importance to economists. It is not ironic that this change in emphasis began to occur circa 1880—when consumption was dramatically increased because of industrialism's success.

It is no wonder, therefore, that organized labor agreed to Taylorism. For it was Frederick Taylor who promised workers incentive pay if they accepted his form of management theory. In exchange for mimicking the dictates and the pace of the machine's movements, the laborer was promised more of the expanding economic pie. If workers would simply allow their work, communities, and actions to be atomized and rationalized according to the efficiency "expert," the meaninglessness of their labor could be pacified by the increasingly ubiquitous green narcotic. More importantly, because of this cult of expertise—that is, a professional chauvinism of knowledge as to what was best for the worker—attempts by emergent unions to share authority with management were negated, thus effectively ensuring both compensatory wages and a class hostility between labor and management. Such expertism in a state-monopolized form was the result of Lenin's adoption of Frederick Taylor's system.[94]

Over the course of the twentieth century, unions gained, sometimes violently, a place in the power structure of the United States. Labor and management settled into adversarial relationships in which economic relations were reduced to a power struggle; the ever-increasing spoils went to the strongest. Justice, or a place at the industrial table of power, was to come from aggregate force and aggression. However, rather than risk capitalism's demise, both management and labor came to accept the rigors of collective bargaining. Indeed, collective bargaining became "the instrument par excellence for obtaining the highest possible pecuniary gains for the consumption-conscious members."[95] The notion of reconciliation, or structural codetermination, sounds strange to such a view. Can it be any wonder, therefore, that the decade that has just passed has witnessed so many casualties in American labor?

Unions, when operative, have grown into a sometimes harsh modern force. The conflict mode of bargaining, in part, has forced secular unions to monopolize collective agreements for a particular trade association. Unions, in the main, have not recognized religious ultimacies in their development; and furthermore, those with religious convictions have not been given a right to share equal representation at the bargaining table. At least in Canada the Christian Labor Association of Canada (C.L.A.C.) has won the right to represent a variety of tradespeople who cannot agree with the materialistic assumptions of either the Marxist or capitalistic unions.

Moreover, on 13 November 1970, the Ontario Legislative Assembly voted in favor of Bill 167. Any employee who "because of religious conviction or belief object[ed] to joining a trade union or objects to the paying of dues or other assessments to a trade union" was allowed to pay an equivalent amount to a registered Canadian charity.[96] This civil rights case not only dramatizes the full extension of a Christian worldview into the realm of labor relations; it also increases the freedom of association for all laborers. The myth that only one union can best represent a community of workers has been effectively dismissed by the "ministry" of the Christian Labor Association.

It seems in keeping with the emphasis upon majority rule in democracy that officials represent religiously undifferentiated people who nevertheless have in common the desire for increasing economic security. The concept of the simultaneity of norm realization (stressing as it does the harmony and richness of ethical demands) stands in sharp relief next to this ideology of self-interest, self-sufficiency, and majoritarian rule. The modern union movement believes that by the one-person, one-vote, and one-agency method a community of laborers, called a union, can attain their ends. This myth can be sustained in America precisely because religion has been accepted as a private, compartmentalized phenomenon and because individual wishes are thought to be best represented by majority decisions. But does a majority vote really represent the wishes of the more fundamental communities who place their hope in more collective ultimacies? This structural question is never raised.

We might see a lessening of the adversarial system if the reconciliation of labor and management were accompanied by a more or less full codetermination in decision making.[97] Have we not learned from the Japanese, albeit from their paternalism, that management and labor can more or less harmoniously coexist in peace and productivity? The notion of reconciliation seems relevant to the relationship between labor and management.

If the destructive consequences of the adversary system are to be lessened, labor, like management, must rediscover the notion of office as service and mutuality. Given the relative authority that both labor and management have in industrial operations, each side must negotiate on the grounds that both parties are necessary. Both parties can and do render a service to each other, to the customer, and to the public. Any myopic preoccupation with short-term objectives and profit margins that excludes a broader view of public

responsibility and the well-being of all concerned is deeply troubled, as the present state of affairs amply attests.[98]

Labor should consider four foci for its task. First and foremost,
labor must be directed to some ultimacy. For the Christian, the
worship of God should be the basic orientation of labor. Worship
cannot, therefore, stay at the door of the church; if it does, it ceases
to be worship. "Man is responsible to God in all things; in WHETHER
he works, in HOW he works, and to what PURPOSE he works."[99]
Secondly, worker creativity must be recognized as something
greater than the efficiency of the machine. (The practical effect of
this statement, as we shall shortly see, suggests a redefinition of
the work place.) By this standard, worker dignity, mutual worker
cooperation, various worker needs, and work-pace are also
stressed. Thirdly, while work implies legitimate rewards known as
wages, it must be recognized that wages are but one avenue of
reward. Fourthly, if some of the monotony, authoritarian discipline, stifling of worker initiative and alienation is to end, labor-
management reconciliation must be started.

Reconciliation could occur if labor and management shaped
every phase of planning and authority, salary, capital modernization, benefits and risks. If wage demands were excessive, for example, management could open its books to the union to show how
such demands, if met, would hurt the business and/or price it out
of competition. Concomitantly, if unions were asked to make wage
concessions, then based upon open books, management would also
have to sacrifice. Thus, both parties would shoulder the responsibility and share the benefits of the industrial process.

It seems inevitable—now that the United Auto Workers has accomplished it—that union representatives would sit on a company's
board of directors. Moreover, this notion of limited codetermination, linked as it is with responsibility and trust, could be extended
to the extensive sharing of necessary information on such topics
as future technological innovation, plans for capital modernization,
and competition. Such a plan would stimulate worker involvement
and hence responsibility. If such a plan could be initiated, absenteeism, worker alienation, excessive wage demands, and poor product
quality would be addressed. In the case of contemporary Pittsburgh, had the Monongahela Valley workers attained codetermination fifteen years ago, job quality, technological displacement,
future investment structures, and capital modernization, as well as
wage demands commensurate with production quotas, could have
been negotiated. The cost of the adversarial system is not only

the millions of dollars spent on unemployment benefits, but more importantly, the devastation of countless lives and an entire economic region.

The net effect of promoting a model of codetermination is to offset the incorporation of labor and, alternatively, to regain some of labor's created dignity and integrity. The win-lose scenario of modern industry must be replaced by a more conciliatory mode. It seems to me that both parties have a stake in the achievement of this goal.[100]

Obviously, this microstrategy will not solve all labor problems, or even a very significant share of them. Another agency, related to labor and management but not represented by these interests per se, needs to become part of—not determine—the labor process. An institution is needed that has sufficient power to require a proportional distribution of public benefits and responsibilities. Since unions cannot act *juridically* in the public interest, although they can and must act *economically* in the public interest, it is necessary that the state act juridically in the public interest. "Public interest then is a political integrating principle binding all supra-arbitrary standards together."[101] That is, the state has the positive task of ensuring justice through the judicial encouragement of legal space for all societal institutions, persons, and organizations. Traditional capitalism, on the other hand, argues one-sidedly for economic organizations which are able to balance off each other's economic interest through an exchange of power. The state must enter the bargaining process to ensure economic peace and enforce contracts so that prosperity may go on unabated. Contrary to this, our view holds that the state is to ensure that all communities' economic and extra-economic interests receive legal room for expression. This view does not represent a simple progressivism, moreover. The state is not a "neutral" party trying to arrange a balance of power between "countervailing powers." The state has the positive task of integrating the demands of justice as defined by the needs of relevant social institutions. For example, courts may rule that a management's investment plans or a union's wage demands are unjust in the sense that society's several institutions' interests are not served. Or, alternatively, economic institutions could press for complete legal room for *all* economic and supraeconomic parties.[102] Such was the case with the C.L.A.C.

This view of the state is not a socialist one. While the state attempts to recognize the interests of the whole community, it does not symbolize, manage or control the whole or internal workings of economic interests. According to the social model outlined earlier in this chapter, there are a variety of spheres, represented by societal communities, that are themselves capable of further division, and whose basic integrity and activity can not be fundamentally determined by the state. At best, and this is crucial, the state can only legally recognize and adjudicate their interests. Socialism's attempt to ensure distributive justice is dashed against the rocks of the reality of societal communities' interests. The capitalistic foes fare little better, as distributive justice in a liberal regime not only fails to succeed through the monolithic representative trade associations, but is defined through a managerial bureaucracy—or, alternatively, through individualistic initiative—whose capacities have proven socially ineffectual to ensure a fuller measure of social justice.

It seems wise to suggest that a national council of economic advisors be created, the representatives of which would be elected from various relevant economic communities; its job would be to democratically solicit and create consensus on a national economic agenda. On this national board it seems wise that representatives of employers, unions, government, consumers, environmentalists, the disenfranchised, banking and the Federal Reserve System be present. The intent of such a diverse body would be to formulate a national policy for the fair and even distribution of all requisite responsibilities and benefits. To the extent that such a policy can be implemented, distributive justice will be served. Particularly deep, but hopefully not endemic, problems, like homelessness, could receive special, though not permanent, attention.

It is clear that new values and ultimacies must be negotiated for the work-world. For if management

> were to accept their employee's fixation with work simply as a means to wages, comfort, convenience, and status, it would amount to an acceptance of an increasingly hedonistic and apathetic partner in the enterprise.[103]

To this end Texas Instruments, in 1970, enacted employee codetermination. This involved three novel approaches. First, it allowed full employee participation in *all* discussions that concerned job-related problems. Next, line foremen were actively encouraged to solicit worker comments on product and work improvement. Finally, top management contractually commited itself to full mutuality in regard to the basic directions of the business.[104]

Contrary to Taylor's atomization of worker communities, the General Motors plant in Lordstown, Ohio has encouraged basic worker teams to flourish. Such teams are made up of four members. Two laborers do on-line work, while the other two coach, check, encourage, and plan for a better job. Later the roles are reversed. While the Vega (the original product of the plant) (was) less than the top of the line, product improvement in the 1970's has been credited to improved worker concentration, rest and socialization, and increased worker responsibility.

A different perspective should be applied to plant construction. Sites should be constructed so as to maximize management and labor's social, psychological, and technological needs. The Volvo plant in Kalmar, Sweden is one example. The plant was constructed, contrary to Taylor's rationalization of the work place, in the shape of a star so as to maximize worker solidarity and interchange. Each point of the star represented a specialized function of auto assembly. A team of fifteen to twenty-five workers worked at each point. There was no particular emphasis on the assembly line, and all parts were centrally located. The car was assembled in full view of all concerned, with workers rotating jobs. Each worker was subject to the discipline of worker groups and production schedules. The quality of the 1970s Volvo is lasting testimony to the success of such a method.[105]

Finally, labor, while slow in picking up the gauntlet of reform, has taken some initial steps. In Bolivar, Tennessee, laborers in a General Motors plant initiated codetermination after a history of absenteeism, wildcat strikes, poor product quality, and class hostility. After initial testing periods, workers were able to both improve the quality of the products and manufacture them in seven hours. This left the union and management with the question of what to do with the extra hour, or "earned idle time." After trying and rejecting card playing, going home, and simple idleness, the union decided to initiate an educational time. Over a period of time, 200 classes on various subjects were offered, allowing many workers to receive their high school diplomas.[106]

Ultimately such successes inspire the full confession of one's faith because of the depths of the issues involved. Thus Gary R. Gemmill exclaims,

> work is NOT a curse brought about by humankind's fall from grace; it is a curse we have inflicted upon ourselves. Organizations are created by humans and can be changed by them. It is time for each of us to begin to reclaim . . . personal power and to nurture courage in ourselves . . . to pursue uncertain paths.[107]

That this secular confession—and the valuable insights that stand behind it—is not Christian is of no immediate concern to us. For here in honesty and a measure of wisdom are positive suggestions for the reformation of the workplace. Such confessions come from the heart, though their confessors would obviously deny such notions. Given the Evangelical absence from the reformation of the workplace, such confessions of faith are partially warranted, and are rebukes to Christian conformity to Mammon.

STRUCTURE OF CAPITAL

Can anything be said of the structure, that is the identity, meaning, and formation of capital? Let us canvass the contours of this question with broad brush strokes.

In modern enterprise the term capital is hard to associate with any one function. Are "capitalists" owners, managers, directors, single entrepreneurs, or shareholders? The term capital, in reality, touches upon all of these definitions.[108] Capital as wealth has traditionally been treated as a homogeneous aggregate stock or supply of wealth needed to fuel the economic process. The elements of capital are oftentimes called money units; the rewards of capital are profits. A return on monies earned from capital is as necessary as a fair wage because it, too, can contribute to the production process. Thus, I do not agree with Marx that labor is the sole origin of value; capital has a unique place in wealth creation. I want to argue, however, that capital has a social responsibility and a social context,[109] and that capital-ism is the exaggeration of the wealth-producing function of capital at the expense of the social context and responsibility.

The nature and use of capital have greatly changed since the nineteenth century. Then, profit ascendancy, fueled by gain, provided the primary impetus for activity. While industrial growth occurred, its importance was secondary to that of profits. But following the Civil War, starting with Standard Oil, American business began moving to a more monopolistic stance, with economic expansion occupying an increasingly important place in operations. Corporations emerged with an increasing monopolization of market share. Competition also shifted from being predominantly competition in pricing to being competition in technological innovation and advertising. A balance of "countervailing" powers concomitantly emerged among government, management/capital, and unions. An ambivalent partnership of mutual support and antagonism resulted. For although government acts as industry's watchdog, it nevertheless supports business with numerous tax concessions and subsidies. This contradictory relationship of support and supervisions promotes a kind of pragmatism which tends to stress market regulation at certain times even while it subsidizes certain markets if "public welfare" is perceived to be threatened. In either case, no internal principal, beyond pragmatic situational needs, can be discerned. We would like to suggest that principles can be developed which would effect a more stable stance for the business-government relationship.[110]

In my opinion, capital, indeed all wealth, should be designed to meet a variety of agendas. As a vehicle for greater responsibilities and options, capital allows us to open up life's possibilities and to meet needs. Capital has this task because it presupposes, for its proper functioning, a variety of social institutions and cultural activities. Stable families, public tax monies, educational efforts, and personal emotional health serve as the soil in which the functions of capital grow. Thus, by the very social nature of the capital formation process, a social debt is incurred—a debt which any community has a right to claim. This debt, while including economic compensation, goes beyond economic activity to include a demand that capital, indeed all social institutions, provide for an increased sense of personal, social, and cultural benefit. Freedom defined as autonomy lessens these ties and responsibilities and, therefore, helps to destroy life.

The modern economist must also recognize that capital has *non*-private sides to its function. There is a state, municipal, associated, and donor capital.[111] A problem arises, however, when managers demand a nearly autonomous use of profits, thus denying their social context. Although capital, when circulating, does indeed benefit many social communities, the autonomy of capital can violate the social trust present in a social context. Accordingly, if capital autonomously withdraws from a social setting from which it has benefited, suffering results. It seems responsible to suggest, therefore, that public-legal pressure be brought to bear on capital so that when it must withdraw, social cohesion is promoted. With it so removed, I see no reason for continued governmental intervention.

By ignoring the social matrix, traditional individualistic capitalism forced the unionization of labor:

> Modern industry drew the antithesis between classes. The individualistic structure of society reduced labor to a commodity and focused the good will of the entrepreneur to the forces of unbridled competition. Given the way the entrepreneur structured his enterprise the individual-

ism was bound to give way to the dictates of struggle, power and violence.[112]

In response to individualism, the modern concept of countervailing powers has formed a diverse power structure constituted by internecine communities who at the same time maintain an individualistic a priori.[113]

I would argue, however, that "society," pace Marx, cannot be defined too narrowly in an orientation production process that inherently divides people. Marx's belief in the latent hostility of classes is only partially true. In reality, social groupings exhibit much more mutuality than Marx's theories would allow. Society manifests an intertwining of intercommunal (church, family, state, school) associations and interpersonal (buyer-seller, publicist-consumer, candidate-voter) relationships. Their partial coordination and at times necessary mutuality testify not only to the partial inherent interdependence of society but to the myth of self-sufficiency as well. Ironically, as society increased in complexity during the past century, entrepreneurs became more dependent upon a variety of social factors for capital formation. Labor, developed land, educational institutions, and an ethos supporting difficult work conditions were among the social factors supporting the capital formation process. That these processes were often exploited testifies, however, to the truth of Marx's analysis.

Social interlacing or interdependence can be honored while maintaining the internal integrity of business. For this reason the variety of communities that surround a business enterprise must be allowed to fulfill their own function without surrendering to capital functions. Investors, for example, should expect a rate of return on their investment, but never at the expense of the process of capital formation and the functions of other economic communities like labor. Managers should be encouraged to order industrial operations or work in such a way so as to maximize responsibility among workers, consumers, and the environment without state monopolization or control.

It would be more holistically profitable for management and owners and labor to define business' basic goal as the production of overall surplus rather than as the gaining of profit. Surplus means that as a consequence of the production process, labor, potentional resources, overhead, and capital modernization have their respective needs for continued prosperity met. The maintenance of our natural and human resources includes the perpetuation of future stock or future economic possibilities. Production and consumption must never usurp the rights of families, say, to be loving, of schools to educate, and of people to be secure in their jobs now or in the future. Nor must it be allowed to define nature as "natural mineral wealth." While owner-managers must economize to compete, their choices for savings in time, space, and resource allocation ought to acknowledge the full costs of doing business. Failure to do so only endangers the very foundation of the business enterprise. "Fruitful production involves, then, a balancing of costs [the loss of potential resources] and benefits [the increase in fruitfulness]."[114] This mode of preservation suggests that the value represented in consumed goods must not exceed the future value of disposable or usable stock. For some commodities like oil, this process would be possible. For some products like wood, preservation could be such that a net increase in dispositional stock could be affected if reforestation exceeded consumption. If a national policy of energy consumption stressed energy diversification, conservation, and disposable stock replacement wherever possible, this balance might occur.

Owner-managers must broaden their definitions of cost. Although these people are not the only ones benefiting from business—hence not the only ones who should shoulder the burden—they are the ones who initiate and coordinate the business process and therefore must bear at least the initial responsibility for a wider view of cost.

There is and will be great resistance to this broader definition of cost; after all, how can one account for pollution in market costs? The problem is one of measurement; diseconomics (such as pollution) resist quantification. But if a firm refuses to install "scrubbers" or smokestack cleaners, the pollution costs will only be shifted to surrounding social entities (homes, schools, hospitals); one cannot argue that pollution has *no* cost. A more proper question remains: who will pay for a given cost? To this end, we suggest several new definitions of costs which include, but are not confined to, economic terms.

1. *Direct Cost:* This is the immediate effect and damage done to buildings because of corrosion and excessive wear.
2. *Indirect Cost:* This is the cost imposed upon the environment.
3. *Complementary Costs:* The expenses occurred as a result of the ramifications of direct costs. For example if a farmer's land is polluted with chemicals and he eats the food and gets sick, the hospital costs are complementary.

4. *Induced Costs:* Costs that are necessary to prevent further direct costs in the future.
5. *Indirectly Induced Costs:* Costs that arise as a result of a secondary agency, usually government, and its need to clean up.[115]

Obviously our definitions of costs would entail, if enacted, a much more modest definition of growth.

> Economic growth is the net addition to the potential stock of available resources, as qualified by the necessity to preserve all the human and non-human possibilities of persons or entities surrounding the business enterprise.[116]

If, for example, corporate managers were to choose a more capital-intensive form of development, one which stressed increased space, energy, and layoffs, due compensation would have to be made, because costs would be incurred for many. For the workers, a portion of the money gained in contract disputes could be set aside for job retraining necessitated by market forces. This retraining program should be codetermined by labor, management, and adjudicated by government.

This model does not argue against economic growth. It does suggest, however, that growth be coordinated with other societal needs. And, furthermore, it suggests that economic growth projects should have a variety of social needs in mind at the moment of their initiation, not as a charitable afterthought. Responsible profit is that surplus which helps a community attain a variety of norms simultaneously in daily life. Alternatively, suffering—say, that of families destroyed by the industrial process—indicates a form of irresponsible profiteering because there is a further breakdown in social cohesion. Likewise, responsible competition is that competition which broadens the definition of product quality beyond the factors of price and value. A firm should boast not only of getting a quality product to market, but of maintaining a favorable net fertility, or disposable stock ratio. This definition of profit and growth admittedly contains noneconomic factors in its construction. However, reality demands a recognition of extra economic factors. For "if the pursuit of profit is the sole criterion of proper economic behavior, then there is no way to distinguish productive activity from robbery."[117]

Executive salary is another problem that needs to be discussed in light of contemporary union decline. By what criteria are executive salaries determined? Traditionally, scarcity, performance, and ability have been given as rationales for rising salaries. However, these legitimate answers hide more difficult problems. How are such attributes to be justly quantified? What are the limits of such salaries? How much of the actual pay represents the results of mere executive salary demand as opposed to results in the market and talent? What is the effect of rising management salaries upon business morale and consumer costs? Is it just to advocate, as some companies did recently, that the union take a wage cut while executive salaries rose over ten percent.

Perhaps it would be helpful to consider whether such salary demands are a contributing factor to union hostility. If so, perhaps market performance and labor's motivation would be increased if worker morale increased. And perhaps worker morale would increase if executive salaries could be mutually negotiated—just as union salaries are negotiated. Secondly, executive merit pay should only be advanced after a sufficient wage floor has been set under the lowest three positions, as determined by union pay scales. Thirdly, while income should increase with responsibility, it might be appropriate if managerial responsibility were made more accountable as measured by overall enterprise improvement. To the extent that managers are responsible for economic surplus in a more holistic manner, they should be rewarded. Penalties should be executed if the opposite occurs. To facilitate this possibility we suggest that all salaries be subject to a more broadly representative board of directors, one which includes union members and consumer advocates.

More importantly, we need to expand the nonmonetary incentives of executive work. J. T. Mitchell, president of English Cooperative Wholesale, with a one hundred-million-pound annual turnover, was asked about his incentives for receiving a salary of only two thousand pounds per year. He said, "I enjoy the respect of my colleagues. I possess great power. I have a great faith in the cooperative ideal."[118] Similarly, George W. Goethals, builder of the Panama Canal, had little trouble in finding competent engineers who were willing to work at more reasonable wages because these engineers enjoyed a great level of esprit de corps.[119] Likewise, Dr. Harry Steenbock, the man who pioneered the popular usage of vitamin D, refused a company's offer of two million dollars for the patent rights. He chose rather to give the patent rights to the University of Wisconsin, which used the royalties to subsidize fellowships for nutritional scientists.[120] There are many extraeconomic incentives for work.

In keeping with the model of sphere sovereignty, a view that respects the integrity of each area of life, the alternative between a state-mandated wage and a mere market-determined wage seems to be unacceptable. Both views restrict the broader scope of economic responsibility. In the latter case, economic responsibility is determined by the market, which too often forgets a variety of social responsibilities, while in the former case a supposedly all-knowing governmental agency sets wages.

To bring about a more just distribution of salaries, governments can help by creating legal room in the business for a variety of "weaker groups," with "weakness" describing any group that lacks full access to economic burdens and responsibilities. Thus, the state must also combat abuse of power or opportunity, as in oligopolies, that threatens a more equitable participation. It is not the government's job to say, "too much"; the legal ground for such an objection cannot be sustained by the simple fact of greater income. However, when power or opportunity reduces intercommunal or interindividual relationships, government must step in to give all parties room to pursue their God-given callings.[121] Thus, when speculation artificially drives up land prices to the point where farmers and marginal landowners are driven to despair, government must step in to prevent a loss of land. This intervention should not include land redistribution. Instead, it could impose an increased tax on speculative revenues. This tax would increase conservation, disposable stock upkeep, and farmer retraining.

Our model suggests a number of practical strategies that could be adopted to help create a more responsible investment climate. I favor, with modifications, the basic contours of former president Reagan's "incentive zones." According to this notion, businesses would be given tax breaks to set up business in certain predetermined troubled areas. Provided that the enforcement of pollution laws and the maintenance of minimum wage standards are maintained, such a plan could provide for an increased circulation of capital.[122] Any business locating in such zones would be subject to community action councils (the lawyers for which would be paid with public funds) and businesses would have to locate in the designated community for three years before receiving full incorporation benefits. Furthermore, we would argue for preferential supply and sales practices. F. W. Woolworth, for example, targeted Harlem for a two-million-dollar outlet store. The property for the store is owned by Harlem Freedom Associates. Local citizens have acted as trustees for the income, and black contractors have built the store.[123]

Many businesses suffer because the basic direction of a business is set by a board of directors who represent narrow managerial interests. We maintain that any basic community internally affected by business should help set basic policy. Consumer advocates, for example, have deepened business responsibility. Increased shareholder responsibility is an example of growing economic responsibility. Moreover, businesses located in such zones should be mandated, by shareholders, to plow a greater portion of the profits back into the business for product quality and capital upkeep. Maintenance of capital stock, of course, presupposes sufficient capital supply. A "starter" business or "mom-and-pop" businesses would have to be judged differently.

Since the evolution of large-scale business in the mid-nineteenth century, large-scale finance has emerged as a necessity. The emergence of savings and loan banks is good insofar as they circulate capital, encourage savings, and promote opportunity. Dwelling House Savings and Loan Association of Pittsburgh, Pennsylvania is a good model. Located in the Hill District of Pittsburgh, an impoverished section of town, it was founded by Robert R. Lavelle in the late 1950s. It has grown from a bank with $500,000 in assets to one with over $12,000,000. A promotional brochure explains the business's basic purpose:

> Most banks are in business to lend at the highest possible interest with the lowest possible risk. Unfortunately this means that the poor, the black, and other minorities rarely receive mortgage money to buy and own their own homes. Dwelling House attempts to reverse the traditional banking rule—by lending to people who may not be "good risks," at the lowest practical interest rate. Our goal is to approach people with respect and through encouragement and patient financial counseling, to help them become good risks. This follows God's command to serve the poor and the needy.... Home ownership leads to increased civic involvement, political pressure for adequate police and fire protection, and incentive for businesses to locate in the area.[124]

Dwelling House accomplishes this unusual goal by cutting costs and maximizing loan opportunities. By cutting advertising expenses, lowering salaries, minimizing facilities and not enacting high-interest certificates of deposit, Lavelle can afford to lend money on the average for 10½%, even when the prime rate is much higher (e.g., 20% in the late 1970s). Of course, savers cannot expect to make above 5½% earnings on passbook savings. Disrupting the cycle of poverty, however, as Lavelle does by encouraging home ownership, makes a 5 to 5½% return on passbook savings a rich investment.

Although Dwelling House is located in a crime-infested area of Pittsburgh, it follows the saying, "Christ was always with the poor," and despite its location knows how to turn a profit. Although it is one of the city's smallest S and L's, it is one of the most profitable in Pittsburgh as measured by its return on average assets. In fact, it has the ninth-best record in America for profitability,[125] a remarkable record given today's banking climate. Its profitability is due in large part to its unwillingness to terminate delinquent borrowers. Indeed he gives free financial counseling to borrowers so they may be encouraged to meet their obligations. When Lavelle started in banking, home ownership in the Hill section of Pittsburgh was 12%. The City Planning Department of Pittsburgh has now established it at 29%, with Lavelle claiming that it is at 40%.[126]

As a real estate agent also (the bank and real estate activities are separate by law), Lavelle has had to fight for this "ministry." In the late sixties he filed a class-action suit to secure advertising space in the MultiList. At that time black realtors and listings were "redlined," or segregated into forbidden zones by whites, thus preventing equality of sales. While fighting his case all the way to the United States Supreme Court, Lavelle received threats and obscenities for his action. Just before reaching the high court's docket, the case was dropped because of a shifting climate on race relations. With this historic act, blacks were permitted advertising space—a first in America.

We have only hinted at the specific economic definition and function of capital. We save this most crucial question for the last part of our discussion of capital. The economic definition of capital usually includes such things or qualities as material resources, money value, money sums available for loan or purchase, or the present value of future income. Capital resources can be used in a variety of more or less productive circumstances, and they in turn can define other fundamental assets such as land and labor.

Combinations of wealth-capital are said to form capital's structure, which in turn is related to its entrepreneur-oriented functions and related functions.[127] Prices are supposed to signal the proper combinations and the size of wealth-capital formations, with the combinations manifesting the order and function of capital. Here, at the most elementary level, we begin to realize difficulties. "Capital" can have no function apart from human responsibility. Only capitalists can have responsible or irresponsible functions. Capital is not the active agent; it is only the means and context of economic responsibility. This traditional capitalistic model presupposes autonomous, mechanistically functioning parts that allegedly come to equilibrium because of price signals and apart from responsible human agents. Capitalists are only responding to market signals, it is thought.

Similarly, capital goods cannot possibly derive their deepest and broadest meaning from their price and market functions alone.[128] Capital is intertwined with many other important factors, including labor and land, and upon such additional factors as entrepreneurial talent and social communities. Capital goods, while defined, inter alia, in an economic manner, nevertheless depend upon a socially located, whole citizen to realize their economic potential. A separation of a responsible, socially located citizen from "capital's function" is impossible. But this separation and alienation inevitably results from the pricing theory of value, a central presupposita of modern economics. Accordingly, the value of non-economic, non-market goods—like nature—are not inherently valued until a market price is signaled. Consequently, inherent value is separated from economic view if a resource does not enter the market. Similarly, if a resource does not have a price, it cannot be valued. The negative consequences of this myopia can hardly be overestimated.

Surely the unique meaning of capital comes to fruition when it assumes its place within the production process. A reductionism occurs, however, when the various functions of capital are abstracted from their intereconomic and social contexts. This abstraction leads, in turn, to a focus upon the importance and place of capital[129] to the detriment of other factors of production.

Capitalism therefore results. In it capital serves as the nodal or central point of the production process. Labor and the environment or land tend to be defined in relationship to wealth-producing potentials. The reality of this reductionism can be seen in the traditional designations of labor as a "factor of production" and land as a "free gift of nature," whose significance can not be determined prior to market entry.[130]

Clearly, capital and its owners or managers can not be isolated and exaggerated. A theory of value and distribution needs to be developed that more fully reflects not only the real cost, as we have argued, but the reality of other social costs and primary economic factors. Such a project is surely one of the most challenging and demanding of the field, even while it is the most necessary!

LAND

We have looked at the broad contours of a rethinking of labor and capital. Now let us turn our attention to the subject of land and its proper use. In so doing, we are guided by the broad norm of stewardship. As we have argued, stewardship applies to capital in the way the manager-owner treats the labor. One's claims to being a good steward are spurious if labor abuse is present. The call to be stewardly means the manager must be fruitful in developing production and in the maintenance of capital and dispositional stock. Labor, at the same time, is called in stewardship to exchange capital-depleting wages for meaningful, rewarding work. Now we shall see how stewardship builds a more proper view of land usage.

The term "steward" comes from the Greek *oikonomia,* from which the modern term "economics" is derived.[131] The steward was to manage a given estate so as to provide holistic development for those who lived on the estate; one was not to abuse the workers in the process. Crucial for the identity of the steward was the fact that the property did not belong to the steward; one was not an owner but was a husbandman. Thus the property was not "private" in the sense that it could not be used at the steward's autonomous discretion. The land was first of all the Lord's, to dispose of as he saw fit. God has given the land to humanity for fruitfulness, to be carefully cultivated for the mutual benefit of fellow stewards.

Land, in the scope of the biblical drama, is not only a gift but a necessary element of salvation. Any worldview, such as that we have seen among Evangelicals, which attempts to deny the importance of land as redemption's context misunderstands the Scriptures because of an otherworldly emphasis, while falling prey to a de facto capitalistic orientation in land management.

A standard economic dictionary defines land as the "free gifts of nature."[132] But as with capital, this definition does justice neither to the real cost of business nor to the contours of our interdisciplinary argument.

Land represents a sign of promise and fulfillment and will lead, when consummated, to the context of God's redemption of earth through his kingdom. This is the faith side of a view of land. Land is biologically founded, at the same time, upon the concept of ecosphere; plants, animals, water, rocks, and dirt, etc. are the basic strata of life and are, as such, inestimably valuable. This biological basis of our existence also is a symbol for wholeness, joy, rootedness, and coherence. No person living can sustain life without a commitment to land. Land becomes the basis of historicity, the context of unfolding time and communal identity. Thus,

> Humanness . . . will be found in belonging to and referring to that locus in which the particular historicity of a community has been expressed

and to which recourse is made for purposes of orientation, assurance, and empowerment.[133]

To move back to the mode of faith discourse: we see that land is rooted in the covenant and promise of God. In Genesis, chapter 11, the destruction of the land in the Deluge narrative is the culmination of God's frustration with generations of rebellion. Thus, the promise of a homeland to Abraham and his descendants, some chapters later, can be interpreted as nothing short of the initiation of a sign of redemption in the fullest possible sense. Furthermore, when God liberated the children of Israel from the land of oppression, they were expelled into the "wilderness," a land of chaos, threat, vulnerability, the area of no context. The wilderness, while a place of testing, was nonetheless a place of direct provision. Each person gathered as much as he could eat because Yahweh was absolutely faithful and loyal.

Once Israel crossed the Jordan River into the land of promise, years of wandering, precariousness, and rootlessness gave way to a time of trust and security. Once in the land, however, "the central temptation of the land became coveting" another's land and possessions. In the land of promise, Israel's place became a gift—and a sign of responsibility and stewardship.[134] Land was never considered private property, because it was a gift from God and thus not ultimately owned.

The sabbatical system, or the system of cultural rest, was given to Israel by God for rest and replenishment, not for incessant production. (Academics also enjoy the fruits of this system of seven-year rest.) The Sabbath meant that production and desire were to be restricted. Each week could begin with a day of rest because Israel was always promised enough. In such a society, land was to be a source of care for one's neighbor as well as for the poor and widowed.[135] Land was not to be sold to the highest bidder nor defined *primarily* by its wealth-producing capacities. More importantly, all natural and legal boundaries for land were to be respected (Proverbs 23:10, 11). It is not accidental, for instance, that Jezebel, the preeminent symbol of evil in the Old Testament, handled land like a piece of commercial property and not as convenantal dispositional stock.[136]

Israel's exile demonstrates God's displeasure with economic greed and political injustice. Such a view of God's displeasure can be found in Abraham Lincoln's Second Inaugural Address of 4 March 1865, in which he warns of God's judgment but pleads for his mercy. Nor is this vision of judgment without relevance for American Evan-

gelicals, so confident that America is "God's New Israel." Perhaps
Evangelicals might want to consider the possibility that their fall
from public grace, increasingly occurring during this century,
maybe as much a result of God's judgment for their siding with
capitalism as it is the result of the increasing realization of secular
America that Evangelicalism has had no unique socioeconomic insights to offer American identity.[137]

In our opinion, it is not improper to speak of a promised land,
for "the land of Israel is rooted in Yahweh's very character as a
convenant Maker and Keeper."[138] What was said to ancient Israel,
however, may be said to all other people: those not claiming special
status should be treated as justly as those who do claim special
status; and if this statement is not forthcoming, as is often the case,
then the claim to special status must be forfeited.

Returning to our chronicle of redemptive history, we note that
a process of Hellenization took over. Accordingly, a religiously
syncretistic worldview set in, circa 200 B.C., whereby Israel lost its
particularity. This phase of redemptive history approximates
Evangelicalism's accommodation to Industrialism's secularization
process, in my opinion. The process of the Hellenization of Israel
and the Mammonization of Evangelicalism are remarkably similar:
"Hellenization set a pattern for the 'knowing,' uncaring rich to take
advantage of the trusting, helpless poor."[139] Jerusalem, the city of
promise, became no better than Alexandria, the polis of reasonable
civility.

"The meek shall inherit the earth"—so Christ proclaims to startle
the satisfied (Matthew 5:5). This theme seems so ironic. How can
those who trust, who do not grasp and strive after, inherit a commodity that only seems to belong to the aggressive? How can
women in male-dominated cultures sing any songs of hope?[140] The
answer is profoundly simple. Christ has come, for those of faith, to
enfranchise the disenfranchised. The way to land is to sacrifice the
desire for wealth and status, so that one may gain all with Christ.
Not so ironically, the need to sacrifice is built into the heart of
capitalism, as we see each time an entrepreneur postpones gratification for the sake of a risky investment.

We have belabored this theme of land in an attempt to demonstrate that property is not autonomously private, nor wealth acquisition without sacrifice. All land carries with it responsibilities not
only for production but for compassion as well. Land and its fruits
are to be shared, following the tenets of responsible stewardship,
among the weakest of groups. The homeless, perhaps the weakest
group in our culture, must become enfranchised.

Currently, land is being biologically abused in many ways, so we face ecological challenges. Perpetual abuse of the land not only diminishes energy potential, but creates a real threat to all life. Certainly water is a necessary part of human life. If it is endangered we face manifold ramifications. "Almost all of America's 246 water basins are polluted, mostly by topsoil erosion from farming."[141] Logging, mining, construction, and electrical power plants are close to farming in terms of water abuse. Each year, furthermore, over seven million tons of oil are added to the oceans of our world. Thus, while converting resources to energy use, the destruction of our necessary water supplies is occurring.

Because acid rain continues to pollute our land, air pollution has once again gained national attention. The air we breathe is polluted at the rate of 4.8 pounds per American citizen per day![142] Fossil fuels, used to power our cars, when combined with water in the atmosphere produce a dangerous sulfuric acid. When this mixture is combined with ozone gases, a compound similar to tear gas is formed. This compound is the largest element in smog which, when falling to earth in showers, forms acid rain. Already three hundred lakes in the Adirondack Mountains are so acidified that fish cannot live there.[143]

Our topsoil has also become abused. "In 1978, each American produced an average of 20 tons of solid waste per year, 109 pounds per day. . . . In 1980, some 750,000 producers in the United States created about 63 million tons of wsate."[144] We are producing even more today. In light of such abuses to landfill sites, which are often poorly treated and inspected, our discussion about capital's costs for doing business becomes more relevant.

Clearly, the world faces a problem in its use of nonrenewable resources. Every second, the world uses thirty thousand gallons of oil, with the United States using about one-third of that. And although Americans total only five percent of the world's population, they use twenty-seven percent of its production materials.[145] Thus, the problem of overconsumption and waste creation is a real one. This plight is multiplied when we stop to consider that much of the world emulates American production standards. This constant drain on the products of land and its capacity to hold our wastes, if continued at its present rate, would cause us to run out of arable land by the year 2050, even if we double production capacities and hold the population in check.[146] Clearly, an international policy of land stewardship is needed.

We have argued throughout this work that the secular need to dominate nature in autonomy is fueled by a misguided faith which

equates freedom with exploitation. Human freedom to pursue production and consumption must be limited by the wider contexts of
natural and human needs and limits. Stewardship cannot be pursued after exploitation has occurred. Rather, laws and consensus
must be established that enable humanity and nature to pursue
their own destinies before, during, and after the production process. The balancing of various public interests by government can
no longer be counted upon to ensure land quality. Moreover, the
free market will certainly not guarantee the long-term viability of
land defined as free, autonomous property, available to the highest
bidder.

Public-legal distinctions must be made with respect to the various aspects of land use. This will mean that many forests, wetlands,
swamps, and agricultural lands are protected by law from exploitation. Stewardship rights must be made to harmonize with personal
property rights. This will not mean, of course, that all lands will be
nationalized. It may mean, for example, that suburban mall expansion may have to be limited through zoning. It is not an undue
restriction on business to require all enterprises to recognize existing land structures, or to seek a balanced environment for human
and nonhuman life.

Hopefully, the ecological crises that we now face, particularly
with ozone damage, will convince us of the value of land before it
reaches the market or production process. Humanity finds only a
small part of the meaning and purpose in life in economic activities;
land and its many uses must be protected if we are to thrive. Ecological disaster has been caused in part by technological activity,
and further technological activity cannot provide the complete solution to our land problem. It seems more reasonable to suggest
that stewardship be seriously considered as a land ethic.

A tighter form of city planning comprises an important part of
the answer to our land-abuse dilemma. Zoning land according to
kind of land and use should minimize interzone destruction and
maximize harmony. Strict pollution standards should be enforced
so that one region's coal pollution does not disturb another region's
recreational facilities.[147] Pressure should be put on local governments to preserve historic and aesthetic sites, with the preservation funds being drawn first from those industries whose pollution
causes the greatest corrosion, then from the willing public. I do not
find gentrification a plausible form of historical preservation, if for
no other reason than that through it inner-city erosion is simply
shifted to another area. Zones emphasizing multifaceted development—recreation, residential, aesthetic—should harmonize with

those of a primarily commercial nature. Farm land, especially, should be protected from urban sprawl as that land becomes increasing expensive and poorly treated.[148]

Zoning seems wise because land is not merely "mineral wealth"; it does have its own quality, which should be legally recognized. Communities, states, and nations need to develop a long-range land use strategy which includes both preservation and conversion to economic and noneconomic use. Public justice should recognize the identity and function of many different forms of land.

Existing zoning values emphasize accessibility, demand, and commercial exchange.[149] Perhaps these patterns can be replaced by strict maintenance of all noneconomic patterns. When businesses are zoned, their borders should be bounded by noncommercial centers whose identities need to be maintained. If such businesses (along with hospitals and churches, for example), were centrally located, their expansion would be limited. Public spending should also be monitored in this regard. Spending on highways represents an unproportionally large amount of money. Monies should be restricted for the facilities for private cars and given to more affordable means of public transportation. Nonpolluting, noncongestive, space-saving monorails might be a consideration in this regard.

One last word about land. Nowhere does the religious character of land definition appear more striking than in the contrast of Native American and white American conceptions of "mineral wealth." To understand the significance of the difference is to appreciate more fully the need for a change in current land policies. Commenting on the difference, the World Council of Churches summed up the feelings of the world's indigenous peoples:

> Our land is more valuable than money. . . . We can not sell the life of our people and animals. . . . It was put here by the Great Spirit and we can not sell it because it does not belong to us.[150]

The Native American in particular has shown us that land represents a place of service, right, and identity. Certainly, Americans could have tolerated this concept—could even have learned from it—more. Justice implies the freedom for individuals, associations, and peoples to associate in any form, so long as that form promotes the internal well-being of a defined group (such as the Native Americans) and does not do violence to national security. No land must be given up without due compensation and legal consent. Upon occasion, courts have recognized this right. On 30 December 1982, the U.S. District Court of Oregon upheld the terminated Klamath Indian tribe's claims to full rights to their land. The court, in so doing, would not allow the tribe's original rights to over seven hundred thousand acres to be overturned without due consent and compensation. Thus, the court maintained that no unilateral action could undo treaty rights previously agreed upon. This was a large victory for a small tribe, a victory of justice that should have come much sooner.[151]

This verdict also recognizes, albeit much too late, an important fact that begs for our attention: economic incorporation does not bring peace and prosperity; still less does it bring happiness and multifaceted riches.

8

Conclusions

We have attempted to delineate the profound religious merger of Evangelical Protestantism and the Industrial Revolution in the nineteenth century. It has been stressed, contrary to the position of conventional wisdom, that this synthesis was of a religious nature.

Industrialism comprised naturalistic, materialistic, "scientific," and mechanistic components. A technological imperative, born of the desire to dominate nature in the name of freedom, became the complement of a Deism which defined God's relationship to the creation in very mechanistic terms. If the Deity would not control culture, then humanity had to. The materialistic emphasis of Industrialism, or the attempt to define happiness in terms of production and consumption, became the incentive for this worldview.

Evangelicals, on the contrary, defined their worldview in supernatural, theological, moral and metaphysical categories. The universe for the Evangelical was not a closed system but a marvelously open series of events manifesting the glory of God, albeit in a dualistic manner. "Happiness," in this schema, was obtained by obedience to God's moral law as manifest in natural law and the Scriptures. The supreme happiness could only be found in heaven with Christ.

In spite of all of these real differences, a deeper current of unity was apparent. This root unity has been attributed to a religious merger; "religion," again, being defined as the act of service that units the depth dimension of life to that which is believed to be ultimate, secure, and beyond question. As such, religious activity unites various modes or aspects of human activity and refers such activity to that which is believed to be unconditional. This process is operative equally for persons and cultures, as we have shown through our study of the two nineteenth-century worldviews.

In the context of our discussion of religion, idolatry or false religious service was defined by the New Testament designation "Mammon," or the processes of monied-autonomy made ultimate. We have used the term "Gold" synonymously with Mammon. We at-

218

tempted to show, more philosophically, how an incorporating culture sought to define social life by the standards of economic doctrine: human labor as a "factor of production," nature as "mineral wealth," and happiness as utility maximization.

Industrial adherents were active and practical about their beliefs. Their faith in their own autonomy endeavored to envision and embody their confession for cultural reality. This was accomplished, concretely, through a worldview. Thus, a certain progression from a religiously operative belief in autonomy (hence the need for voluntarism) proceeded to trust humanity in faith for cultural possibilities and ended in a view of the world with many of these possibilities being realized as economic "progress." Progress, in turn, became the enthusiast's slogan not only for the gilded age of Industrialism but for the antebellum portion of nineteenth-century millennial Evangelicalism as well. People in both positions increasingly believed that religion was a compartmentalized, personal phenomenon.

The concept of religion is a vague one if it is not tied to recognized basic cultural values we have called presupposita. Several presupposita, or religiously based presuppositions, held these two worldviews together. Democratic individualism, the efficacy of natural law for the mechanism of the market, the acceptance of the maximization of gaining and giving, as well as the notion of free will, were among such presupposita. Of lesser import, though no less of a cohesive force, were the shared values of moral and economic discipline, technical manipulation of the natural environment, and a feverish yet republican expansion of the domain of the "chosen people" under the Manifest Destiny, as well as the necessity of self-help. The shared optimism of a certain portion of this era was able to arise, moreover, because Evangelical-revivalism had come to a truncated view of human sin. Concomitantly, the scope of the Evangelical worldview was increasingly internalized and personalized, leaving it impotent to discover economic alternatives. This problem was compounded by postbellum Evangelicalism's increasing emphasis on an otherworldly gospel—an emphasis which did not, however, prevent many Evangelicals from becoming enthralled by the fruits of Industrialism.

This support of capitalism did not begin with the Civil War. Finney's Whig voluntarism, affirmation of the profit motive, and use of morality for social cohesion became an attempt, conscious or otherwise, to meet the perceived needs of a turbulent society. Revivalists and industrialists came to need each other; the former needed money, the latter legitimation.

The economic thought of Wayland formed yet another component of the industrial-Evangelical link. In the wholesale attempt to create a Christian economic ethic according to the terms of classical theorists like David Ricardo and Adam Smith, Wayland showed how the synthesis would be both theoretical and practical. Following this lead, the postbellum pastor Russell Conwell attempted to reform capitalism along the lines of a democratic, Populist platform. Being a person of the people, Conwell feared the monied aristocracy while touting manifold economic opportunities or "acres of diamonds".

When the Evangelicals did minister to the casualties of Industrialism, they often did so by treating symptoms and not the causes. The Salvation Army admirably served (and continues to serve) a variety of social castoffs. The noteworthy and commendable compassion and sacrifice manifested by the Army—like many Evangelical ministries—were after the market acts, however. The Evangelical church has been good at offering aid and help after the fact to a society remade by Industrialism. The current agonies suffered by, say, the homeless testify to the need to think of the vulnerable *before* market operations begin.

There seem to be additional deep currents that unite Industrialism and Evangelicalism. Postmillenialism is perhaps the best example of a form of Evangelicalism that confused the materialistic progress of capitalism with the coming of the kingdom of God. As conversions mounted and technology dazzled the century's believers with new inventions, antebellum Evangelicals mixed their faith in Christ with faith in economic-technological progress. Thus, economic enterprise went hand-in-hand with millennial hopes of Christ's Second Coming. The "American System" had Evangelical adherents because it equated and gave concrete expression to the free market and free will, two synonyms for shared American identity. If one were successful under this doctrine, the myth of the self-made, free person was sustained. Given this century's definition of "freedom" as conquest, it is little wonder, therefore, that the Protestant notion of Divine Providence, or God's gracious rule by decree, was changed into a Manifest Destiny which believed it was to conquer "the Garden," or the American wilderness. Concomitantly, stewardship did not mean the responsibility for carefully developing the wilderness so that all might benefit, but became too often synonymous with the exploitation of land, wildlife, and indigenous peoples.

In this land of "freedom," voluntary social control was at a premium. Revivalism provided such a restraint. Thus, Evangelicalism became inherently conservative by its manifest inclination to tame the abuses inherent in industrializing democracy. This conservative force, along with the desire to affirm the above-mentioned values, helped secure cultural space for a time for Evangelicals. Thus, they settled into a comfortable alliance with Industrialism, thinking the republic was in all ways prospering.

American culture was divided between the forces of rational control over physical resources and spiritual control over the private-moral resources of the nation. As long as this precarious dualism could be held together, Industrialism and Evangelicalism could agree upon the boundaries of mutual influence and control. Industrialism took, increasingly, the outer world of culture; Evangelicalism gradually retreated to the inner world of piety, morality and faith. As the secularization of American culture grew in intensity, this synthesis and its rough boundaries became more precarious. As a result, Evangelicalism found itself on the cultural defensive, without a place to stand. The reactionary conservatism that sprung from marginalization was only intensified by the emergency of Protestant liberalism as a denominational force that sought to compete for the layman's attention in the major Protestant sanctuaries.

Evangelicals furthered their own secularization by too often accepting a definition of religion that was, at its core, private and personal. Their very self-definition incorporated notions of religion. Publically located revivals did take place, but all too often their goal was the cultivation of virtues that were of a primarily personal and individual nature. Furthermore, when Evangelicals such as Russell Conwell sought to influence public policy, they often did so under the umbrella of the institutional church. The ecclesiasticism so entailed could do little to withstand the onslaughts of secularization, especially in an urban, ethnically pluralistic setting.

Timothy Smith, in *Revivalism and Social Reform in Mid-Nineteenth-Century America,* maintains that Evangelicals acted as a progressive force for ameliorative social change. There can be no doubt that to varying degrees their attempt has been partially successful. At the same time, however, a rather sinister transformation has been going on. By their thought forms, methods of evangelization, and basic religious tenets and related values, Evangelicals have profoundly deepened the process of secularization. The notion of individualism is a case in point. A basic, autonomous, fundamental building block—an individual—is thought to be the basis of society in both capitalism and Evangelicalism. This severed, isolated image differs dramatically from the organic "body" image of people presented by the scriptures, an image that stresses the connective, inter-relatedness, and interdependent nature of human existence. Scriptures call us "members," not "individuals." Furthermore, Fundamentalism, insofar as it has added its shrill voice of protest to secularization, has supported the forces of economic modernity even while resisting scientific modernity. Caught in a world of swirling changes, the more reactionary Fundamentalists have often defined their economic ethic in reaction to socialistic modernity. Unfortunately, few new alternatives can be developed when one's self-definition arises from conflict. Thus, Evangelicalism and Fundamentalism have served the Christ of culture, to use H. Richard Niebuhr's typology.

It has been argued that Evangelicals can claim no support for their economic ethic from classical Christian theorists. In the measure that Evangelicals have departed from such theory, however, they have severed themselves from the tradition of the Reformation, a tradition they claim to uphold. The degree of departure has been highlighted by classical Christianity's repudiation of the principles of acquisitiveness and related values. Luther and Calvin, especially, rose up against the forces of proto-capitalism and the acquisitiveness that prompted it. Moreover, these Christian theorists envisioned society less as a competing beehive and more as a kingdom of interdependent persons. Their concomitant hatred of individualism and greed is especially apparent in Luther's disdain for the Fugger monopoly, a disdain hardly shared by many postbellum Evangelical free-market enthusiasts.

While we have criticized Evangelicalism's failure to resist economic secularization, we do not believe that Protestant liberalism has escaped this process either. In supporting progressivism's reformist impulses and various forms of socialism, the Social Gospel in particular and Protestant liberalism in general have struggled unsuccessfully, in our opinion, to find a long-lasting third way out of the capitalistic/socialistic dilemma. Nowhere is this more apparent than in Protestant liberalism's support of the notions and ethos of American secular democratic liberalism and mainline Protestantism's implied acceptance of a spirit of technological rationalization, complete with experts, mandates, and fragmentation. Protestantism's bureaucratic tendencies manifest in councils, edicts and declarations, closely parallels our federal government's tendency to excessive bureaucratization.

When Evangelicalism tried to provide a serious academic alternative to modernity, it chose a philosophy that was heavily laced with rationalistic assumptions and logical antinomies. Scottish Common Sense Realism's use of proportions (conceived of as individual building blocks of knowledge), sacred/secular dualisms, and the artificial elevation of human reason eventuated in the equation of theory with belief, and belief (almost) with the force of scripture. Though attempting to defend itself against the critique of modern thought, Common Sense Realism believed in an a priori of modern thought: the sufficiency of reason to adjudicate ultimate truth. Thus, while Common Sense Realism sought to be true to theological doctrines, it philosophically and economically undermined the classical Christian faith, as can be seen in Wayland's fusion of realism and capitalistic presupposita.

We would like to think that these problems would have been addressed in a meaningful way by Evangelicals in the twentieth century. There has been some fine work done by some Evangelical theorists. But these first fruits need to be expanded upon and developed more fully.

As Protestant liberals and moderates have gained control of the major denominations, Evangelicals have fallen into a peripheral role. As mainline edicts have come that contradict the inherent conservatism of much of Evangelicalism, a pent-up backlash has often manifested itself in the membership's flight from major denominations to more conservative churches. With the Reagan election, its associated conservatism, and the retreat of New Deal political platforms in the 1980s, the notion of the free market has returned to dominate thought. Furthermore, as Americans have reeled from Watergate, Vietnam, Iranian hostage-taking, and the whirl of technological change, a retreat to personal peace and prosperity has seemed a most appealing course. As a result, the Evangelical preaching in this era has all too often fallen prey to the same tones of personalism and implicit materialism characteristic of the nineteenth century. One need only listen to the gospel of success communicated through portions of the "electronic church" to appreciate the modern results of our thesis.

The implications for culture in this work are many; we will mention only a few. A new ecumentical spirit must grip the Catholic and Protestant agenda. We need rigorous thought and careful reflection. Tested alternatives to capitalism and socialism would be offered. As long as the Church continues to condone American capitalism, it will be both "in" and "of" the world, and hence offer no healing alternative to its culture. The plight of our nation's troubled landscape demands action. To address this situation, the process of evangelization—to be "born again"—must include new principles for economics and for business. Full interdependence, sacrifice, stewardship, the dignity of labor, the harmonization of capital with other modes of production, and government coordination (not domination) of a national economic agenda are principles whose time have arrived.

Society will have to resolve the antinomies of capitalism if it is to experience a greater measure of true happiness. The role of government as combined advocate/watchdog of business should give way to a view that harmonizes business needs with other social responsibilities. As outlined in our last chapter, responsible business could reconcile the efficiency/justice debate by a stewardly worldview in which business fruitfulness goes hand-in-hand with a more complete, and harmonized, view of social progress.

This agenda cannot and must not be shouldered by the Evangelicals. The process of secularization has long since left the Evangelicals as a minority. Americans, in all our valued religious diversity, must now come to grips with the exaggerated place of money in our lives. There are some hopeful signs, however. The national debate beginning to surface around the use of our "peace dividend" is a good one. It forces us to rethink our spending values and priorities. Perhaps now savings, our ravaged infrastructure, and a variety of other domestic programs can receive due attention. Until we do address these problems, our difficulties—not the least of which are current levels of homelessness, poverty, and personal and national debt—will remain, however. A national agenda must be developed that addresses these desperate problems.

True critique, inspired by a realistic vision of one's own limitations, can, in the long run, offer hope for those who are willing to struggle with the issues. Ultimately, we need not feel any mania about our projects of "reformation." If to any degree reality is fabricated by grace, and if absolutization is something that cannot stand as it is, then Mammon will fall, or at least change in time. Our job is simply to support and to defend those things which we know to be true. This is one of the glowing contributions that Protestantism has made to Western civilization: our works do not save us, however responsibly done.

Notes

Introduction

1. We capitalize Industrialism to show that it represents, like Evangelicalism, more ultimate commitments. Industrialism, as we will see, is the practical expression of at least three major social revolutions: the scientific and the technological revolutions as well as the advent of classic capitalism.

2. Christ juxtaposes in Matthew 6:24 the service of God and Money, or Mammon, as two mutually exclusive ultimate commitments. So striking are their antipathies that he demands one should "hate" or "love" God or Mammon. He seems to imply that Mammon can be served with love or entire devotion as an ultimacy. For contemporary constructions using similar notions, see R. H. Tawney, *The Acquisitive Society* (New York: Harcourt, Brace and Company, 1948); Reinhold Niebuhr, *The Children of Light and the Children of Darkness* (New York: Charles Scribner's Sons, 1944), esp. 86–118; Bob Goudzwaard, *Capitalism and Progress* (Grand Rapids, Mich.: William B. Eerdmans Publishing Company, 1979), esp. 7ff. What we are saying about "Mammon" may equally be applied to the term "Gold."

3. For a discussion of a discernible theological core of basic beliefs, with noteworthy divergences, see David F. Wells and John D. Woodbridge, eds., *The Evangelicals: What They Believe, Who They Are, Where They Are Changing* (Grand Rapids, Mich.: Baker Book House, 1975).

4. George M. Thomas, *Revivalism and Cultural Change: Christianity, Nation Building, and the Market in the Nineteenth-Century United States* (Chicago: University of Chicago Press, 1989), 4, 5, 7, 8, 9. Douglas W. Frank, *Less Than Conquerors* (Grand Rapids, Mich.: William B. Eerdmans Publishing Company, 1986), 36–37.

5. George Marsden, *Fundamentalism and American Culture* (New York: Oxford University Press, 1980).

6. Ernest Sandeen, *The Roots of Fundamentalism* (Chicago: University of Chicago Press, 1970).

7. Paul Johnson, *A Shopkeeper's Millennium: Society and Revival in Rochester, 1830* (New York: Hill and Wang, 1978); William G. McLaughlin, *Revivals, Awakenings, and Reform* (Chicago: University of Chicago Press, 1978).

8. Timothy L. Smith, *Revivalism and Social Reform* (Nashville: Abington Press, 1957).

9. Frank, *Conquerors,* 37.

10. Henry F. May, *Protestant Churches and Industrial America* (New York: Harper and Brothers Publishers, 1967), 6.

11. In fairness to May, he does make a distinction between the "Social Gospel" and conservatives. A lack of theological reflection keeps him, however, from ex-

panding on this difference (something that we ourselves can do only marginally because of space restraints), and showing why conservative theology often led to conservative economics. Much to our amazement, May likens Unitarians to conservative social Christians on points of theology and basic religious beliefs. See May, 168.

12. Aaron Abell, *The Urban Impact on American Protestantism* (Cambridge: Harvard University Press, 1943), 5.

13. For a survey of this belief in a neoorthodox and secular form, see William J. Abraham, *The Coming Revival: Recovering the Full Evangelical Tradition* (New York: Harper and Row, 1984), 9ff.

Chapter 1. Religion Defined

1. In this era Evangelicalism was obviously vocal at times about its faith. However, it did increasingly accept this basic subject/object schema. For an evaluation of this process as it pertains to Industrialism, see Bob Goudzwaard, *Capitalism and Progress: A Diagnosis of Western Society* (Toronto: Wedge Publishing Foundation, 1979), 1–11. Cf. Jeremy Rifkin with Ted Howard, *The Emerging Order: God in the Age of Scarcity* (New York: G. P. Putnam's Sons, 1979), 30–35 on the Lockean notion of "toleration" and the truncation of religion in the West.

2. For a deeper analysis of this form of religion, see Paul Tillich, *What is Religion?* ed James L. Adams (New York: Harper and Row, 1969), 62–65, 67–69, 118–20.

3. Peter Berger, *The Sacred Canopy: Elements of a Sociological Theory of Religion* (New York: Doubleday, 1967), 3. For his treatment of "religion," cf. 3, 26–28, 35, 36, 65, 71, 178.

4. For an analysis of this problem as it pertains to Protestantism, see James H. Olthuis, "Must the Church Become Secular?" in James H. Olthuis et al., *Out of Concern for the Church* (Toronto: Wedge Publishing Foundation, 1970), 117–21.

5. R. H. Tawney, *Religion and the Rise of Capitalism: A Historical Study* (Gloucester, Mass.: Peter Smith Inc., 1962), 279.

6. Samuel P. Hays, *The Response to Industrialism: 1885–1914* (Chicago: The University of Chicago Press, 1957), 72.

7. For an antebellum and postbellum account of this spirit of activism as it pertains to voting and business ethics, see John L. Hammond, *The Politics of Benevolence: Revival Religion and American Voting Behavior* (Norwood, N.J.: Ablex Publishing Corp., 1979), 73f.

8. As reprinted in John Pollock, *Moody Without Sankey: A New Biographical Portrait* (London: Hodder and Stoughton, 1963), 50. Cf. K. L. Latourette, *A History of the Expansion of Christianity,* vols. 3–4, *The Great Century* A.D. *1800–1914: Europe and the United States of America* (New York: Harper and Row, 1941), 38.

9. A mode is one of fifteen fundamental ways of being in the world. As such, it is not a "thing" or a substance or a "what," but more a "how." For example, number, space, motion, organic life, emotional feeling, logical distinction, cultural development, symbolic signification, social interaction, economic value, aesthetic suggestiveness, law, commitment and the certainty of faith comprise the aspects of reality or ways of being-in-the-world for man. Since their intrinsic nature is given in reality, these modes have meaning which is simultaneously irreducible and interconnected, so that an inseparable coherence is manifest. However, while reality has inchoate meaning, its cultural expression depends upon human en-

deavor. Cf. Herman Dooyeweerd, *Roots of Western Culture: Pagan, Secular and Christian Options,* trans. John Kray, ed. Mark VanderVennen and Bernard Zylstra (Toronto: Wedge Publishing Foundation, 1979), 30, 40f., 214, 217, and Tillich, *What is Religion?* 65–67, 80–83.

10. Paul Tillich, *Biblical Religion and the Search for Ultimate Reality* (Chicago: University of Chicago Press, 1955), 8. For a more detailed description of the structures for reality, cf. Herman Dooyeweerd, *A New Critique of Theoretical Thought,* vol. 3 (Philadelphia: The Presbyterian and Reformed Publishing Co., 1969).

11. Benjamin Ward, *The Conservative Economic Worldview* (New York: Basic Books, 1979), 4.

12. Goudzwaard, *Capitalism and Progress,* 11.

13. Paul Tillich, *Theology of Culture,* ed. Robert C. Kimball (New York: Oxford University Press, 1959), 7, 8.

14. Paul Tillich, *The Protestant Era,* trans. James L. Adams (Chicago: University of Chicago Press, 1948), 281. We have found no explicit reference to capitalism as a religion in Tillich. We do believe, however, that it is consistent with his thoughts, as seen in this quote, to refer to capitalism as a religion and support such a claim with Tillich's work.

15. Hays, *Industrialism,* 2.

16. The word "Mammon" can be translated as "money." However, it can also denote an object of worship, allegiance or loyalty. Cf. Matthew 6:24 f. in the King James Version.

17. Roland Robertson, *The Sociological Interpretation of Religion* (New York: Schocken Books, 1970), 47. Cf. 34–51, 238–39.

18. Hays, *Industrialism,* 3.

19. Dooyeweerd, *New Critique,* vol. 1, 57. Cf. Paul Tillich, *What is Religion?* 59f.

20. Berger, *Sacred Canopy,* 28. For his reference to religion as one of man's functions, cf. 3, 26, 27, 65, 71.

21. Ibid., 28f.

22. Such presupposita, of course, affect subsequent logical analysis just as depth commitment affects subsequent cultural expression. The reader may object to the designation "presupposita" as jargonistic. We use this term rather than presupposition because it denotes a religious presupposition. We have rejected the term presupposition because the Kantian root of this word implies a logical foundation and thus begs the question of origin and mooring. Presuppositions are founded upon more ultimate presupposita.

23. John M. Keynes, "Economic Possibilities for Our Grandchildren," in *Essays in Persuasion,* (New York: Harcourt, Brace, 1932), 372.

24. Ibid., 371, 372.

25. Paul Tillich, *Ultimate Concern: Tillich in Dialogue* (New York: Harper and Row, 1965), 8. We, following Tillich, believe that there is an ultimate reality. The Infinite, or God, must never be equated with the finite, or, in our case, economic realities. Idolatry occurs when the truly infinite is united with, or identified with, the finite of life.

26. Hays, *Industrialism,* 1. Emphasis added.

27. Jim Fowler and Sam Keen, *Life Maps: Conversations on the Journey of Faith* (Minneapolis: Berry Winston Press, 1978), 24, 25. We use "environment" here, and not "commitment," because ultimate commitments affect one's environment even as faith affects cultural development.

28. For fuller analysis of this phenomenon, see Dooyeweerd, *Roots,* 90–108.

29. Bernard Mandeville, *The Fable of the Bees: or, Private Vices, Public Benefits*

(1714; Harmondsworth: Penguin Books, 1970), 63'–75 as quoted by Goudzwaard, *Capitalism,* 28.

30. See, especially, St. Augustine, *The City of God* (New York: Random House, 1950), bk 5, 150.

31. For a modern version of this argument, see Dooyeweerd, *New Critique,* 2, 294f.

32. Thus, Dooyeweerd following and depending upon an Augustinian analysis. See ibid., 295.

33. Wilford C. Smith, *Faith and Belief* (Princeton: Princeton University Press, 1979), 118. Emphasis added.

34. Dooyeweerd, *New Critique,* vol. 2, 304.

35. Robert L. Heilbroner, *The Worldly Philosophers: The Lives and the Ideas of the Great Economic Thinkers,* 4th ed. (New York: Simon and Schuster, 1972), 35. This term is also used in Dooyeweerd, *Roots,* 107, 217. It represents an attempt to explain the philosophical-anthropological assumptions that composed capitalism's view of people. Capitalism argued that our deepest needs were material and economic in nature. Agreeing with such a reductionistic anthropology, Marx could only argue that the worker and not the capitalist should control the means of wealth and production. Cf. Rifkin, *Order,* 23.

36. For the relationship of Deism to capitalism's notion of the laws of supply and demand, see Goudzwaard, *Capitalism,* 20f., 42f., 61f. For the relationship of the Industrial Revolution to Deism, see Goudzwaard, 61–63.

37. D. Roper, *A Christian Philosophy of Culture* (Potchefstroom: Potchefstroom University, South Africa, 1982), 43. The attempt here is not to draw rigid lines of demarcation. Rather, while moving from basis to comprehensiveness; we are attempting to show the integrality yet distinctiveness of religion and science.

38. Al Wolters, *Creation Regained* (Grand Rapids, Mich.: William B. Eerdmans Publishing Company, 1985), 2.

39. Abraham Kuyper, *Calvinism: Six Lectures Delivered in the Theological Seminary at Princeton* (New York: Fleming H. Revell Co., n.d.), 9f. Cf. Glifford Geetz, *The Interpretation of Culture* (New York: Basic Books, 1973), 127. It is interesting to note that Kuyper used concepts analogous to Geertz's almost one hundred years before Geertz.

40. Kuyper, *Calvinism,* 59. Cf. Tillich, *What Is Religion?* 126.

41. For Kuyper's reliance upon Calvin for his definition of religion, see *Stone Lectures,* 46–98, especially 52, 53. For Calvin's definition of religion as a universal phenomenon, see his *Institutes of the Christian Religion,* 2 vols., ed. John T. McNeill, trans. Ford L. Battles (Philadelphia: The Wesminster Press, 1967), 1.3.1, 1.4.1, and 1.12.1.

42. Kuyper, *Christianity and the Class Struggle,* trans. Dirk Jellema (Grand Rapids, Mich.: Piet Hein Publishers, 1950), 18, 29.

Chapter 2. An Introduction to the Evangelical-Industrial Worldview

1. In his *Life and Letters,* Darwin shows his indebtedness to the work *Malthus on Populations* by suggesting that it was Malthus who first discovered the principle that, in the struggle for existence, only the strongest organism will survive. See P.G. Fothergill, *Historical Aspects of Organic Evolution* (London: Hollis and Carter, 1952), 108.

2. John R. Everett, *Religions in Economics* (Philadelphia: Porcupine Press, 1982), 11.

3. Ibid., 11.

4. Quoted in ibid.

5. Edward L. Youmans et al., *The Culture Demanded by Modern Life* (New York: D. Appleton and Co., 1867), 48.

6. This is an extract taken from a speech delivered by Fiske at the Herbert Spencer Banquet on 9 November 1882. Reported in John Fiske, *Herbert Spencer on the Americans* (New York: Houghton Mifflin, 1894), 55.

7. John Fiske, *Through Nature to God* (New York: Houghton Mifflin, 1899), 133.

8. Everett, *Economics,* 13.

9. Maurice R. David, *Sumner Today: Selected Essays of William Graham Sumner* (New Haven: Yale University Press, 1940), 339. Cf. Sumner's *The Challenge of Facts,* ed. Samuel Keller (New Haven: 1914), especially chs. 1, 2, 11.

10. Sumner, *The Challenge of Facts,* 410, 415.

11. Sumner, *The Forgotten Man and Other Essays,* vol. 1 (New Haven: Yale University Press, 1918), 92.

12. Everett, *Economics,* 20. On Sumner's version of the power of natural law, see his *The Forgotten Man,* 472–75.

13. Everett, *Economics,* 20.

14. Ibid., 20.

15. Ibid., 201.

16. Whatever validity it may have had initially, the Puritan or Protestant work ethic had, by this time, been thoroughly secularized.

17. Lester P. Ward, *Dynamic Sociology,* vol. 2 (New York: D. Appleton and Co., 1863), 2.

18. On his adherence to the American notion of progress, especially as it applies to science, capital formation and technology, see ibid., 663.

19. Rush Welter, *The Mind of America: 1820–1860* (New York: Columbia University Press, 1975), 4.

20. Ibid., 40.

21. Ibid., 44.

22. Ibid., 156, 157.

23. Ibid., 157.

24. Ibid., 131. One is struck by the similarity between the spirit of this secularized quote and the apostle Paul's quote on the Christian virtue of love. See 1 Corinthians 12:4–12 (AV).

25. Welter, *The Mind,* 413f. Cf. Robert S. Michaelsen, "The American Gospel of Work and the Protestant Doctrine of Vocation" (Ph.D. diss., Yale University, 1951), and Ruth Douglas, "The Protestant Doctrine of Vocation in Presbyterian Thought of the Nineteenth Century" (Ph.D. diss., New York University, 1952).

26. Welter, *The Mind,* 21. Cf. Marie Ahearn, "The Rhetoric of Work and Vocation in Some Popular Northern Writings Before 1860" (Ph.D. diss., Brown University, 1965.)

27. Calvin Cotton, "Junius Tracts" 7:7, 15. As cited by Welter, *The Mind,* 150. His emphasis.

28. Welter, *The Mind,* 150.

29. *Life of P.T. Barnum By Himself* (New York: Houghton and Mifflin, 1855), 150f.

30. These remarks are taken as a synopsis from his autobiography.

31. Welter, *The Mind,* 155.

32. This imagery is suggested by Walter, *The Mind,* 337.

33. See Genesis 1:26–31 (AV). For a fuller discussion, see Perry Miller, *Errand Into the Wilderness* (Cambridge: Harvard University Press, 1956), 236f.

34. Charles W. Upham, "Kansas and Nebraska," *North American Review* 80:166 (January 1855): 125.

35. Perry Miller, *The Life of the Mind of America* (New York: Harcourt Brace and World, 1965), 190f.

36. This term is meant to designate the tendency of orthodoxy to define the heart of Christian experience in terms of its creedal formulations. For a survey of this growing tension between orthodoxy and revivalism, cf. John C. VanderStelt, *Philosophy and Scripture: A Study of Old Princeton and Westminster Theology* (Marlton, N.J.: Mack Pub. Co., 1978) and George M. Marsden, *The Evangelical Mind and the New School Presbyterian Experience* (New Haven: Yale University Press, 1970).

37. Sydney E. Ahlstrom, ed., *Theology in America: The Major Protestant Voices from Puritanism to Neo-Orthodoxy* (Indianapolis: Bobbs-Merrill, 1967), 57.

38. Charles Finney, *Memoirs* (New York: A. S. Barnes, 1876), 340.

39. John Wesley, *A Plain Account of Christian Perfection* (1776; London: Epworth Press, 1952), 50f. On American similarities, cf. Charles Finney, *Lectures on Systematic Theology,* ed. J. H. Fairchild (1846; New York: 1878), 115f., 200–281.

40. Finney, *Lectures on Revivals on Religion* (New York: Leavitt, Lord and Co., 1835), 21, 102.

41. Cf. Timothy L. Smith, "Righteousness and Hope: Christian Holiness and the Millennial Vision in America, 1800–1900," in *American Quarterly,* 31 (Spring 1979): 31–33 and George M. Marsden, *Evangelical Mind,* 7–58.

42. Miller, *The Life,* 41, 42.

43. Ibid., 301. We will more fully define millennial optimism shortly.

44. Arthur M. Schlesinger, Jr., *The Age of Jackson* (Boston: Little, Brown, 1950), 350f.

45. Ibid., 314 on Adam Smith's inspirational effect upon Jacksonian democracy. It is also important to note, however, that Evangelical revivalism often clashed with several followers of Jacksonian America on other "moral" matters like temperance and Sabbath-keeping. See John L. Hammond, *The Politics of Benevolence,* 62f.

46. Timothy L. Smith, *Revivalism and Social Reform in Mid-Nineteenth Century America* (Nashville: Abington Press, 1957), chs. 1, 3, 5, 10, 14.

47. On Finney's activism, see Marsden, *Fundamentalism and American Culture: The Shaping of Twentieth-Century Evangelicalism, 1870–1925* (New York: Oxford University Press, 1980), 86.

48. This important fact will be discussed more fully when we survey the ties between British and American Evangelicals. See, for now, Clark Kitson, *Church Men and the Condition of England: 1832–1885* (London: Methuen, 1973).

49. Miller, *The Life,* 299, 300.

50. John Hammond, *Benevolence,* ix.

51. Paul C. Nagel, *This Sacred Trust: American Nationality, 1798–1898* (New York: Oxford University Press, 1971), 25.

52. Miller, *The Life,* 49, quoting evangelist-pastor Eli Smith.

53. For an evaluation of this revival, as told through the recollections of revivalist Stephen Tyng, Sr., see Stephen Tyng, Jr., *He Will Come; or, Meditations Upon the Return of Lord Jesus to Reign Over the Earth* (New York: Houghton and Mifflin, 1878).

54. Miller, *The Life,* 91.

55. For a postbellum Fundamentalist's account of this position, see footnotes

on Revelation 20:4, in C. I. Scofield, *The New Scofield Reference Bible* (New York: Oxford University Press, 1967), 1373, 1374.

56. Nagel, *Sacred Trust,* 29.

57. Welter, *The Mind,* 266.

58. Ibid., 263, quoting the "Home Missionary" 19:5 (September 1846): 117 a–b. Cf. Rockne M. McCarthy et al., *Disestablishment the Second Time,* foreword by Martin Marty (Grand Rapids, Mich.: Eerdmans, 1982), 15–72.

59. Welter, *The Mind,* 267–70.

60. Cf. John Markoff and Daniel Regan, "The Rise and Fall of Civil Religion: Comparative Prospectives," in *Sociological Analysis* 42 (Nov. 1981), 333–52, especially 340, and Robert N. Bellah, *Beyond Belief: Essays on Religion in a Post-Traditional World* (New York: Harper and Row, 1970) 168–89.

61. Clifford Edward Clark, *Henry Ward Beecher: Spokesman for Middle-Class America* (Chicago: University of Illinois Press, 1976), 70f.

62. Nagel, *Sacred Trust,* 82, 83.

63. John U. Nef, *War and Human Progress: An Essay on the Rise of Industrial Civilization* (Cambridge: Oxford University Press, 1952), 103.

64. Howard M. Jones, *The Age of Energy* (New York: Viking, 1971) 104.

65. This phrase was suggested by Miller, *The Life,* 290.

66. As cited in ibid., 289.

67. Jones, *The Age,* xii.

68. Cf. ibid., 463f., and Leo Marx, *The Machine in the Garden: Technology and the Pastoral Ideal in America* (New York: Oxford University Press, 1964), especially Marx's discussion of Twain and Henry Adams.

69. Alan Trachtenberg, *The Incorporation of America: Culture and Society in the Gilded Age* (New York: Hill and Wang, 1982), 42.

70. Cf. Jones, *The Age,* 143, 146, 150–53 and Beecher's "Tendencies of American Progress," in *The Original Plymouth Pulpit,* vol. 5 (Boston: Pilgrim Press, 1871), 203–19.

71. *The Galbraith Reader,* ed. Lovell Thompson (Ipswich, Mass.: Gambit Press, 1977), 285.

72. Jones, *The Age,* 149.

73. As reported in Harvey Wish, *Society and Thought in Modern America: A Social and Intellectual History of the American People from 1865,* 2d ed. (New York: Hill and Wang, 1982), 12.

74. From Alan Trachtenberg, *The Incorporation of America,* 12.

75. Ibid., 12.

76. Jones, *The Age,* 159.

77. Ibid. On individualism and the American culture in this era, see Steven Lukes, *Individualism* (Oxford: Basil Blackwell, 1973), 123, 124 and Yehoshua Arieli, *Individualism and Nationalism in American Ideology* (Cambridge: Harvard University Press, 1964).

78. Trachtenberg, *Incorporation,* 3, 5.

79. Ibid., 42–45 as he cites Wright's speech before an 1882 American Social Science Association convention.

80. For a discussion of this theme as it relates to postbellum anxieties, see Loren Baritz, *City on a Hill* (New York: Oxford University Press, 1964), 91–156.

81. As cited in Trachtenberg, *Incorporation,* 102.

82. Cf. Richard V. Pierard, *The Unequal Yoke* (New York: J. B. Lippincott, 1970), 25–40 and Marsden, *Fundamentalism,* 282, 283.

83. Marsden, *Evangelical Mind,* 180–98.

84. "The Second Coming of Christ," in *The Best of B.L. Moody,* ed. Wilbur M. Smith (Chicago: University of Chicago Press, 1971), 193, 194.

85. What follows is taken from *The Scofield Reference Bible,* ed. C. I. Scofield (1909; New York: Oxford University Press, 1967). There the periods are referred to successively on pages 3–4, 7, 19, 94, 1162, 1359, and 1373.

86. Ibid., 14, 15 notes. Cf. 1002, 1373, notes.

87. Ibid., 1359–1373, notes. For a more detailed view of these themes, one that we will more fully investigate in subsequent analysis, see Timothy P. Weber, *Living in the Shadow of the Second Coming: American Premillennialism, 1875–1925* (New York: Oxford University Press, 1979).

88. See C. Allyn Russell, *Voices of American Fundamentalism* (Philadelphia: Presbyterian and Reformed Publishing Co., 1976), 145–50.

89. See Marsden, *Fundamentalism,* 78.

90. Cortland Myers, "The Holy Spirit in His Relation to City Evangelization," in *The Holy Spirit in Life and Service: Addresses Delivered before the Conference on the Ministry of the Holy Spirit Held in Brooklyn, NY Oct., 1894,* ed. A. C. Dixon (New York: Houghton and Mifflin, 1895), 129, 130.

91. See Marsden, *Fundamentalism,* 85.

92. R. H. Tawney, *Religions and the Rise of Capitalism: A Historical Study* (Gloucester, Mass.: Peter Smith Press, 1962), 280.

93. Marsden, *Fundamentalism,* 86. See especially note 4, p. 252.

94. Cf. Marsden, *Fundamentalism,* 48, 49, 54, 61, 83; Pierard, *Unequal Yoke,* 28–40 and J. Howard Pew, "Social Issues and Politics: Are Churches Going Too Far?" in *U.S. News and World Report* 48 (25 April 1960): 135. This is not to say, however, that Fundamentalists supported monopolistic capitalism.

95. See Ernest Sandeen, *Roots of Fundamentalism* (Chicago: University of Chicago Press, 1970), 190f. for the relationship of these volumes to the development of the Fundamentalist identity vis-à-vis Protestant liberalism.

96. Lyman Stewart, *The Fundamentals: a Testimony to the Truth* (Chicago, 1910–1915). On superficial treatment, cf. Arthur T. Pierson, "Our Lord's Teaching About Money" 10:39–47 and Robert Speer, "Foreign Missions or World-wide Evangelism" 12:73. For a fuller review, to which I am indebted, see Marsden, *Fundamentalism,* 118–23. For a major exception to the tenor of these documents and for a less militant stance against possible exceptions to capitalism, see Charles Erdman, "The Church and Socialism" 12:108–19.

97. Richard Hofstadter, *Anti-Intellectualism in American Life* (New York, 1962).

98. Francis Wayland, *The Elements of Intellectual Philosophy* (New York: Sheldon and Co., 1854), 17.

99. John Vander Stelt, *Philosophy and Scripture* (Marlton, N.J.: Mack Publishing Co., 1978), 303–14.

100. Wayland, *Elements,* 87.. Cf. 96, 97, 180.

101. Vander Stelt, *Philosophy and Scripture,* 284–302. The term "Old Princeton" refers to Princeton Theological Seminary's basically Calvinistic-Fundamentalist stance in the late nineteenth century. As such, it stood opposed to theological Protestant liberalism, while abhorring Dispensationalism's hermeneutics and Pentecostalism's version of sanctification.

102. Walter E. W. Ellis, "Social and Religious Factors in the Fundamentalist Modernist Schisms Among Baptists in North America, 1895–1934" (Ph.D. diss., University of Pittsburgh, 1974), 132–78.

103. Liston Pope, *Millhands and Preachers: A Study of Gastonia,* introduction

by Richard A. Peterson and N. V. Demerath III (1942; New Haven: Yale University Press, 1965), 332.

104. Cf. Robert E. Wenger, "Social Thought in American Fundamentalism 1918–1933" (Ph.D. diss., University of Nebraska, 1973), 50–72 and Donald G. Mathews, *Religion in the Old South* (Chicago, 1977). Although the scope of Wenger's historical survey exceeds ours, his thesis is nevertheless relevant to this point.

Chapter 3. American Industrialism

1. R. H. Tawney, *Religion and the Rise of Capitalism* (New York: Mentor Books, 1926), 25 suggests this phrase.

2. Ibid., 26.

3. Ibid., 33. Cf. Robert L. Heilbroner, *The Making of an Economic Society* (Englewood Cliffs, N.J.: Prentice-Hall, 1962), 53.

4. Robert L. Heilbroner, *The Worldly Philosophers* (New York: Simon & Schuster, 1972), 22f.

5. Heilbroner, *Economic Society,* 31f. Cf. John Huizinga, *The Waning of the Middle Ages* (New York: Anchor Books, 1954).

6. Heilbroner, *Economic Society,* 38.

7. Quoted in Jan Veenhof, "Nature and Grace in Bavinck," trans. Albert M. Wolters (Toronto, Ont.: Institute for Christian Studies, 1968), 6, 7. Veenhof's article contains extracts from the large work by Herman Bavinck, *Revelatie en Inspiratie.*

8. I hesitate to use the term "class" as a synonym for vocation, as the definition and origin of modern class structure remains too exclusively tied to the production process, demonstrating yet another marked example of Industrialism's power.

9. Bob Goudzwaard, "Syllabus in Economic History" (Toronto, Ont.: Association for the Advancement of Christian Studies, 1980), 35 (Mimeograph). Of course, this diagram does not exhaust all medieval vocational possibilities. Its intent is simply to suggest how the nature/grace hierarchical schema affected, in principle, "official" economic life.

10. For these and parallel philosophical tensions, see Frederick Copleston, *A History of Philosophy,* vol. 2, *Medieval Philosophy Augustine to Scotus* (New York: Image Books, 1962), 132–55.

11. Heilbroner, *The Worldly Philosophers,* 25. Cf. Tawney, *Religion,* 35.

12. Heilbroner, *The Worldly Philosophers,* 30, Tawney, *Religion,* 30–39, and Bob Goudzwaard, *Capitalism and Progress* (Grand Rapids, Mich.: Wm. B. Eerdmans Publishing Co., 1979), 5f., 65–67.

13. Heilbroner, *The Worldly Philosophers,* 31, Tawney, *Religion,* 40f., and Heilbroner, *The Making of an Economic Society,* 37.

14. The above analysis, including the religious idiom, was taken from Oscar Handling, *A History of America* (New York: Holt, Rinehart and Winston, 1968), 5.

15. For an analysis of the technological imperative as it was related to the Kantian definition of freedom and the subsequent economic revolution, see Herman Dooyeweerd, *Roots of Western Culture,* 150f. Cf. Tawney, *Religion,* 62, 63.

16. For the relationship of critical reason, earthly utopian secular fantasies, and the pending economic revolution, cf. Goudzwaard, *Capitalism,* 36f.

17. Francis Bacon, *Novum Organum,* bk. 1, aphorism 2, as quoted in Jeremy Rifkin, *The Emerging Order: God in the Age of Scarcity* (New York: G. P. Putnam's Sons, 1979), 27.

18. Jacques Ellul, *The Technological Society,* trans. John Wilkinson (New York: Vintage Books, 1964), 49. Cf. John B. Bury, *The Idea of Progress: An Inquiry Into Its Growth and Origin* (New York: MacMillan, 1932), 173, 174.

19. R. H. Tawney, *The Acquisitive Society* (New York: Harcourt, Brace and World, 1920), 31.

20. See Egbert Schuurman, *Reflections on the Technological Society* (Toronto, Ont.: Wedge Publishing Company, 1977), 35–40.

21. This term, so capitalized, is used by Otto Gierke, *Natural Law and the Theory of Society 1500–1800,* trans. Ernst Barker (Boston: Beacon Press, 1960), 35.

22. Cited in Henry W. Spiegel, *The Growth of Economic Thought* (Englewood Cliffs, N.J.: Prentice-Hall, 1971), 230.

23. Adam Smith, *An Inquiry Into the Nature and Causes of the Wealth of Nations,* trans. Max Lerner (1776; New York: The Modern Library, 1965), 423f.

24. It has been generally held that Smith's descriptions were accurate for a proto-industrial situation. For a refutation of that notion, see Hla Myint, *Theories of Welfare Economics* (London: London School of Economics and Political Science, 1948); Joseph A. Schumpeter, *History of Economic Analysis* (New York: Oxford University Press, 1954). Cf. Arnold Toynbee, *The Industrial Revolution* (Boston: Beacon Press, 1956), 59f.

25. Otto Gierke, *Natural Law,* 106f. Cf. Heilbroner, *Philosophers,* 21, 25.

26. On the relationship of materialistic philosophy and the classical school of economics, see John A. Hobson, *Economics and Ethics: A Study in Social Values* (New York: D. C. Heath, 1929), 102–5.

27. Benjamin Ward, *The Conservative Economic World View* (New York: Basic Books, 1979) 11f., and Heilbroner, *Economic Society,* 48.

28. Heilbroner, *Economic Society,* 58, and Gierke, *Natural Law,* 135f.

29. Arnold Toynbee, *Industrial Revolution,* 61.

30. Heilbroner, *Economic Society,* 61. Cf. Smith, *Wealth,* 135f.

31. Please note the "ex" in extensive. It points to the "thorough" and "utterly dominating" character of the modern factory. See *The Random House Dictionary: College Edition,* ed. Laurence Urdang (New York: Random House, 1968), 459.

32. Heilbroner, *Economic Society,* 82, 83.

33. On labor as a consumable product, see Smith, *Wealth,* vii–viii, and especially 31–33.

34. Tawney, *Religion,* 118–28, especially 127.

35. Ibid., 33, 44. (On Tawney's description of the modal reductionism and "idolatry," see 43, 44.)

36. Jeremy Bentham, *The Principles of Morals and Legislation* (1789; New York: Hafner Publishing Company, 1962), 1.

37. Bentham believed that communities were fictitious bodies composed of individuals. See ibid., 3.

38. We have not said that one must consume immediately. One may save, and, therefore, delay gratification for another day. Markets, however, tend to favor a more shortsighted view of consumption and production. See *The Galbraith Reader,* ed. Lowell Thompson (Ipswich, Mass.: Gambit Press, 1977), 393–99. On the necessity and morality of consumption in utilitarianism, see Goudzwaard, *Capitalism,* 31f.

39. John A. Hobson, *Economics and Ethics, A Study in Social Values* (New York: D. C. Heath, 1929), 108. To be fair to later utilitarian scholars, John S. Mill tried to extend this calculus to qualities of life like justice and beauty. However, the diffi-

culty of quantifying such abstractions only deepened the problem. Cf. Theodore Roszak, *The Making of a Counter Culture* (New York: Doubleday, 1969), 1–3.

40. Toynbee, *Industrial Revolution,* 63. For a thorough treatment of the interrelationship of evolving technology in the scientific revolution, sociocultural changes on the European continent, and nascent industrialization, see Margaret Jacob, *The Cultural Meaning of the Scientific Revolution* (New York: Alfred A. Knopf, 1988).

41. This discussion was taken, in part, from John L. Hammond and Barbara Hammond, *The Rise of Modern Industry* (New York: Harper and Row, 1975), 139f.

42. Ibid., 232.

43. Alan Trachtenberg, *The Incorporation of America: Culture and Society in the Gilded Age* (New York: Hill and Wang, 1982), 3.

44. See Sidney Ratner, James Soltow and Richard Sylla, *The Evolution of the American Economy* (New York: Basic Books, 1979), 182–200; for similarities and differences between the two revolutions, see Nathan Rosenberg, *Technology and American Economic Growth* (New York: Harper and Row, 1972), 59f.

45. United States Congress, *American State Papers and Finance,* vol. 3, 1815; quoted in Robert W. Fogel, *Railroads and American Economic Growth: Essays in Econometric History* (Baltimore: Johns Hopkins University Press, 1964), 122. By 1820 the number had risen to 200,000. It must also be noted that the American iron industry did not begin to rapidly modernize until 1830.

46. Thomas Jefferson to Paul Allen (biographer of Lewis, 18 August 1813), *Letters From the Lewis and Clark Expedition, 1783–1854,* ed. Donald Jackson (Urbana: University of Illinois Press, 1962), 625. In a moment of unguarded religious hope, Thomas Jefferson once tied the lands that Lewis and Clark were exploring to his dream for an agrarian ideal. That same year, 1813, he said, "Those who will labor the earth of the West are the chosen people of God, if he ever had a chosen people of God. . . . They will be the stewards of our land." See People's Bicentennial Commission, *Voices of the American Revolution* (New York: Bantam Books, 1975), 160.

47. Walter Prescott Webb, *The Great Plains* (New York: Ginn and Company, 1959), 143f.

48. William Goetzmann, *Exploration and Empire: The Explorer and the Scientist in the Winning of the American West* (New York: Alfred A. Knopf, 1966), 180, 263, 264.

49. Michael Ames, "Missionaries Toil for Souls and Survival," in *The American West Publishing Company,* ed. Donald E. Bower, 10:1 (Jan. 1873): 28, 29.

50. Frederick J. Turner, *The Frontier in American History* (1920; New York: Holt, Rinehart and Winston, 1965), X, 3, 6, 15, 212f., 306.

51. Trachtenberg, *Incorporation,* 12–15. Cf. Ernest Lee Tuveson, *Redeemer Nation: The Idea of America's Millennial Role* (Chicago: The University of Chicago Press, 1968), viii, 95, 96, 143.

52. Walter Prescott Webb, *The Great Plains,* 185–89.

53. Turner, *The Frontier,* 7.

54. Ibid., 17.

55. Cf. Tuveson, *Redeemer Nation,* vii.

56. Lord Herbert of Cherbury on visiting America and riding with the U.S. Cavalry on the Great Plains. See Webb, *Plains,* 493.

57. Goetzmann, *Exploration,* 391f. Cf. Turner, *The Frontier,* 16f. and Trachtenberg, *Incorporation,* 30, 31.

58. Cf. Trachtenberg, *Incorporation,* 26, 27 and Francis Paul Prucha, *American*

Indian Policy in Crisis: Christian Reformers and the Indian, 1865–1900 (Norman: University of Oklahoma Press, 1976), 297, 298.

59. Richard J. Dodge, *The Hunting Grounds of the Great West* (London: Chatto and Windus, 1877), 2.

60. George Rogers Taylor and Irene D. Neu, *The American Railroad Network, 1861–1890* (Cambridge: Harvard University Press, 1956), 5.

61. United States Census Office, "Report on American Transportation," *Tenth Census of the United States,* vol. 4 (Washington D.C. 1883), as quoted in Fogel, 127.

62. Robert W. Fogel, *Railroads and American Economic Growth,* 3, 5. Cf. Taylor and Neu, *American Railroad,* 1, 2.

63. Cf. Robert C. Black, III, *The Railroads of the Confederacy* (Chapel Hill: University of North Carolina Press, 1952), and Thomas Weber, *The Northern Railroads in the Civil War, 1861–1865* (New York: King's Court Press, Columbia University, 1952).

64. Taylor and Neu, *American Railroad,* 57.

65. Fogel argues extensively against W. W. Rostow's theories of the stages of economic growth and their relationship to the developing railroad. Fogel maintains that the railroad was but *one* factor in economic development, while Rostow maintains that rails were *the* factor of industrialism. Cf. Fogel, *Railroads,* 129f., and W. W. Rostow, *The Stages of Economic Growth* (Cambridge: Harvard University Press, 1960), 55f.

66. Taylor and Neu, *American Railroad,* 6.

67. Following Fogel, *Railroads,* 47f., by social savings we mean the savings engendered by shipping by rail as compared with any other means of transportation.

68. Ibid., 224, 225.

69. Trachtenberg, *Incorporation,* 19.

70. Prucha, *American Indian,* 133.

71. Ibid., 47–49, 82, 232.

72. Ibid., 75f. It must be noted that Grant's secretary of the interior was Charles Finney's son-in-law.

73. Ibid., 89. Park Street Church, pastored by the late president of the prominent Evangelical divinity school, Gordon-Conwell, has been a strong Evangelically-led congregation for many decades. It was the place where in 1831 William Lloyd Garrison preached on abolition, having been forbidden to speak elsewhere in Boston.

74. Ibid., 168. It must be said that Evangelicals were not the only ones so influenced. Proto-liberal Henry Ward Beecher once said of the relationship of civilization to the "(Indian)" worldview, "Christianity is not merely a thing of churches and school-houses. The post-offices are a Christian institution; the railroad with all of its corruption is a Christian power . . ." "Indians and Progress," *Lake Mohawk Conference Proceedings* 1885, 51–52. In Prucha, *American Indian,* 160.

75. Prucha, *American Indian.* See also Merrill Gates, "Land and Law as Agents in Educating Indians," *Report of the Board of Indian Commissioners,* 185, 26. In Prucha, *American Indian,* 153.

76. "The Annual Meeting Report," *The Women's National Indian Association,* 12, in Prucha, *American Indian,* 148; cf. William G. McLoughlin, ed., *The American Evangelicals, 1800–1900; An Anthology* (New York: Harper and Row, 1968), 13f.

77. Trachtenberg, *Incorporation,* 23. It must be said in fairness that some other Evangelicals opposed this notion. Cf. Prucha, *American Indian,* 245f.

78. Prucha, *American Indian,* pp. 262f.

79. Ibid., 389.

80. Carl N. Degler, *The Age of the Economic Revolution* (Glenview, Ill.: Scott, Foresman and Company, 1977), 1.

81. For the development of the term "corporation" as applied to the interrelationship of the individual to society, and for the restriction of the term, almost exclusively, to *economic* matters, see Sander Griffioen, "Facing the New Corporation" (Toronto, Canada: Association for the Advancement of Christian Scholarship, 1981). Cf. Richard J. Barber, *The American Corporation* (New York: Dutton and Company, 1970).

82. Cf. A. A. Berle and G. C. Means, *The Modern Corporation and Private Property* (New York: Macmillan, 1932) and William C. Kessler, "Business Organization and Management," in Harold F. Williamson, ed., *The Growth of the American Economy* (New York: Prentice-Hall, Inc., 1964), 602–15.

83. Unless otherwise designated, capital is defined, rather redundantly, as any good used to make secondary goods. In an even broader sense, capital is any income-producing commodity used for productive rather than consumptive purposes. Cf. Muriel Hidy, "The Capital Markets," in Williamson, *American Economy*, 256 and Ratner et al., *Evolution*, 219.

84. Henrietta M. Larson, *Jay Cooke, Private Banker* (Cambridge: Harvard University Press, 1936).

85. Thomas C. Cochran, "Business Organization and the Development of an Industrial Discipline," in Williamson, *American Economy*, 293. Cf. Goudzwaard, *Capitalism*, 94f.

86. Joe S. Bain, "Industrial Concentration and Anti-Trust Policy," in Williamson, *American Economy*, 621.

87. For a definition of the process of "watering stock," see G. Bannock, R. E. Baxter and R. Rees, *The Penguin Dictionary of Economics*, 2d ed. (New York: Penguin Books, 1979), 460.

88. Louis C. Hunter, "The Heavy Industries," in Williamson, *American Economy*, 484.

89. David Brody, *Steelworkers in America* (Cambridge: Harvard University Press, 1938), 56. It must also be noted that the initial success of U.S. Steel was not due to the needs of the private sector, but to the Navy's demands for thick armor plate for warships.

90. Daniel Nelson, *Managers and Workers: Origins of the New Factory System in the United States, 1880–1920* (Madison: University of Wisconsin Press, 1975), 23.

91. On the postbellum improvement of occupational safety, see Nelson, *Managers*, 25f. On Jones and Laughlin's safety record, see John A. Fitch, *The Steelworkers* (New York: Macmillan, 1910) 198, 199. As a former employee and resident respectively of Chatham College, Pittsburgh, Pa., I have often found it to be divinely ironic that my wife and I lived in the former Laughlin mansion and, thereby, could afford to do graduate work on a critique of Industrialism!

92. Trachtenberg, *Incorporation*, 57.

93. Carroll D. Wright, paper given before the American Social Service Association, 1882. As cited in Trachtenberg, *Incorporation*, 42.

94. For a further review of this process, see Edward C. Kirkland, *Industry Comes of Age*, vol. 6 (New York: Holt, Rinehart and Winston, 1962), 150f. and Nathan Rosenberg, *Technological American Economic Growth* (New York: Harper and Row, 1972).

95. F. B. Copley, *Frederick Taylor, Father of Scientific Management*, vol. 2 (New York: Harper and Brothers, 1923), 857, 867, 878.

96. F. W. Taylor, "On the Art of Cutting Metals," in *Transactions of the American Society of Mechanical Engineers,* vol. 28 (New York: Macmillan and Company, 1906), 50f.

97. Sudhir Kakar, *Frederick Taylor: A Study in Personality Innovation* (Cambridge: Harvard University Press, 1970), chs. 6–9.

98. Robert H. Guest, "Scientific Management and the Assembly Line," in *Technology and Change,* ed. John G. Burke and Marshall C. Eakin (San Francisco: Boyd and Frasier, 1979), 100.

99. Kakar, *Frederick Taylor,* 61–65.

100. Guest, "Scientific Management," 65f.

101. John T. Flynn, *God's Gold: The Story of Rockefeller and His Times* (New York: Harcourt, Brace and Company, 1932), 64. While he did not earn money for this calendar year, he did earn one large sum of money before his sixteenth birthday, from which he paid his expenses.

102. The term "stewardship" is a crucial one in our subsequent analysis. For the moment, however, note that Rockefeller associated this term with charity in general and church-giving in particular. Cf. Allan Nevins, *The Heroic Age of American Enterprise* (New York: Scribner's Sons, 1940), 660–69.

103. His text and my quotation are taken from the King James Version of the Bible.

104. This may appear to be an overscrupulous attitude on our part; after all, Rockefeller had no formal theological training. But why did Rockefeller accept such an equation of the term "business" with "vigilance"? Cf. John Murray, "The Epistle to the Romans" in *The New International Commentary on the New Testament,* ed. F. F. Bruce (Grand Rapids, Mich.: William B. Eerdmans Publishing Company, 1971), 130; and *A Greek-English Lexicon of the New Testament,* ed. William F. Arndt and F. Wilbur Gingrich (Cambridge University Press, 1957), 771. For a synopsis of Rockefeller's sermon, see Flynn, *Gold,* 110.

105. This argument is based, in part, upon the insights of the "Revisionist" school of economics. Though the weaknesses of this school are several in our opinion, those insights point to the crucial role played by the entrepreneur in the process of capital formation. See Nevins, *Heroic Age.* For a critique of Nevins and this school, and Rockefeller's alleged "obsessive-compulsive" personality, see Ferdinand Lundberg, *The Rockefeller Syndrome* (Secaucus, N.J.: Lyle Stuart, 1975), 46f., 48f., 113f., and 118f.

106. Matthew Josephson, *The Robber Barons: The Great American Capitalists, 1861–1901* (New York: Harcourt, Brace and World, 1933), 267.

107. Nevins, *Heroic Age,* 665–70, cites this widely agreed-upon figure as the total wealth accumulated by Rockefeller in his lifetime.

108. Flynn, *Gold,* 296.

109. Ibid., 35.

110. Josephson, *Robber Barons,* 325.

111. As reprinted in Flynn, *Gold,* 306. Cf. Ferdinand Lundberg, *Syndrome,* 118, 177, especially 152–55.

112. John Hobson, *Economic and Ethics,* 102. Cf. Flynn, *Gold,* 401.

113. Andrew Carnegie, "Wealth and Its Uses," in *The Empire of Business* (New York: Doubleday, n.d.), 135–40. It was Rockefeller who said, in a moment of honesty, that Mammon unites and gives direction to church functions. "It is the church's unappeasable appetite for funds to support its vast array of secular activities and its costly ritualistic services which makes it a slave of Mammon." See Flynn, *Gold,* 397.

114. For the interrelationship of Carnegie, "theosophy," industrial acquisitiveness, and worldview, see John K. Winkler, *Incredible Carnegie: The Life of Andrew Carnegie 1835–1919* (New York: Vanguard Press, n.d.), 4f.

115. For a fuller justification of this thesis, see Daniel T. Roger, *The Work Ethic in Industrial America 1850–1920* (Chicago: University of Chicago Press, 1978), 12–17.

116. Thomas Carlyle, *Past and Present* (New York: Charles Scribner's Sons, 1843), 183.

117. Roger, *Work Ethic,* 19, 20.

118. Norman Ware, *The Industrial Worker, 1840–1860* (Boston: Houghton Mifflin, 1924).

119. On wage slavery and capital intimidation, see John R. Commons et al., *A History of Labor in the United States,* vol. 2 (New York: Macmillan, 1921), 15f.

120. For a realistic, graphic, and moving account of the incorporation of Slovak labor in Pittsburgh in the early postbellum period see Thomas Bell's best-selling novel, *Out of The Furnace* (1941; Pittsburgh: University of Pittsburgh Press, 1981).

121. As reprinted in Roger, *Work Ethic,* 32.

122. Commons, *Labor,* 47.

123. Roger, *Work Ethic,* 48. Cf. Sedley Taylor, *Profit Sharing Between Capital and Labor* (London: Kegan, Paul, Trench Company, 1884).

124. John A. Fritch, *The Steel Workers* (New York: Russell Sage Foundation, 1911), 207–14. Cf. Martin A. Foran, *The Other Side* (Washington: Gray and Clarkson Company, 1886), for a balanced treatment of how labor and management viewed profit-sharing.

125. Selig Perlman, *A Theory of the Labor Movement* (New York: Macmillan, 1928), 160f, 197.

126. Commons, *Labor,* 330. It is interesting to note, however, that membership across the country in all unions continued to climb to 300,000 workers, or 21% of the labor force, during this time of corruption.

127. Ibid., 359–62.

128. In 1901, Antoni Wawryznski came to America without his family, after almost seven years of searching for any work opportunities in Poland and the rest of Europe. After crossing the Atlantic in a dysentery-infested, theft-ridden boat run by an unscrupulous captain, he arrived in Baltimore with little if any money. He eventually made his way to the American Sheet and Tube Company in Farrell, Pennsylvania, and worked seven days a week at ten cents an hour. At that rate it took him several years to save enough money to send for his family. By the time they arrived, the various relationships had been all but destroyed. Broken by separation, ill health, and poverty, his wife Anna became an indirect victim of industrialism. This all-too-typical story is the history of my paternal grandparents. For a similar story of emigrant labor, see Bell's *Out of The Furnace.*

129. For the radical shift in worldview caused by immigration, see Oscar Handlin, *The Uprooted* (Boston: Little, Brown, 1951), 21–98.

130. Carroll D. Wright, "Factory System as an Element in Civilization," *Journal of Social Science* 16 (1882): 125. Cf. Wright, "The Ethical Influences of Inventions," *Social Economist* 1 (1891): 269–75.

131. For a review of the success of the A.F.L. circa 1890 onward, see Perlman, *Labor Movement,* 207f. For the internecine views of labor theorists on the incorporation of American labor, see Perlman, *Labor Movement,* 230f; Roger, *Work Ethic,* 66–72; and Common, *Labor,* 315–40.

132. For such a survey, see Norman J. Ware, *The Labor Movement in the United*

States, 1860–1895 (1929); Terrance Powderly, *The Path I Trod,* ed. Harry J. Carmen (New York: Columbia University Press, 1940).

133. While leading the Knights, Powderly implored President Grover Cleveland to stop the wholesale gifts of land to these and other industries; Powderly argued instead for a system of cooperative farming for settlers and small businesses. Terrance Powderly to Grover Cleveland, 12 April 1887, *The Path,* 223, 224.

134. Powderly, *The Path,* 271.

135. Powderly's confession of faith included the centrality of Christ's person and work of redemption, the denial of papal infallibility, a hatred of sacerdotalism, sacramentalism as a vehicle for faith, and the parity of church and union as vehicles of God's grace for the world. See ibid., 50–52, 60, 64, 75, 213, 196, 264f., 327, and 328. Interestingly, the Polish National Church is centered in Scranton, Pa.; it also tried to be Catholic while rejecting papal infallibility.

136. Powderly, *The Path,* 266.

137. George Gunton, *Wealth and Progress* (New York: D. Appleton and Company, 1887), 318. Cf. 205–7, 325 and 383.

138. Thomas Nixon Carver, *The Religion Worth Having* (New York: MacMillan, 1914), 5f.

Chapter 4. Classical Christian Theorists

1. Goudzwaard maintains that Augustine's view of divine providence grew out of a synthesis of Stoic and Christian elements. See his *Capitalism and Progress,* 16f.

2. As reprinted in Waldo Beach and H. Richard Niebuhr, eds., *Christian Ethics* (New York: The Ronald Press, 1955), 132.

3. For a further etymological study of this term, see the excellent study by R. H. Barrow, *Introduction to St. Augustine and the City of God* (London: Faber and Faber, 1950), 23.

4. Ibid., 25.

5. For further discussion of the relationship of "heart" to Augustine's historiography, see Frederick Copleston, *A History of Philosophy: Medieval Philosophy,* vol. 2, pt. 1 (New York: Image Books, 1962), 101f.

6. Barrow, *St. Augustine,* 36 as he quotes Augustine's *City of God,* bk. 16, ch. 28. Hereafter in the notes, references to the *City of God* will give the book number, followed by a slash and then the chapter.

7. Cf. Barrow, *St. Augustine,* 25f. and Augustine 12/6, 12/1 (see also 16/28 and 16/1). Copleston, *Medieval Philosophy,* 102f.

8. Barrow, *St. Augustine,* 92 and Augustine 19/13.

9. Ibid., 52 and 5/15.

10. Augustine located the origin of private property in the fall, thereby revealing his Neoplatonism. Cf. Goudzwaard, *Capitalism,* 17. As with his views on sexuality, Augustine here seemed to manifest certain dualistic tendencies and hence could not unambiguously call the creation very good.

11. Barrow, *St. Augustine,* 42–45.

12. For a further discussion of what I shall call "ecclesiasticism," see Ernst Troeltsch, *The Social Teaching of the Christian Churches,* vol. 1, trans. Olive Wyon (New York: Harper and Row, 1960), 260f.

13. Ibid., 221f.

14. See R.H. Tawney, *Religion and the Rise of Capitalism* (New York: Mentor Books, 1954), as he quotes Thomas Aquinas, 38.

15. Troeltsch, *Social Teaching*, 314f.

16. For a fuller discussion of avarice, see also Tawney, *Religion*, 39–54 and Troeltsch, *Social Teaching*, vol. 1, 316f.

17. Tawney, *Religion*, 44, 45. For Aristotle's case against usury, see his *Politics*, trans. B. Jowett (Oxford: Clarendon Press, 1885). For Aquinas' statements on usury, see his *Summa Theologica*, trans. the Fathers of the English Dominican Province (London: R.T. Washbourne, 1911–25), secunda secundae, quaest. 78.

18. Aquinas, *Summa Theologica*, quaest. 78.

19. Extreme asceticism represents but one consistent result of the dualistic tension between nature and grace. Bodily and economic functions became so deprecated under this schema that the functions per se were thought to be evil. Underlying this notion was a denial of the "very goodness" of creation. However, even when such extremism was not evidenced, as in the thought of Aquinas, economics was at best a handmaiden to theology. On the medieval tension between nature and grace, see Goudzwaard, *Capitalism*, 10, 12, 26, Dooyeweerd, *Roots*, 111–47, and Troeltsch, *Social Teaching*, 237–40.

20. Martin Luther, "An Open Letter to the Christian Nobility of the German Nation," in *Three Treatises*, trans. C. M. Jacobs (Philadelphia: Fortress Press, 1965), 24, 25 and *Works of Martin Luther* (1915; Philadelphia: Muhlenberg Press, 1943).

21. See Tawney, *Religion*, vol. 2, 85, 86.

22. Ibid., 81.

23. Actually, Luther disliked the unproductiveness of many monks.

24. Roy Pascal, *The Social Basis of the German Reformation* (New York: Augustus M. Kelly Publishers, 1971), 184, 185.

25. Althaus, *Martin Luther*, 108f. Cf. Pascal, 190.

26. Althaus, *Martin Luther*, 101, quoting Luther's *Werke*, 15, 466 who was referring to the medieval Rockefeller, Jakob Fugger. Emphasis added.

27. Ibid., 109, 110 and 15, 296.

28. For more of Luther's antipathy to German monopolies and especially Fugger in the social context of his day, see Pascal, *German Reformation*, 3–21.

29. As quoted in Robert N. Crossley, *Luther and the Peasants' War* (New York: Exposition Press, 1974), 60. It is interesting to note in this context that Luther came from farmers' stock.

30. Paul Althaus, *The Ethics of Martin Luther*, trans. Robert C. Shultz (Philadelphia: Fortress Press, 1972), 39 as he quotes Luther's *Werke*, 10, 299, 308, 309, 402.

31. Troeltsch, *Social Teaching*, vol. 2, 66, 67.

32. Ibid., 568f and 874f.

33. John Calvin, *Institutes of the Christian Religion*, vol. 4, ch. 20, trans. Ford Battles, ed. John T. McNeill (Philadelphia: Westminster Press, 1967), 2.

34. André Bieler, *The Social Humanism of John Calvin*, trans. Paul T. Fuhrmann (Richmond, Virginia: John Knox Press, 1940), 18. Cf. W. Fred Graham, *John Calvin the Constructive Revolutionary* (Virginia: John Knox, 1971), 77f.

35. Quoted in Bieler, *John Calvin*, 8. See also Calvin's commentary on 1 Timothy 6:17–19.

36. Bieler, *John Calvin*, 51 as he cites Calvin's commentary on Matthew 25:24. An excellent summa of Calvin's works is his collected *Opera: Joannis Calvin Opera qual supersunt omnie*, ed. Johann Baum, Edward Cunitz and Edwards Reus (1864; Brunswick, Germany: Schwetschke Press, 1957).

37. Cf. his *Institutes*, bk. 3, ch. 10, 6.

38. Waldo Beach and H. Richard Niebuhr, *Christian Ethics* (New York: The Ronald Press, 1955), 273, 290.

39. Calvin, *Institutes*, bk. 3, 10, 5. Cf. Beach and Niebuhr, *Christian Ethics*, 285.

40. Beach and Niebuhr, *Christian Ethics*, pp. 284–86 and Calvin's *Institutes*, bk 3, ch. 7, sec. 5.

41. See Graham, *John Calvin Revolutionary*, 50f. for a fuller discussion of Geneva. During the year 1558 Calvin welcomed 360 refugees seeking asylum. Such an influx strained local labor conditions, whereupon Calvin persuaded the municipal authorities to float a state loan so that local velvet and cloth mills could create new jobs.

42. Graham, *John Calvin Revolutionary*, 121. Note should be made of Calvin's acceptance of a just rate of usury. Cf. John T. Noonan, *The Scholastic Analysis of Usury* (Cambridge: Harvard University Press, 1957), 192 for Calvin's departure from scholastic practice on usury.

43. Commentary on Psalms 15:5, 55:12; see also Calvin's commentary on Ezekiel 18:8; and *Opera* xxviii.

44. Bieler, *John Calvin*, 69. Here he cites Calvin's sermon on Deuteronomy 15:11–15.

45. Ibid., 67, 68, as he cites Calvin's sermon 44 in the *Harmony of the Gospels* on Matthew 3:3–10.

46. Ibid., 66, 67, as he cites Calvin's sermon on Deuteronomy 15:11–15.

47. Cf. Roger Fenton, *A Treatise on Usury* (London: William Appley, 1911), 60, and *Institutes*, bk. 3, ch. 7, 5 where Calvin speaks of economic reality as interconnected even as the body is integrally intertwined: "No member has this power for itself nor applies it to its own private use; but each pours it out to the fellow members. Nor does it take any profit from its power except what proceeds from the common advantage to the whole body."

48. Bieler, *John Calvin*, 47.

49. Ibid., 53, citing Calvin's commentary on Matthew 3:9, 3:10. Cf. Graham, *John Calvin Revolutionary*, 71.

50. Graham, *John Calvin Revolutionary* 86.

51. Bieler, *John Calvin*, 39, 40. Graham, *John Calvin Revolutionary*, 110f.

52. Graham, *John Calvin Revolutionary*, 128–44.

53. Tawney, *Religion*, 91. Cf. Beach, *Ethics*, 269–72; e.g., "The Christian life, as Calvin sees it, is a continuous and hard struggle to realize in every sphere of existence the consequence of the new beginning."

Chapter 5. A Transatlantic Intermezzo

1. G.M. Trevelyan, *English Social History* (London: Methuen, 1944), 509.

2. Ibid., 531–34.

3. Ibid., 509.

4. Kenneth Latourette, *A History of the Expansion of Christianity*, vol. 4 (New York: Harper Brothers, 1941), 11.

5. E.R. Norman, *Church and Society in England, 1770–1970* (Oxford: Clarendon Press, 1976), 40f.; and G. Kitson Clark, *Churchmen and the Condition of England, 1832–1885*, (London: Methuen, 1973), xx.

6. Latourette, *Expansion of Christianity*, 12, 13; and Trevelyan, *English History*, 548.

7. Trevelyan, *English History*, 546.

8. Ibid., 570. The reader may remember that we cited Manchester, in chapter 3, as one prototypical English industrial center.

9. J. E. Orr, *The Second Evangelical Awakening in Great Britain* (London: Marshall, Morgan and Scott, 1945), 76, 149; and Norman, *Church and Society,* 33.

10. H. McLeod, *Class and Religion in the Late Victorian City* (Hamden, Conn.: Archon Books, 1975), 54, 55.

11. K. S. Inglis, *Churches and the Working Class in Victorian England* (London: Routledge and Kegan Paul, 1963), 9, 86.

12. Norman, *Church and Society,* 50, 125.

13. Jan Harm Boer, *Missionary Messengers of Liberation in a Colonial Context* (Amsterdam: Rodopi Press, 1979), 24; and McLeod, *Class and Religion,* 10, 11, 282.

14. Inglis, *Working Class in Victorian England,* 106; and McLeod, *Class and Religion,* 110, 148.

15. Normon, *Church and Society,* 52–54.

16. Inglis, *Working Class in Victorian England,* 93.

17. Ibid., 76–79.

18. Latourette, *Expansion of Christianity,* 3:14f., 4:274–77; and J.H. Kane, *Understanding Christian Missions* (Grand Rapids, Mich.: Baker Book House, 1974), 142.

19. Clark, *Condition of England,* 72, 73. Norman, *Church and Society,* 139, 142.

20. David Bowen, *The Idea of the Victorian Church: A Study of the Church of England, 1833–1889* (Montreal: McGill University Press, 1968), 335–38. Cf. Charles G. Finney, *Memoirs* (New York: Fleming H. Revell Co., 1876), 386–414, 455–470.

21. Charles G. Finney, *Lectures on Revivals of Religion,* ed. William G. McLoughlin (Cambridge: Harvard University Press, 1960), viii–ix.

22. For an interesting discussion of the interrelationship of American and British Holiness movements, see Richard Carwardine, *Transatlantic Revivalism: Popular Evangelicalism in Britain and America, 1790–1865* (Westport, Conn.: Greenwood Press, 1978), 39, 40, 121–23, 144, 145, 182, 183, 190, 191, 199, 200.

23. Latourette, *Expansion of Christianity,* 14; Norman, *Church and Society,* 150–51, 124; McLeod, *Class and Religion,* 106; and especially E.R. Wicklam, *Church and People in an Industrial City* (London: Butterworth Press, 1957), 200.

24. See Carwardine, *Transatlantic Revivalism,* xiv.

25. Anthony F. C. Wallace, *Rockdale: The Growth of an American Village in the Early Industrial Revolution* (New York: Alfred A. Knopf, 1978), 264–408.

26. Carwardine, *Transatlantic Revivalism,* 70, 71, 96, 116, 117.

27. Wallace, *Rockdale,* 338–42, and Albert Post, *Popular Free Thought in America, 1825–1850* (New York: Simon and Schuster, 1974).

28. Wicham, *Industrial City,* 97–106.

29. Carwardine, *Transatlantic Revivalism,* 159.

30. Carroll S. Rosenberg, *Religion and the Rise of the American City: The New York City Mission Movement, 1812–1870* (Ithaca: Cornell University Press, 1971), 187.

31. Carwardine, *Transatlantic Revivalism,* 26 cites a variety of British and American Evangelicals who held this view. For further specifics, see William C. Conant, *Narratives of Remarkable Conversion and Revival Incidents* (New York: Derby and Jackson, 1858), as cited frequently by Carwardine.

32. For a more detailed sketch of the evolution of modern philanthropy as it pertains to Rockefeller, see E.R. Brown, *Rockefeller's Medicine Men: Medicine and Capitalism in America* (Berkeley: University of California Press, 1979), 13–59.

33. I am suggesting that the function and organization of charity evolved during

the course of this century. I will show the effects of such evolution in the latter part of this chapter.

34. Carwardine, 29, quoting a letter evangelist Freeborn Garrettson wrote to his American colleague William Kidd, 11 November 1799.

35. Carwardine, *Transatlantic Revivalism,* 29.

36. Ibid., 33.

37. Ibid., 39–42. I do not mean to imply that the Methodist denomination was the only Protestant body to experience this connection. The intent is only to highlight one representative example of this liaison. Presbyterians, Baptists, Congregationalists and certainly Anglicans experienced similar ties. See Carwardine, 13–17, 61–63, 71–73, 76–80, 90, 91, 145, 146, 169, 170.

38. For an excellent summary of the ways in which this New School movement affected the Presbyterian church, see George M. Marsden, *The Evangelical Mind and the New School Presbyterian Experience* (New Haven: Yale University Press, 1970), x–xii, 7–30.

39. W. W. Rostow, *British Economy in the Nineteenth Century* (Oxford: Oxford University Press, 1948), 125.

40. Carwardine, 83, quoting Alan D. Gilbert, "The Growth and Decline of Nonconformity in England and Wales, With Special Reference to the Period Before 1850" (D. Phil. thesis, Oxford University, 1973).

41. Harold Begbie, *Life of William Booth, The Founder of the Salvation Army,* vol. 1 (London: Wordsworth Press, 1920), 9, 61, 62.

42. Carwardine, *Transatlantic Revivalism,* 111.

43. Ibid., 116, 117, quoting *The Wesleyan Revivalist, by a Local Preacher in the Wesleyan Connection* (London: Castle Conington, 1840), 45, 46; and Wickham, *Industrial City,* 97–106.

44. James Caughey, *A Voice From America: or, Four Sermons Preached by the Rev. J. Caughey, the Great American Revivalist,* 2d ed. (Manchester, 1847), 13.

45. Carwardine, *Transatlantic Revivalism,* 123.

46. Cf. James Dixon, *Methodism in its Origin, Economy and Present Position* (London: James Nisbet Company, 1843), 163–66.

Chapter 6. Case Studies

1. Basil Miller, *Charles G. Finney: He Prayed Down Revivals* (Grand Rapids, Mich.: Zondervan Pub. Comp., 1942), 23, 24.

2. Ibid., 74, 75. Cf. Whitney R. Cross, *The Burned-over District* (Ithaca: Cornell University Press, 1950), 155f.

3. Miller, *Charles G. Finney,* 90.

4. Ibid., 94.

5. Charles G. Finney, *Lectures on Revivals of Religion* (1835; New York: Fleming H. Revell Comp., 1868), 14. Cf. his *Lectures to Professing Christians* (New York: Smith and Valentine, 1837), 180, 181.

6. Finney, *Lecture on Revivals,* 12.

7. For his views on slavery, see ibid., 272, 273. For his "personalistic" definition of sin, see ibid., 34–44.

8. Finney, *Lectures on Revivals,* 351, 358. Cf. 17, 33, 349, 356.

9. Ibid., 375.

10. Ibid., 166, 167. Emphasis added. We do not deny, of course, that Finney fought for many just social causes. His predominant emphasis upon the salvation

of the soul, as metaphysically superior to the body, restricted a more consistent and integral revival vision for social renewal.

11. Ibid., 137.

12. Ibid., 137, 144. Emphasis in original. Cf. his *Lectures to Professing Christians*, 22.

13. Finney, *Lectures on Revivals*, 143; see also 281–83.

14. Lewis Tappan to Benjamin Tappan, 14 March 1828, quoted in Charles C. Cole, *The Social Ideas of the Northern Evangelists, 1820–1860* (New York: Octagon Books, 1966), 169.

15. Finney, *Lectures on Revivals*, 421.

16. Charles G. Finney, *Lectures on Systematic Theology* (Oberlin, Ohio: James F. Fitch, 1846), 300; cf. 456f., 479f.

17. Finney, *Professing Christians*, 187.

18. Ibid., 20.

19. Ibid., 96; see also 97, 105–7.

20. Charles G. Finney, *Sermons on Important Subjects* (New York: John S. Taylor, 1836), 203, 205.

21. Ibid., 209.

22. Ibid., 264.

23. Cole, *Social Ideas*, 191.

24. Finney, *Systematic Theology*, 2.

25. Ibid., 4–6.

26. Ibid., 205, 212.

27. Ibid., 16. Finney's capitalization of "free will" is telling.

28. Ibid., 23. In this statement we can see, contra Cole, *Social Ideas*, 191, that Finney did not hold to a natural law theory for market operations.

29. Finney, *Revivals*, 443, 444.

30. Cf. Finney's *Sermons on Gospel Themes* (Oberlin: E. J. Goodrich, 1876), 308ff.

31. Ibid., 52, 53.

32. Ibid., 58–59.

33. Cole, *Social Ideas* 168. Cf. Cross, *The Burned-over District*, 155, and Charles G. Finney, *The Character and Claims and Practical Workings of Freemasonry* (Chicago: Ezra Cook Publishing Comp., 1887), 193.

34. Charles G. Finney, *Memoirs of Reverend Charles G. Finney* (New York: Fleming H. Revell Co., 1876), 297.

35. Ibid., 437; see also Cross, *The Burned-over District*, 154–56, 168, 169.

36. Cross, *The Burned-over District*, 72.

37. Paul E. Johnson, *A Shopkeeper's Millennium: Society and Revivals in Rochester, New York, 1815–1837* (New York: Hill and Wang, 1978), 27.

38. Ibid., 32. Cf. Luckman and Berger, "Social Mobility and Personal Identity," *European Journal of Sociology* (1964), 337.

39. Johnson, *Shopkeeper's Millennium*, 32.

40. For a fuller study of Finney's new measures in Rochester, see Johnson, *Shopkeeper's Millennium*, 97–102, 108; and Cross, *The Burned-over District*, 161, 165–69, 183.

41. Johnson, *Shopkeeper's Millennium*, 102. Cross, *The Burned-over District*, 216, 270, 273; and Finney, *Memoirs*, 287f.

42. Johnson, *Shopkeeper's Millennium*, 106; see also 107.

43. Ibid., 133. See also note 54, pp. 201, 202, for an elaboration of this thesis,

cf. Cross, *The Burned-over District,* 79, 116, and Oscar Handlin, *America* (New York: Holt, Rinehart and Winston, 1968), 400–403.

44. Johnson, *Shopkeeper's Millennium,* 137.

45. Joseph F. Flubacher, *The Concept of Ethics in the History of Economics* (New York: Vintage Press, 1950), 332. Here he is citing M. J. L. O'Connor, *Origins of Academic Economics in the United States,* 8f., 80.

46. Francis Wayland, Jr., and H. L. Wayland, *A Memoir of the Life and Labor of Francis Wayland, D.D., LL.D.,* vol. 1 (New York: Sheldon and Co., 1867), 16.

47. Ibid., 25.

48. Ibid., 52.

49. Ibid.

50. Ibid., 124f. It is worthy of note, however, that Wayland seemingly contradicts this semi-Calvinistic view several times; see sermon 6, "The Fall of Man," in Francis Weyland, *Salvation by Christ* (Boston: Gould and Lincoln Co., 1859), 84–86, 88–91.

51. Wayland and Wayland, *Memoir,* 154.

52. Ibid., 198.

53. Ibid., 277, 278.

54. Francis Wayland, Jr., and H. L. Wayland, *A Memoir of the Life and Labor of Francis Wayland, D.D., LL.D.,* vol. 2 (New York: Sheldon and Co., 1867), 72.

55. James O. Murray, *Francis Wayland* (New York: Houghton Mifflin, 1891), 281. Cf. *Memoir,* vol. 2, 238.

56. Wayland and Wayland, *Memoir,* vol. 2, 133.

57. Ibid. Cf. Francis Wayland, Sr., *The Limitations of Human Responsibility* (New York: D. Appleton and Co., 1838), 167f.

58. Wayland, Sr., *Limitations,* 167.

59. Francis Wayland, *The Elements of Intellectual Philosophy* (New York: Sheldon Company, 1854), 17.

60. Ibid., 21–29, 137–40, 180–279.

61. John C. Vander Stelt, *Philosophy and Scripture* (Marlton, N.J.: Mack Pub. Co., 1978), 303–14.

62. Ibid., 87. Cf. 96, 97, 180.

63. Wayland and Wayland, *Memoir,* 1:88.

64. Wayland, *Intellectual Philosophy,* 87; see also Otto Gierke, *Natural Law and the Theory of Society: 1500–1800,* trans. Ernest Barker (Boston: Beacon Press, 1960), 128.

65. Francis Wayland, *The Elements of Moral Science* (Bsoton: Gould, Kendall and Lincoln, 1842), 127; cf. 36, 111, 125.

66. Wayland, *Intellectual Philosophy,* 87.

67. Wayland, *Moral Science,* 137.

68. Ibid., 139.

69. Ibid., 219.

70. Ibid., 233; see also Gierke, *Natural Law,* 104, 130, 131.

71. Wayland, *Moral Science,* 346, 347. It is interesting to note here that Wayland allowed for civil disobedience. See also his *Moral Science,* 350 and "The Duty to the Civil Magistrates," part 3, in *Salvation by Christ* (Boston: Gould and Lincoln, 1859), 376–86.

72. Gierke, *Natural Law,* 128; see also Wayland, *Moral Science,* 219, and Arthur M. Schlesinger, Jr., *The Age of Jackson* (Boston: Little, Brown, 1950), 414.

73. Francis Wayland, *The Elements of Political Economy* (1837; Boston: Gould and Lincoln, 1872), 16.

74. Ibid. Emphasis in original.

75. Ibid., 19. Cf. 20, 24.

76. Ibid., 16–19. On the classical view of labor theory of value, a view that was shared in part by Karl Marx, see Mark Blaug, *Economic Theory in Retrospect* (Cambridge: Cambridge University Press, 1978), 39–45, 112, 113.

77. Wayland, *Political Economy,* 32, 19, 24. Cf. Goudzwaard, *Capitalism and Progress,* 25.

78. Jeremy Bentham, *The Principles of Morals and Legislation* (New York: Hafner Publishing Co., 1962), 1.

79. Ibid., 31. Emphasis in original.

80. Ibid., 3.

81. Goudzwaard, *Capitalism and Progress,* 31. Cf. Tawney, *Religion and the Rise of Capitalism,* 202.

82. Wayland, *Political Economy,* 33.

83. Ibid., 57.

84. See his "The Perils of Riches" in his *Sermons to the Churches* (New York: Blakeman Co., 1858), 213, 218, 220, 238, 239.

85. Wayland, *Political Economy,* 108; cf. 93–98, 113, 125.

86. Ibid., 389.

87. Cf. Reinhold Niebuhr, "How Philanthropic Is Henry Ford?" in *Love and Justice,* ed. D. B. Robertson (Philadelphia: Westminster Press, 1958), 98, 100, 101, 104, 108.

88. Wayland, *Political Economy,* 106, 33.

89. Ibid., 376.

90. Ibid., 373, 374.

91. Ibid., 125.

92. Ibid., 131.

93. Ibid., 40, 41.

94. Aaron Abell, *The Urban Impact on American Protestantism, 1865–1900* (London: Archon Books, 1962), 157.

95. Robert E. Cooley, "The Inside View," in *The Gordon-Conwell Contact,* Gordon-Conwell Seminary, 13:2 (April 1983): 2.

96. Agnes R. Burr, *Russell H. Conwell and His Work* (Philadelphia: John C. Winston and Co., 1926), 60f.

97. Ibid., 133f. It must be kept in mind that while Conwell did not write this book, it was nevertheless an "official" biography. Without doubting Conwell's sincerity or his evangelical credentials, we are raising the possibility that his conversion was due, in part, to uniquely nineteenth-century virtues.

98. Ibid., 227, 228.

99. Ibid., 228.

100. Ibid., 279. For a confirmation of this assessment by a local newspaper, cf. 264.

101. Ibid., 269.

102. Ibid., 367.

103. Russell H. Conwell, "Abraham Lincoln," in his *Sermons for the Great Days of the Year* (New York: George H. Doran Co., 1922), 42.

104. Russell H. Conwell, *Why Lincoln Laughed* (New York: Harper and Brothers, 1922), 19, 20.

105. Much to his advisors' alarm, Lincoln welcomed a jester by the name of Artemus Ward to the White House. Apparently Ward, like Mark Twain, had an

uncanny ability to satirize even the gravest of Washington politicos. Lincoln characterized such yarns as "fresh spring water." Cf. ibid., 62–74, especially 73.

106. Conwell, "New Year and Debt," *Sermons,* 9.

107. Ibid., 21; see also his *Borrowed Axes and Other Sermons* (Philadelphia: The Judson press, 1923), 4, 10, 113, 118.

108. John Murray, *The Epistle to the Romans, The New International Commentary on the New Testament,* ed. F. F. Bruce, (Grand Rapids, Mich.: William F. Eerdmans Pub. Comp., 1977), 155, 156. Cf. Donald Guthrie, *The Pauline Epistles* (Chicago: Inter-Varsity Press, 1968), 45. Note that both are Evangelical commentaries; they therefore have the same loyalties as Conwell.

109. Conwell, "Graduation Thoughts," *Sermons,* 152.

110. Conwell, "The American Flag," ibid., 170. Cf. "George Washington Day," ibid., 57–69.

111. Robert Shackleton, "The Story of the Acres of Diamonds," in Russell H. Conwell, *Acres of Diamonds* (New York: Harper and Brothers, 1915), 160f.

112. Russell H. Conwell, *Acres of Diamonds,* 18.

113. Ibid., 18, 19; see also 31.

114. Ibid., 21.

115. Abell, *Urban Impact,* 164. For a study of the "institutional church movement," see Abell, 137–65.

116. Burr, *Russell H. Conwell,* 291.

117. For the role that some clergy played in medicine and legitimization, see E. Richard Brown, *Rockefeller's Medicine Men* (Berkeley: University of California Press, 1979).

118. Abell, *Urban Impact,* 155, 156; Burr, *Russell H. Conwell,* 308f; and J. Wilbur Chapman, "Bethany Church of Philadelphia," in *Chautauquan* 12 (Jan. 1891), 470–73. John Wanamaker's Presbyterian heritage complemented the ecumenical outlook of Conwell's philanthropy.

Chapter 7. Alternatives to the Problems at Hand

1. This phrase was taken from Bob Goudzwaard, *Capitalism,* 66, 205f.

2. A portion of this definition was taken from Al Wolters, *Creation Regained* (Grand Rapids, Mich.: William B. Eerdmans Publishing Company, 1985), 12–21.

3. Langdon Gilkey, *Maker of Heaven and Earth* (New York: Anchor Books, 1964), 79. Cf. Emil Brunner, *The Christian Doctrine of Creation and Redemption,* trans. Olive Wyon (Philadelphia: Westminster Press, 1974), vol. 2, *Dogmatics,* 9.

4. Gilkey, *Heaven and Earth,* 19.

5. Ibid., 57.

6. Karl Heim, *The World: Its Creation and Consummation,* trans. Robert Smith (Philadelphia: Muhlenberg Press, 1962), 75. This definition admittedly raises some profound ontological and epistemological questions that touch upon aspects of scientific methodology, Christology, the nature and origin of evil, etc. To adequately deal with these topics would require an effort that goes far beyond the scope of this study. On the epistemological questions surrounding sovereign decree, ontological order, and cognition, see chs. 6 and 7 in Augustine, *On the Trinity,* vol. 3 of *Nicene and Post-Nicene Fathers of the Christian Church,* ed. Philip Schaff, 1st ser., 8 vols. (New York: Scribner, 1888), and Dooyeweerd, *New Critique,* vol. 1, 5f. On the irresistibility of sovereign decrees vis-à-vis evil and on the parasitic nature of evil (i.e., the derivative, dependent, and referential nature of evil), see

Augustine, *Confessions,* bk. 1, ch. 2, and his *City of God,* bk. 13, ch. 16; and Dooyeweerd, *New Critique,* 507. On the crucial relationship of Christ to the creation, see Augustine, *Confessions,* bk. 5, ch. 4, 81f. in the Schaff edition.

7. G. C. Berkouwer, *The Providence of God* (Grand Rapids, Mich.: Wm. B. Eerdmans Pub. Co., 1952), 5. I, therefore, have no objections to evolution of any kind, if that term connotes change or development.

8. For a more complete definition of the covenant of creation as providence, see Herman Bavinck, *Our Reasonable Faith,* trans. Henry Zylstra (Grand Rapids, Mich.: Wm. B. Eerdmans Publishing Co., 1956), 49.

9. Ibid., 34. God, of course, is not a male, as this language seems to indicate. The Scriptures seem to be full of "masculine" and "feminine" images. See, for example, Job 38:29. The point at issue here is that God's identity transcends our gender differences. Once one grasps that fact, any gender term can be used.

10. Brunner, *Creation and Redemption,* 12.

11. Alfred North Whitehead, "Science in the Nineteenth Century," in *Science in the Modern World* (New York: Free Press, 1953), 107.

12. On the relationship of the universality and the specificity of God's revelation, especially as it pertains to Christ and the Scriptures, see Berkouwer, *General Revelation* (Grand Rapids, Mich.: Wm. B. Eerdmans Pub. Comp., 1955), 285f.; Bavinck, *Our Reasonable Faith,* 38, 39; and Al Wolters, "The Centre and the Circumference," in *Vanguard* 10:2 (April 1980): 5f. Basically, we believe that general revelation gives the contours of understanding which were obscured by sin. Christ, the Word made flesh, came to rectify the force of sin and thus restore creational clarity to our cultural task. To aid us in this regard the Scriptures were given to us, as a repositivization and focusing of general revelation, to enable us fully to worship the Second Adam and thereby assume the dominion lost by the first Adam due to sin.

13. Herman Dooyeweerd, "De Structure der Rechtsbeginsellen de Methode der Rechtswetenschap in het Licht det Wetsidee," in *Scientific Contributions* (Amsterdam: Free University Press, 1930), 237, 207.

14. Gilkey, *Heaven and Earth,* 164.

15. Augustine, *Confessions,* bk. 11, ch. 3, 13f.

16. Gilkey, *Heaven and Earth,* 195.

17. For Dooyeweerd's dependence upon Augustine's definition of time and meaning, see L. Kalsbeek, *Contours of a Christian Philosophy,* ed. Bernard Zylstra and Josina Zylstra (Toronto: Wedge Publishing Co., 1975), 72–103, and David Hugh Freeman, *Recent Studies in Philosophy and Theology* (Philadelphia: Presbyterian and Reformed Publishing Co., 1962), 33–55.

18. James Olthuis, "The Reality of Societal Structures" (Toronto: Institute for Christian Studies, n.d.), 13 (mimeographed). Cf. Dooyeweerd, *New Critique,* vol. III. For a critical view of societal spheres, see John P. Chaplin, "Dooyeweerd's Theory of Public Justice" (Master of Philosophy thesis, Institute for Christian Studies, 1983), 20–50.

19. Kalsbeek, *Contours,* 353, cf. 84–94.

20. We shall develop this term more fully in subsequent analysis. For the moment, by stewardship we mean the human ability and responsibility to care for, develop and justly administer the affairs of the creation. Implied, of course, in this definition is a sacred trust. See Goudzwaard, *Capitalism,* 211f.; cf. Augustine, *City of God,* bk. 11, ch. 24.

21. Wolters, *Creation,* 36. Cf. Brunner, *Creation and Redemption,* 25f.

22. Cf. Goudzwaard, *Capitalism*, 72–79, and David Lyon, *Karl Marx* (Downers Grove, Ill.: Inter-Varsity Press, 1979), 99–126.

23. Wolters, *Creation*, 41–43. Cf. John Calvin, *Commentary on the Epistle to the Romans* (Edinburgh, Scotland: Calvin Translation Society, 1844), 27, 28.

24. Gilkey, *Heavens and Earth*, 47.

25. We have repeatedly used the term Ultimacy to refer to a god-like reference point. In the Scriptures the God of Abraham, Isaac and Jacob, who revealed and culminated his covenant in Christ, is not philosophically so designated. Our point here is simply to elucidate the universal function served by Jehovah or Another.

26. For the Christian notion of stewardship as it applies to creational development, see Al Wolters, "The Foundational Command: 'Subdue the Earth'" (Toronto: Institute for Christian, 1973), and G. C. Berkouwer, *Man: The Image of God* (Grand Rapids, Mich.: Wm. B. Eerdmans, 1962), 54, 71.

27. For a fuller treatment of the covenant of creation as it applies to the various topics mentioned, see Meredith G. Kline, *By Oath Consigned* (Grand Rapids, Mich.: Wm. B. Eerdmans Publishing Co., 1968), 30, 33, 31f., 37, 84–89, and Bavinck, *Reasonable Faith*, 49.

28. Revelation 21:1. "And I saw a new heaven and a new earth," says John the Apostle, "for the first heaven and the first earth were passed away . . ." For a Reformational critique of dispensational premillennialism, see Cornelis Vanderwaal, *Search the Scriptures*, vol. 10 (St. Catherine's, Canada: Paideia Press, 1979), 110f. and his *Hal Lindsey and Biblical Prophecy* (St. Catherine's: Paideia Press, 1978).

29. Len Scheffczyk, *Creation and Providence*, trans. Richard Strackan (New York: Herder and Herder Company, 1970), 34. For a masterful exegesis of the various pertinent passages surrounding a renewed creation, see Scheffczyk, 21–46.

30. It is interesting to note in this regard that Immanuel Kant had his own version of this doctrine which he developed in *Zum ewigen Frieden* (Toward perpetual peace).

31. Scheffczynk, *Creation*, 27. I am treading on very sensitive ground. I am speaking about the particular center of the Christian religion—Christ. I recognize the obvious: no other worldview shares this center. I must not surrender my commitment to my center, for then my worldview changes. At the same time, I must speak to a pluralistic audience. Particularity and pluralism are the twin responsibilities of all worldviews. I await help from colleagues as we wrestle with this difficult issue.

32. Richard B. Gaffin, Jr., ed., *Redemptive History and Biblical Interpretation: The Shorter Writings of Geerhardus Vos* (Phillipsburg, N.J.: Presbyterian and Reformed Publishing Co., 1980), 59–90.

33. *Confessions*, bk. 8, 10, 11. It must be noted that Augustine, and Calvin after him, have been charged with a personal soteriological determinism which does not necessarily lead to a social determinism for reasons we have outlined. To fully deal with this charge requires more space than this project permits. However, the outlines of this problem are to be found in the questions surrounding freedom and necessity.

34. Berkouwer, *Man: The Image of God* (Grand Rapids, Mich.: Wm. B. Eerdmans Pub. Co., 1956), 122–24, as quoting Kant, *Die Religion innerhalb der Grenzen der blossen Vernunft*, 35–38, 49–55.

35. Calvin, *Institutes*, bk. 2, ch. 1, 5–7.

36. For the Puritan position on this doctrine, the one which Finney encoun-

tered, see H. Shelton Smith, *Changing Conceptions of Original Sin: A Study in American Theology Since 1750* (New York: Charles Scribner's Sons, 1955), 1–9, and Iain H. Murray, *The Puritan Hope* (London: The Banner of Truth Trust, 1971), 3, 4, 10, 83–103.

37. For the evolution of the Revivalist's view of sin, similar to those of proto-Protestant liberalism, see Smith, *Original Sin,* 20, 23, 53, 140–143, 146, 147, 161, 162.

38. Albert Galin and Albert Descamps, *Sin in the Bible,* trans. Charles Schaldenbrand (New York: Descles Co., 1964), 17.

39. R. K. Harrison, *Introduction to the Old Testament* (Grand Rapids, Mich.: Wm. B. Eerdmans Publishing Co., 1969), 1007–9.

40. Galin and Descamps, *Sin,* 17.

41. Ibid., 18.

42. Herman Ridderbos, *The Coming of the Kingdom,* trans. H. de Jongste, ed. Raymond O. Lorn (Philadelphia: Presbyterian and Reformed Publishing Co., 1969), 215.

43. Herman Ridderbos, *Paul: An Outline of His Theology,* trans. John R. DeWitt, (Grand Rapids, Mich.: Wm. B. Eerdmans Publishing Co., 1975), 115. Cf. G. C. Berkouwer, *Sin* (Grand Rapids, Mich.: Wm. B. Eerdmans Publishing Co., 1977), 501f.

44. Wolters, *Creation,* 47–48.

45. For a further elucidation of this "evil," or alienation in Marx, see Johan Van Der Hoeven, *Karl Marx: The Roots of His Thought* (Toronto: Wedge Publishing Foundation, 1976), 63–68.

46. Dietrich Bonhoeffer, *Creation and Fall* (1937; New York: Macmillan, 1959), 65. Cf. Berkouwer, *Sin,* 18: "The question of the origin of evil is illegitimate for the simple reason that a logical explanation assigns a sensibleness to that which is intrinsically nonsensical, . . . a certain order to that which is disorderly."

47. For a summary of the classical position and Augustinian critique, see Berkouwer, *The Providence of God* (Grand Rapids, Mich.: Wm. B. Eerdmans Publishing Co., 1951), 254f.

48. Augustine, tract One, para. 13, *In Joannis Evangelium,* as cited in Berkouwer, *Sin,* 264.

49. Berkouwer, *Sin,* 266.

50. Dooyeweerd, *New Critique,* vol. 1, 63.

51. Herman Bavinck, *Reformed Dogmatics,* 118.

52. Bonhoeffer, *Creation and Fall,* 66, 68.

53. Dooyeweerd, vol. 2, 33. With certain reservations we point to the alternatives of the late E. F. Schumacher, namely "intermediate technology," and the increasing resistance, in certain parts of the Third World, to a simple-minded equation of total technological cultural transformation with "progress." For First World Resistance to a technological society, see Egbert Schuurman, *Technology and the Future,* trans. Herbert Morton (Toronto: Wedge Publishing Foundation, 1980) and Schumacher's *Small is Beautiful* (New York: Harper and Row, 1973).

54. For an excellent summary and critique of Kuyper's doctrine of common grace, see S. U. Zuidema, "Common Grace and Christian Action in Abraham Kuyper," in *Communication and Confrontation* (Toronto: Wedge Publishing Foundation, 1972), 52–105.

55. Ridderbos, *Paul,* 73.

56. Geerhardus Vos, *Biblical Theology* (Grand Rapids, Mich.: Wm. B. Eerdmans Publishing Co., 1948), 55, 48. Here he is explaining Genesis 3:16f.

57. Gustavo Gutiérrez, *A Theology of Liberation*, trans. and ed. Caridad Eagleson and John Eagleson (New York: Maryknoll Books, 1973), 155, 157, 158.

58. Cf. Gutiérrez, *Liberation*, 169 and Al Wolters, *Gospel*, 82. Both authors are using, from different starting points, Calvin's classic distinction found in his *Institutes*, bk. 1, ch. 5, p. 6.

59. Reinhold Niebuhr, *The Children of Light and the Children of Darkness* (New York: Charles Scribner's Sons, 1944), 10.

60. Wolters, *Creation*, 59.

61. I am not arguing for a soteriological universalism. While this will become more clear shortly, my intent is simply to suggest that all humans who respond to the liberating call of Christ can expect to be part of a "groaning creation" that is the telos of Christ's redemptive activity. On the scope of redemption, see Ridderbos, *Paul*, 82f.; Gutiérrez, *Liberation*, 177; and Calvin, bk. 3, ch. 25, p. 7.

62. Gustaf Aulén, *Christus Victor*, trans. A. G. Herbert (New York: MacMillan Publishing Co., 1969), 4.

63. Ibid., 20, 21. For Logos doctrine, see 37. Cf. Vos, *Biblical Theology*, 557–602.

64. Aulén, *Christus Victor*, 27.

65. Berkouwer is correct to call attention to Aulén's caricature of the traditional view. See his *Work of Christ* (Grand Rapids, Mich.: Wm. B. Eerdmans Publishing Co., 1976), 339f.

66. The term "irony" is chosen over that of paradox because of my desire to do justice to the fact of divine freedom at the Incarnation. I find no fundamental dialectical structure, like paradox, that even God must obey. Rather, I see a path freely chosen by God, out of love for His creation, which while appearing to suggest weakness (at the cross, for example) has as its true but hidden (to us) intent the overcoming of all evil.

67. Cf. Genesis 3:14f., especially vv. 18–19, Deuteronomy 21–23, and Galatians 3:13.

68. Berkouwer, *Work of Christ*, 173. Cf. Calvin's *Institutes*, bk. 2, ch. 16, p. 12 and Matthew 26:38.

69. Romans 5:10.

70. Ridderbos, *Paul*, 185.

71. Ibid., 189.

72. Gutiérrez, *Liberation*, 175–77.

73. Herman Ridderbos, *The Coming of the Kingdom*, ed. Raymond O. Zorn, trans. H. De Jongste (Phillipsburg, N.J.: Presbyterian and Reformed Pub. Co., 1969), 19, cf. 23.

74. For the relationship of the concept of the "Son of Man" to its roots in Daniel chapter 7 see Ridderbos, *Kingdom*, 156f.

75. The more traditionally Calvinistic wing of Evangelicalism, it must be noted, has always taken strong exception to Fundamentalism's, and especially Dispensationalism's, excessive futuristic eschatology. See Marsden, *Fundamentalism*, 48f. and notes 4 and 5; and also his *New School Presbyterian Experience*, 189–98.

76. For relevant biblical texts, see John 12:31; 2 Peter 2:5; 1 Thessalonians 4:13–18. For a confirmation of the antiworld exegesis, see Marsden, *Fundamentalism*, 49f.

77. *The Scofield Reference Bible*, ed. C. I. Scofield (1907; New York: Oxford University Press, 1967), 1341, n. 1.

78. Ibid., 1375, n. 3.

79. On the future as the culmination of kingdom and time in Christ, see Rid-

derbos, *The Coming of the Kingdom*, 523f. On the consummation of the new heavens and the new earth, see Meredith G. Kline, *Images of the Spirit* (Grand Rapids, Mich.: Baker Books, 1980), 124. On annihilation, fire and the new earth, see Berkouwer, *The Return of Christ* (Grand Rapids, Mich., 1972), 219–34. Here Berkouwer speaks of final and ultimate creational restoration and renewal. See 224.

80. Ridderbos, *Kingdom*, 188.

81. Gutiérrez, *Liberation*, 171.

82. According to Luke 4:16–20, Jesus choses to begin his ministry, by preaching the gospel to the poor. By announcing the fulfillment of the "acceptable year of the Lord," here interpreted as the "Year of Jubilee," he intends to signal freedom for slaves and a restoration of a share in the land of promise. We believe that this passage, interpreted as broadly as life's many aspects allow, should be the intent of all revivals, worship services and socioeconomic policy.

83. Graham Bennack et. al., eds. *The Penguin Dictionary of Economics* (New York: Penguin Books, 1979), 268.

84. *Vine's Expository Dictionary of Old and New Testament Words*, ed W. E. Vine (New York: Fleming H. Revell Comp., 1981), 163–64.

85. Paul Marshall et al., *Labor of Love: Essays on Work* (Toronto: Wedge Publishing Foundation, 1980), 1. Perhaps even Marshall's distinctions are too economistically defined. Where, after all, does the concept of voluntary service fit into this schema? Voluntary service is difficult to calculate in gross national product determination preciously because its economic function remains latent. Nevertheless, often it is vocational and a "labor of love." If Marshall would subsume voluntary service under the rubric of labor, this placement should be made more explicit—if only to avoid the appearance of economism.

86. This term is taken from W. R. Forrester, *Christian Vocation* (New York: Charles Scribner's Sons, 1953), 186, 199. It refers to Brunner's understanding of creation and its ordinances as the providential bases for a plurality of ordered vocations designated by God for his glory and human fulfillment and benefit.

87. The so-called missionary mandate refers to Christ's last command, before leaving earth, to "teach" and "baptize" all nations in the name of Christ. This command has properly been interpreted by Evangelicals as an impetus for missionary effort. However, because the cultural mandate has been less vigorously obeyed, modern Evangelicalism has tended to formally support prevailing cultural patterns. For the missionary mandate, see Matthew 28:16–20; cf. Luke 24:46–48.

88. On the amelioration of the harshness of work and a general survey of the Old Testament view of work, see Alan Richardson, *The Biblical Doctrine of Work* (London: S. C. M., 1958).

89. See 1 Cor. 4:12; 15:10; 16:16; Eph. 4:28; Gal. 4:11; Phil. 2:16; Col. 1:29; 1 Thess. 3:10.

90. *De civitate Dei*, I/29; XL/25. Cf. Herbert A. Deane, *The Political and Social Ideas of St. Augustine* (New York: Columbia University Press, 1963), 44, 108f.

91. William Tyndale, "A Parable of Wicked Mammon" (1527), in *Doctrinal Treatises and Portions of Holy Scripture* (Cambridge, England: Parker Society, 1848), 98, 104.

92. André Bieler, *La pensée economique et de Calvin* (Geneva: Librairie de l'Université, 1961), 321, as quoted by Marshall, *Labor of Love*, 10.

93. *Institutes*, bk. 3, ch. 10, p. 6 especially n. 8.

94. Daniel Bell, *Work and Its Discontents: The Cult of Efficiency in America* (New York: League for Industrial Democracy, 1970), 41.

95. M. A. Lipset, "The Political Process in Trade Unions," in Walter Galenson,

ed., *Labor Problems in a Christian Perspective* (Grand Rapids, Mich.: Wm. B. Eerdmans Pub. Co., 1972), 229. Some current management theorists still advocate a nonunion workplace. While this approach does have its merits, like an integral view of communication between workers and management, the approach does not seem to address traditional necessary labor concerns: a sense of belonging to a meaningful socioeconomic institution, group identity and political influence, personal security, even in the midst of cyclical disturbances, and international consciousness. See Robert Lewis, William A. Krupman, *Winning NLRB Elections: Management's Strategy and Preventive Programs* (New York: Practicing Law Institute, 1979). See especially pp. 303–24 for a short but constructive labor history.

96. Gerald Vandezande, "Of Strikes and Strife: A Critique of the Status Quo," *Labor Problems* 117 (editor's note). For a history of the C.L.A.C. and its effects upon Canadian Labor, see Richard Forbes, "CLAC: A Novel Approach," *Labor Problems* 117 (1987): 339f. It must be admitted that we find no parallel *structural* movement in management situations. While the Pittsburgh-based "Value of the Person" ministry, headed by Wayne Alderson, stresses the value, dignity, and worth of the individual worker, it leaves the method of production largely intact. Thus, the main agency for change remains unions—organizations not as powerful as management.

97. Ed Vanderkloet, et al., *Beyond the Adversary System* (Toronto: Christian Labor Association, 1976), 17f. One could easily object to these and coming notions as "utopian" if they were not being so fully implemented in several Western democracies. Thus, in the deepest sense, our arguments spring from religious convictions which have manifested considerable cultural fruit. A valuable book—one stressing what we have called the "multifaceted arena" of business—is Vern Terpstra and Kenneth David's *The Cultural Environment of International Business* (Cincinnati: South-Western Publishing Comp., 1991).

98. We are referring to the traditional business school paradigm which trains managers to aim for short-term goals and profit maximization. This paradigm held as long as the American market for cars, for example, was monopolized by Detroit. Once the American consumer was introduced to Japanese autos and Japanese management style—stressing as it does worker cooperation, long-range analysis, and a different view of profits, all of which made for better auto bargains—the results were obvious.

99. Ed Vanderkloet, "Why Work Anyway," in Paul Marshall et al., *Labors of Love*, 39. Emphasis and style in original. The modern trend of "ergonomics" or the "laws of work" represent a helpful trend in labor humanization. See I. A. R. Galer, ed., *Applied Ergonomics Handbook* (Boston: Butterworth, 1987).

100. See Robert R. Blake, Herbert A. Shepherd, Jane S. Mouton, *Managing Intergroup Conflicts in Industry,* as quoted by Werner G. Schmidt, "Christian Ethics in Labor Relations," in Redekop, ed., *Labor Problems,* 141. Although this model has the virtue of including labor in industrial discussion, such discussions are still to be "managed," i.e. conducted by experts whose knowledge of technical matters is thought to exceed the experience of workers. Consequently, a class chauvinism arises that tears at the fabric of the work community with a result that morale and product quality suffer.

101. Herman Dooyeweerd, *New Critique,* vol. 3, 444, 445.

102. For a more thorough investigation of the relationship of government to economic communities, see my "The Gospel, Business, and the State," in *Biblical Principles and Economics: The Foundations,* vol. 1, ed. Richard C. Chewning (Colorado Springs, Colo.: Navpress, 1989), 203–22.

103. W. J. Heisler, ed., *A Matter of Dignity* (University of Notre Dame: John W. Houck Press, 1977), 140.

104. Wm. P. Sexton, "Work Humanization in Practice: What Should Business Do?" in ibid., 140, 141.

105. See David G. Bowers, "Work Humanization in Practice: What Business is Doing," 447f. and Ted Mills, "Leadership from Abroad: European Development in Industrial Democracy," 115f. It must be remembered that Volvos of the 1970s were very affordable (many sold for under $3,000). Only in subsequent years, after a return of mass production, have prices soared. I am aware that my analysis of unions and management is too exclusively tied to North American and European models and examples. I take this tack, hopefully, not out of ignorance but because of the needs and limits of relevancy. For a more global perspective on business' perspective, see Raghu Nath, ed., *Comparative Management: A Regional View* (Cambridge, Mass.: Ballinger Publishing Company, 1988).

106. Irving Bluestone, "Work Humanization In Practice: What Can Labor Do?" 176.

107. Gary R. Gemmill, "Postscript: Toward a Person-Centered Organization" in ibid., 202.

108. Cf. Walter G. Muelder, *Religion and Economic Responsibility* (New York: Charles Scribner's Sons, 1953).

109. By the word "social," interpreted in its broadest possible sense, we are suggesting a variety of cultural institutions and mutually adaptive networks whose function is that of cohesiveness. Culture, as the sum of this social interlacement, is nevertheless the more or less dynamic unfolding of creation under the stewardship of humanity.

110. To thoroughly study the relationship, normative and pragmatic, between government and business would take us too far afield. I am suggesting in my introductory remarks that when the capital function is exaggerated, its processes eventuate in coercion of certain governmental functions. The current phenomenon of "PACs," or political action committees, is an example. To "remedy" this imbalance, government reasserts its autonomy in the form of increasing regulations. See my "The Gospel, Business, and the State," in *Biblical Principles and Business: The Foundations,* Richard C. Chewning, ed. (Colorado Springs, Colo.: Navpress, 1989).

111. William Cunningham, *The Use and Abuse of Money* (New York: Charles Scribner's Sons, 1891). Although this book is hardly "modern," as seen from its publication date, its central accuracy was affirmed for our study's time frame and through the emergence of the modern corporation's need for vast sums of capital.

112. Karl Marx, *Der Historiche Materialismus: Die Frühschritten,* hrg. von S. Landehut und J.P. Mayer (Leipzig: Berlin Press, 1932), as quoted by Dooyeweerd, *New Critique,* vol. 3, 456.

113. See for example *The Galbraith Reader* (Ipswich, Mass.: Gambit Press, 1977), 114–48, especially 129.

114. Bob Goudzwaard, "Toward a Reformation in Economics" (Toronto: Association for the Advancement of Christian Scholarship, 1980), 30.

115. Ibid., 48, 49. Cf. J. Philip Wogaman, *The Great Economic Debate: An Ethical Analysis* (Philadelphia: The Westminster Press, 1977), 93.

116. Goudzwaard, "Reformation in Economics," 33.

117. Joan Robinson, *Freedom and Necessity: An Introduction to the Study of Society* (Winchester, Mass.: Allen and Unwin, 1970), 116.

118. Walter C. Muelder, *Religion and Economic Responsibility* (New York: Charles Scribner's Sons, 1953), 86.

119. Charles W. Beard, *The American Leviathan* (New York: Macmillan, 1930), 379.

120. Muelder, *Economic Responsibility,* 89.

121. Bob Goudzwaard, "Incomes and Their Distributions" (Toronto: Association for the Advancement of Christian Scholarship, n.d.), 6.

122. Our biggest disappointment with this concept concerns the almost exclusively economic character of these zones. Why were hospitals, churches, a variety of schools, families, and law enforcement agencies left out of this package? Perhaps Reagan, like his liberal foes, believes that money—albeit business money—will chase away poverty.

123. Charles Power, *Social Responsibility and Investments* (New York: Abingdon Press, 1971), 197.

124. Dwelling House Savings and Loan brochure: *"Meeting People's Needs"* (5011 Herron Ave., Pittsburgh, Pa. 15219).

125. Rodney Brooks, "Dwelling in the House of Lavelle," *Black Enterprise* 14, no. 11 (June 1984), 146.

126. Ibid.

127. Ludwig M. Lachmann, *Capital and its Structure* (Kansas City: Sheed Andrews and McMeel, Inc. 1978), 56f.

128. Ibid., 53. A highly persuasive critique of the pricing theory of value can be found in "Technology and Economics," in *Responsible Technology,* Stephen V. Monsma ed. (Grand Rapids: Wm. B. Eerdmans, 1986), p. 103–142.

129. See, therefore, ibid., 58.

130. For a further review of the problem of the lack of economic and social responsibility present in various theories about capital and on the reductionism apparent in the function of capital, see Bas Kee, "The Capital Debate and the Economic Aspect of Reality," in *Social Science in a Christian Perspective* (London, England: University Press of America, 1988). An exceptionally helpful book, one which concentrates upon the necessities of a business (especially the social responsibility of capital), is Richard C. Chewning et al., *Business Through the Eyes of Faith* (San Francisco: Harper and Row, 1990).

131. Goudzwaard, *Capitalism and Progress,* 211. Cf. Luke 12:42 and 16:2, and Paul G. Schrotenboer, *Man in God's World* (Toronto: Wedge Publishing Foundation, 1972), 4 where he says, "The Greek term indicates that office or stewardship has to do with managing or administration. In each context where the term is used, the position of managing or administering ... is delegated to man. The office bearer is therefore a representative of his superior."

132. *The Penguin Dictionary of Economics,* 270.

133. Walter Brueggeman, *The Land: Place as Gift, Promise and Challenge in Biblical Faith* (Philadelphia: Fortress Press, 1977), 5.

134. Ibid., 59.

135. We ought particularly to be reminded of how two widows, Ruth and Naomi, were permitted to gather surplus from the fields of Boaz, later becoming enfranchised through marriage, and still later, becoming part of the lineage of King David, upon whose throne Christ sits. See Ruth 2:1–5 and 4:22.

136. Brueggeman, 95. Cf. 1 Kings 18:4; 19:2; 21.

137. For a relationship of claim to special status and convenatal wrath, see Abraham Heschel, *The Prophets* (New York: Harper and Row, 1962), 103–36.

138. Brueggeman, 140. Cf. Ezekiel 36:22–28.

139. Brueggeman, 162.

140. Compare Hannah's song in 1 Samuel 2:1–10 and Mary's song in Luke 1:51–55.

141. John Carmody, *Ecology and Religion* (New York: Paulist Press, 1983), 14.

142. Ibid., 16.

143. Ibid., 19.

144. Ibid., 19, 20.

145. Ibid., 31.

146. Jorgen Randers and Donella Meadows, "The Carrying Capacity of Our Global Environment," in *Toward a Steady-State Economy,* ed. Herman E. Daley (San Francisco: W. H. Freeman Co., 1974), 283.

147. I fully admit that for American companies to construct such pollution control devices might hurt them in the world market. In addition to the broad programs of cost sharing outlined in the last section, I believe it should become governmental policy to initiate international pollution treaties.

148. Theodore W. Patterson, *Land Use Planning* (New York: Von Nostrand Reinhold, 1979), 199.

149. Richard H. Jackson, *Land Use in America* (New York: John Wiley and Sons, 1981), 200.

150. This statement was first made by Indian chief Seattle in 1854 in response to the proposal by the U.S. Government that reservations for Indian tribes be established in the Northwest Pacific Territories. Reprinted in World Council of Churches, *Land Rights for Indigenous People* (Geneva: Oikoumene, Programme Unit on Justice and Service, 1983), 14.

151. Fortunately, we Americans have slowly but surely made progress in recognizing the right of Native Americans to associate as they see fit. Thus, we are more pluralistically and tolerantly treating representatives of Native American government as if they are in fact governmental representatives. See Lamin Sanneh, *Translating the Message: The Missionary Impact on Culture* (New York: Maryknoll Press, 1990), 24–48.

Bibliography

Primary and Secondary Works

Abell, Aaron. *The Urban Impact on American Protestantism, 1865–1900.* London: Archon Books, 1962.

Abraham, William J. *The Coming Revival: Recovering the Full Evangelical Tradition.* New York: Harper and Row, 1984.

Ahlstrom, Sydney E. *Theology in America: The Major Protestant Voices from Puritanism to Neo-Orthodoxy.* Indianapolis: Bobbs-Merrill, 1967.

Althaus, Paul. *The Ethics of Martin Luther.* Translated by Robert C. Schultz. Philadelphia: Fortress Press, 1972.

Arieli, Yehoshua. *Individualism and Nationalism in American Ideology.* Cambridge: Harvard University Press, 1964.

Augustine, Saint, of Hippo. *The City of God.* New York: Random House, 1950.

————. *On The Trinity.* In *Nicene and Post-Nicene Fathers of the Christian Church,* edited by Philip Schaff, vol. 1. New York: Scribner and Sons, 1888.

Aulén, Gustaf. *Christus Victor.* Translated by A. G. Herbert. New York: Macmillan, 1969.

Baritz, Loren. *City on a Hill.* New York: Oxford University Press, 1964.

Barrow, R. H. *Introduction to Saint Augustine and the City of God.* London: Faber and Faber, 1950.

Bavinck, Herman. *Our Reasonable Faith.* Translated by Henry Zylstra. Grand Rapids, Mich.: William B. Eerdmans, 1956.

Beach, Waldo, and H. Richard Niebuhr. *Christian Ethics.* New York: The Ronald Press Company, 1955.

Beacher, Henry Ward. *Patriotic Addresses in America and England from 1850 to 1885.* New York: Fords and Howard, 1891.

Begbie, Harold. *The Life of William Booth, the Founder of the Salvation Army.* 2 vols. London: Wordsworth Press, 1920.

Bell, Daniel. *Work and Its Discontents: The Cult of Efficiency in America.* New York: League for Industrial Democracy, 1970.

Bell, Thomas. *Out of this Furnace.* Pittsburgh: University of Pittsburgh Press, 1981.

Bentham, Jeremy. *The Principles of Morals and Legislation.* New York: Hafner Publications, 1962.

Berger, Peter L. *The Sacred Canopy: Elements of a Sociological Theory of Religion.* New York: Doubleday, 1967.

Berger, Peter L., and Thomas Luckman. *The Social Construction of Reality.* New York: Doubleday, 1967.

Berkouwer, G. C. *General Revelation.* Grand Rapids, Mich.: William B. Eerdmans, 1955.

———. *Man, the Image of God.* Grand Rapids, Mich.: William B. Eerdmans, 1962.

———. *The Providence of God.* Grand Rapids, Mich.: William B. Eerdmans, 1952.

———. *The Return of Christ.* Grand Rapids, Mich.: William B. Eerdmans, 1972.

———. *Sin.* Grand Rapids, Mich.: William B. Eerdmans, 1977.

Bieler, André. *The Social Humanism of John Calvin.* Translated and edited by Paul T. Fuhrmann. Richmond, Va.: John Knox Press, 1964.

Blaug, Mark. *Economic Theory in Retrospect.* Cambridge: Cambridge University Press, 1978.

Boer, Jan H. *Missionary Messengers of Liberation in Colonial Context.* Amsterdam: Rodopi Press, 1979.

Bonhoeffer, Dietrich. *Creation and Fall.* New York: Macmillan, 1959.

Bowen, David. *The Idea of the Victorian Church: A Study of the Church of England, 1833–1889.* Montreal: McGill University Press, 1968.

Brody, David. *Steelworkers in America.* Cambridge: Harvard University Press, 1938.

Brown, D. Mackenzie. *Ultimate Concern: Tillich in Dialogue.* New York: Harper and Row, 1965.

Brown, E. Richard. *Rockefeller's Medicine Men: Medicine and Capitalism in America.* Berkeley: University of California Press, 1979.

Brueggeman, Walter. *The Land: Place as Gift, Promise, and Challenge in Biblical Faith.* Philadelphia: Fortress Press, 1977.

Brunner, Emil. *The Christian Doctrine of Creation and Redemption.* Translated by Olive Wyon. Philadelphia: Westminster Press, 1974.

Burr, Agnes. *Russell H. Conwell and His Work.* Philadelphia: John C. Winston Company, 1926.

Calvin, John. *The Institutes of the Christian Religion.* Translated by Ford Battles. Edited by John T. McNeill. Philadelphia: Westminster Press, 1967.

Carmody, John. *Ecology and Religion.* New York: Paulist Press, 1983.

Carwardine, Richard. *Transatlantic Revivalism: Popular Evangelicalism in Britain and America, 1790–1865.* Westport, Conn.: Greenwood Press, 1978.

Caughey, James. *A Voice from America, or Four Sermons Preached by Reverend James Caughey.* Manchester: no publisher indicated, 1847.

Chewning, Richard C., John W. Eby, and Shirley J. Roels. *Business Through The Eyes of Faith.* San Francisco: Harper and Row, 1990.

Clark, Clifford E. *Henry Ward Beecher: Spokesman for the Middle Class.* Chicago: University of Chicago Press, 1976.

Cole, Charles. *The Social Ideals of the Northern Evangelicals, 1820–1860.* New York: Octagon Books, 1966.

Commons, John R., ed. *A History of Labor in the United States.* 2 vols. New York: Macmillan, 1921.

Conanet, William. *Narratives of Remarkable Conversions and Revival Incidents.* New York: Fleming Revell Company, 1858.

Conwell, Russell H. *Borrowed Axes and Other Sermons.* Philadelphia: The Judson Press, 1923.

———. *Why Lincoln Laughed.* New York: Harper Brothers Publishing Company, 1922.

Copleston, Frederick. *A History of Philosophy.* Vol. 2, *Medieval Philosophy Augustine to Scotus.* Westminster, England: The Newman Press, 1960.

Copley, F. B. *Frederick Taylor: Father of Scientific Management.* 2 vols. New York: Harper and Brothers, 1923.

Cross, Whitney R. *The Burned-over District.* Ithaca: Cornell University Press, 1950.

Crossley, Robert N. *Luther and the Peasants' War.* New York: Exposition Press, 1974.

Curti, Merle, and Roderick Nash. *Philanthropy in the Shaping of American Higher Education.* New Brunswick, N.J.: Rutgers University Press, 1965.

Daly, Herman E., ed. *Toward a Steady-State Economy.* San Francisco: William H. Freeman Company, 1974.

Degler, Carl N. *The Age of Economic Revolution.* Atlanta, Ga.: Scott, Foresman and Company, n.d.

Dixon, James. *Methodism in its Origin, Economy, and Present Position.* London: James Nisbet Company, 1843.

Dooyeweerd, Herman. *A New Critique of Theoretical Thought.* 4 vols. Philadelphia: The Nisbet Company, 1843.

———. *Roots of Western Culture: Pagan, Secular, and Christian Options.* Translated by John Kraay. Edited by Mark Vander Vennen. Toronto: Wedge Publishing Company, 1979.

———. "De Structure der Rechtsbeginsellen en de Method de Rechtswetenschap in het Licht der Wetsidee." [The structure of the principles of justice and the method of jurisprudence in light of the cosmonomic law-ideal.] In *Scientific Contributions.* Amsterdam: Free University Press, 1930.

Ellul, Jacques. *The Technological Society.* Translated by John Wilkinson. New York: Vintage Books, 1964.

Everett, John. *Religion in Economics.* Philadelphia: Porcupine Press, 1982.

Fenton, Roger. *A Treatise on Usury.* London: William Aspley Company, 1911.

Finney, Charles G. *The Character and Claims and Practical Workings of Freemasonry.* Chicago: Ezra Cook Publishing Company, 1887.

———. *Lectures on Important Subjects.* New York: John S. Taylor Company, 1846.

———. *Lectures to Professing Christians.* New York: Smith and Valentine, 1837.

———. *Lectures on Revivals of Religion.* Edited by William G. McLoughlin. Cambridge: Harvard University Press, 1835.

———. *Lectures on Systematic Theology.* Oberlin, Ohio: James M. Fitch Company, 1846.

———. *Memoirs of Reverend Charles G. Finney.* New York: Fleming H. Revell Company, 1876.

Fiske, John. *Herbert Spencer and the Americans.* New York: Houghton Mifflin, 1894.

Flubacher, Joseph F. *The Concept of Ethics in the History of Economics.* New York: Vintage Press, 1950.

Flynn, John T. *God's Gold: The Story of Rockefeller and His Times.* New York: Harcourt, Brace, and Company, 1932.

Fogel, Robert. *Railroads and American Economic Growth: Essays in Economic History.* Baltimore: Johns Hopkins University Press, 1978.

Fothergill, P. G. *Historical Aspects of Organic Evolution.* London: Hollis and Carter, 1952.

Fowler, James, and Keen, Samuel. *Life Maps: Conversations on the Journey of Faith.* Waco, Texas: Winston Press, 1978.

Frank, Douglas W. *Less Than Conquerors.* Grand Rapids, Mich.: William B. Eerdmans, 1986.

Freeman, David H. *Recent Studies in Philosophy and Theology.* Philadelphia: Presbyterian and Reformed Publishing Company, 1962.

Gaffin, Richard, ed. *Redemptive History and Biblical History: The Shorter Writings of Geerhardus Vos.* Philippsburg, N.J.: Presbyterian and Reformed Publishing Company, 1980.

Galbraith, John K. *The Galbraith Reader.* Edited by Lowell Thompson. Ipswich, Mass.: Gambit Press, 1977.

Gelin, Albert, and Albert Descamps. *Sin in the Bible.* Translated by Charles Schaldenbrand. New York: Descles Company, 1964.

Gierke, Otto. *Natural Law and the Theory of Society, 1500 to 1880.* Translated by Ernest Barker. Boston: Beacon Press, 1960.

Gilkey, Langdon. *Maker of Heaven and Earth.* New York: Anchor Books, 1965.

Goetzmann, William. *Exploration and Empire: The Explorer and Scientist in the Winning of the American West.* New York: Alfred A. Knopf, 1966.

Goudzwaard, Bob. *Capitalism and Progress: A Diagnosis of Western Society.* Grand Rapids, Mich.: William B. Eerdmans, 1979.

Graham, Fred. *John Calvin the Constructive Revolutionary.* Richmond, Va.: John Knox Press, 1971.

Gunton, George. *Wealth and Progress.* New York: D. Appleton and Company, 1887.

Gutiérrez, Gustavo. *A Theology of Liberation.* Translated and edited by Caridad Eagleson and John Eagleson. New York: Maryknoll Books, 1973.

Hammond, John, and Barbara Hammond. *The Rise of Modern Industry.* London: Methuen, 1925.

Hammond, John L. *The Politics of Benevolence: Revival Religion and American Voting Behavior.* Norwood, N.J.: Ablex Publishing Company, 1979.

Handlin, Oscar. *A History of America.* New York: Holt, Rinehart, and Winston, 1968.

Harrison, R. K. *Introduction to the Old Testament.* Grand Rapids, Mich.: William B. Eerdmans, 1969.

Hays, Samuel P. *The Response to Industrialism, 1885–1914.* Chicago: University of Chicago Press, 1957.

Heilbroner, Robert. *The Making of an Economic Society.* Englewood Cliffs, N.J.: Prentice-Hall, 1962.

————. *The Worldly Philosophers.* 4th ed. New York: Simon and Schuster, 1972.

Heim, Karl. *The World: Its Creation and Consummation.* Translated by Robert Smith. Philadelphia: Muhlenberg Press, 1962.

Heisler, W. J., ed., *A Matter of Dignity.* Notre Dame: John W. Houck Press, 1977.

Hobson, John A. *Economics and Ethics: A Study in Social Values.* New York: D.C. Heath, 1929.

Huizinga, John. *The Waning of the Middle Ages.* New York: Anchor Books, 1954.

Inglis, K. S. *Churches and the Working Class in Victorian England.* London: Routledge and Kegan Paul, 1963.

Jackson, Richard H. *Land Use in America.* New York: John Wiley and Sons, 1981.

Jefferson, Thomas. *Letters from the Lewis and Clark Expedition, 1783–1854.* Edited by Donald Jackson. Urbana: University of Illinois Press, 1962.

Johnson, Paul E. *A Shopkeeper's Millennium: Society and Revivals in Rochester New York, 1815–1837.* New York: Hill and Wang, 1978.

Jones, Howard M. *The Age of Energy.* New York: The Viking Press, 1971.

Josephson, Matthew. *The Robber Barons: The Great American Capitalists, 1861–1901.* New York: Harcourt, Brace, and World, 1933.

Kakar, Sudhir. *Frederick Taylor: A Study in Personality Innovation.* Cambridge: Harvard University Press, 1970.

Kane, J. H. *Understanding Christian Missions.* Grand Rapids, Mich.: Baker Book House, 1974.

Keynes, John M. "Economic Possibilities for our Grandchildren." In *Essays in Persuasion.* New York: Harcourt, Brace, and Company, 1932.

Kitson Clark, G. S. R. *Church Men and the Condition of England.* London: Methuen, 1973.

Kline, Meredith G. *By Oath Consigned.* Grand Rapids, Mich.: William B. Eerdmans, 1968.

Kuyper, Abraham. *Calvinism: Six Lectures Delivered in the Theological Seminary at Princeton.* Grand Rapids, Mich.: William B. Eerdmans, 1961.

Lattourette, Kenneth L. *A History of the Expansion of Christianity.* Vols. 3 and 4, *The Great Century A.D. 1800–1914: Europe and the United States of America.* New York: Harper and Row, 1941.

Lukes, Steven. *Individualism.* Oxford: Basil Blackwell, 1973.

Lundberg, Ferdinand. *The Rockefeller Syndrome.* Englewood Cliffs, N.J.: Lyle Stuart, 1975.

Luther, Martin. "An Open Letter to the Christian Nobility of the German Nation." In *Three Treatises.* Translated by C. M. Jacobs. Philadelphia: Fortress Press, 1965.

————. *Works of Martin Luther.* Philadelphia: Muhlenberg Press, 1943.

Lyon, David. *Karl Marx.* Downers Grove, Ill. Inter Varsity Press, 1979.

McLaughlin, William G. *Revivals, Awakenings, and Reform.* Chicago: University of Chicago Press, 1978.

McLeod, H. *Class and Religion in the Late Victorian City.* Hamden, Conn.: Archon Books, 1975.

Mandeville, Bernard. *The Fable of the Bees; or, Private Vices, Publick Benefits.* London: 1714; Harmondsworth: Penguin, 1970.

Marsden, George. *Fundamentalism and American Culture: The Shaping of Twentieth Century Evangelicalism, 1870–1925.* New York: Oxford University Press, 1980.

Marx, Leo. *The Machine in the Garden: Technology and the Pastoral Ideal in America.* New York: Oxford University Press, 1964.

May, Henry F. *Protestant Churches and Industrial America.* New York: Harper and Brothers Publishers, 1967.

Miller, Basil. *Charles G. Finney: He Prayed Down Revivals.* Grand Rapids, Mich.: Zondervan Publishing Company, 1942.

Miller, Perry. *Errand Into the Wilderness.* Cambridge: Harvard University Press, 1956.

————. *The Life of the Mind of America.* New York: Harcourt, Brace, and World, 1965.

Muelder, Walter. *Religion and Economic Responsibility.* New York: Charles Scribner's Sons, 1953.

Murray, Iain. *The Puritan Hope.* London: The Banner Truth Trust, 1971.

Myint, Hla. *Theories of Welfare Economics.* London: London School of Economics, 1948.

Nagel, Paul C. *The Sacred Trust: American Nationality, 1798–1898.* New York: Oxford University Press, 1971.

Nelson, Daniel. *Managers and Workers: Origins of the Factory System in the United States, 1880–1920.* Madison: University of Wisconsin Press, 1975.

Nevins, Allan. *The Heroic Age of American Enterprise.* New York: Scribner's Sons, 1940.

Niebuhr, Reinhold. *The Children of Light and the Children of Darkness.* New York: Charles Scribner's Sons, 1944.

Niebuhr, Richard R. *Experimental Religion.* New York: Harper and Row, 1972.

Noonan, John T. *The Scholastic Analysis of Usury.* Cambridge: Harvard University Press, 1957.

Norman, E. R. *Church and Society in England, 1770–1970.* Oxford: Clarendon Press, 1976.

Olthius, James H. "Must the Church Become Secular?" In *Out of Concern for the Church.* Association for the Advancement of Christian Scholarship. Toronto: Wedge Publishing Foundation, 1970.

Orr, James E. *The Second Evangelical Awakening in Great Britain.* London: Marshall, Morgan, and Scott, 1945.

Pascal, Roy. *The Social Basis of the German Reformation.* New York: Augustus M. Kelly, 1971.

Patterson, Theodore W. *Land Use Planning.* New York: Von Nostrand Reinhold Company, 1979.

Perlman, Selig. *A Theory of the Labor Movement.* New York: Macmillan, 1928.

Pierard, Richard. *The Unequal Yoke.* New York: J.B. Lippincott, 1970.

Pollock, John. *Moody Without Sankey: A New Biographical Portrait.* London: Hodder and Stoughton, 1963.

Pope, Liston. *Millhands and Preachers: A Study of Gastonia.* New Haven: Yale University Press, 1965.

Post, Albert. *Popular Free Thought in America, 1825–1850.* New York: Simon and Schuster, 1974.

Powderly, Terrance. *The Path I Trod.* Edited by Harry J. Carmen. New York: Columbia University Press, 1940.

Powers, Charles. *Social Responsibility and Investments.* New York: Abingdon Press, 1971.

Prucha, Francis P. *American Indian Policy in Crises, 1865–1900*. Norman: University of Oklahoma Press, 1976.

Ratner, Sydney; James Soltow, and Richard Sylla. *The Evolution of the American Economy*. New York: Basic Books, 1979.

Redekop, John H. *Labor Problems in a Christian Perspective*. Grand Rapids, Mich.: William B. Eerdmans, 1972.

Richardson, Alan. *The Biblical Doctrine of Work*. London: S. C. M. Company, 1958.

Ridderbos, Herman. *The Coming of the Kingdom*. Translated by H. de Jongste. Philadelphia: Presbyterian and Reformed Publishing Company, 1969.

———. *Paul: An Outline of His Theology*. Translated by John R. Dewitt. Grand Rapids, Mich.: William B. Eerdmans, 1975.

Rifkin, Jeremy, with Ted Howard. *The Emerging Order*. New York: G. P. Putnam's Sons, 1979.

Robertson, Roland. *The Sociological Interpretation of Religion*. New York: Schocken Books, 1970.

Rodger, Daniel T. *The Work Ethic in Industrial America, 1850–1920*. Chicago: University of Chicago Press, 1978.

Rosenberg, Carrol S. *Religion and the Rise of the American City: The New York City Mission Movement, 1812–1870*. Ithaca: Cornell University Press, 1971.

Rosenberg, Nathan. *Technology and American Economic Growth*. New York: Harper and Row, 1972.

Rostow, W. W. *British Economy in the Nineteenth Century*. Oxford: Clarendon Press, 1948.

Russell, C. Allyn. *Voices of American Fundamentalism*. Philadelphia: Presbyterian and Reformed Publishing Company, 1976.

Sandeen, Ernest. *Roots of Fundamentalism*. Chicago: University of Chicago Press, 1970.

Scheffczyk, Leo. *Creation and Providence*. Translated by Richard Strachan. New York: Herder and Herder Company, 1970.

Schlesinger, Arthur M. *The Age of Jackson*. Boston: Little, Brown, 1950.

Schuurman, Egbert. *Reflections on the Technological Society*. Toronto: Wedge Publishing Company, 1977.

Scofield, C. I., ed. *The New Scofield Reference Bible*. New York: Oxford University Press, 1969.

Smith, Adam. *An Inquiry Into the Nature and Causes of the Wealth of Nations*. Translated by Max Lerner. New York: The Modern Library, 1965.

Smith, H. Shelton. *Changing Conceptions of Original Sin: A Study in American Theology Since 1750*. New York: Charles Scribner's Sons, 1955.

Smith, Timothy. *Revivalism and Social Reform in Mid-Nineteenth Century America*. Nashville, Tenn.: Abington Press, 1957.

Smith, Willfred C. *Faith and Belief*. Princeton: Princeton University Press, 1979.

Spiegel, Henry W. *The Growth of Economic Thought*. Englewood Cliffs, N.J.: Prentice-Hall, 1971.

Sumner, Willim G. *The Challenge of the Facts*. Edited by Samuel Keller. New Haven: Yale University Press, 1914.

————. *The Forgotten Man and Other Essays.* New York: D. Appleton Company, 1883.

Tawney, R. H. *The Acquisitive Society.* New York: Harcourt, Brace, and World, 1920.

————. *Religion and the Rise of Capitalism: A Historical Study.* Gloucester, Mass.: Peter Smith, 1962.

Taylor, Frederick, W. "On the Art of Cutting Metals." In *Transactions of the American Society of Mechanical Engineers.* 28 (February 1906): 11f.

Terpstra, Vern, and Kenneth David. *The Cultural Environment of International Business,* 3d ed. Cincinnati: South-Western Publishing Comp., 1991.

Thomas, George M. *Revivalism and Cultural Change: Christianity, Nation Building, and the Market in the Nineteenth-Century United States.* Chicago: University of Chicago Press, 1989.

Tillich, Paul. *Biblical Religion and the Search for Ultimate Reality.* Chicago: University of Chicago Press, 1955.

————. *Dynamics of Faith.* Edited by Ruth N. Anshen. New York: Harper and Brothers, 1957.

————. *The Protestant Era.* Translated by James L. Adams. Chicago: University of Chicago Press, 1948.

————. *A Theology of Culture.* Edited by Robert C. Kimball. New York: Oxford University Press, 1959.

————. *What is Religion?* Edited by James L. Adams. New York: Harper and Row, 1969.

Toynbee, Arnold. *The Industrial Revolution.* Boston: Beacon Press, 1884.

Trachtenberg, Alan. *The Incorporation of America: Culture and Society in the Gilded Age.* New York: Hill and Wang, 1982.

Trevelyan, G. M. *English Social History.* London: Methuen, 1944.

Troeltsch, Ernst. *The Social Teachings of the Christian Church.* Vol. 1. Translated by Olive Wyon. New York: Harper and Row, 1960.

Turner, Frederick J. *The Frontier in American History.* New York: Holt, Rinehart, and Winston, 1965.

Tuveson, Ernest L. *Redeemer Nation: The Idea of America's Millennial Role.* Chicago: University of Chicago Press, 1968.

Tyng, Stephen, Jr. *He Will Come; or, Meditations Upon the Return of the Lord Jesus to Reign over the Earth.* New York: Houghton and Mifflin, 1878.

Van Der Hoeven, Johan. *Karl Marx: The Roots of His Thought.* Toronto: Wedge Publishing Company, 1976.

Vanderkloet, Edward. *Beyond the Adversary System.* Toronto: Wedge Publishing Company, 1976.

Vander Stelt, John C. *Philosophy and Scripture: A Study of Old Princeton and Westminster Theology.* Marlton, N.J.: Mack Publishing Company, 1978.

Vanderwaal, Cornelius. *Hal Lindsey and Biblical Prophecy.* St. Catharines, Canada: Paideia Press, 1978.

————. *Search the Scriptures.* Vol. 10, *Revelation.* St. Catharine's, Canada: Paideia Press, 1979.

Veenhof, Jan. "Nature and Grace in Bavinck." Translated by Albert Wolters. Toronto: Association for the Advancement of Christian Scholarship, 1968.

Vos, Geerhardus. *Biblical Theology.* Grand Rapids, Mich.: William B. Eerdmans, 1948.

Wallace, Anthony F. C. *Rockdale: The Growth of an American Village in the Early Industrial Revolution.* New York: Alfred A. Knopf, 1978.

Ward, Benjamin. *The Conservative Economic World View.* New York: Basic Books, 1979.

Ware, Norman. *The Industrial Worker, 1840–1860.* Boston: Houghton Mifflin Company, 1924.

Wayland, Francis. *The Elements of Intellectual Philosophy.* New York: Sheldon Company, 1854.

————. *The Elements of Moral Science.* Boston: Gould, Kendall, and Lincoln, 1842.

————. *The Elements of Political Economy.* Boston: Gould and Lincoln, 1837.

————. *The Limitations of Human Responsibility.* New York: D. Appleton and Company, 1838.

————. *Salvation by Christ.* Boston: Gould, Kendall, and Lincoln, 1859.

Wayland, Francis, Jr., and H. L. Wayland. *A Memoir of the Life and Labor of Francis Wayland, D.D., LL.D.* 2 vols. New York: Sheldon Company, 1867.

Webb, Walter P. *The Great Plains.* New York: Ginn, 1959.

Weber, Thomas. *The Northern Railroads in the Civil War, 1861–1865.* New York: King's Crown Press, 1952.

Weber, Max. *The Protestant Ethic and the Spirit of Capitalism.* Translated by Talcott Parsons. Foreword by R. H. Tawney. New York: Charles Scribner's Sons, 1958.

Wells, David F., and John D. Woodbridge. *The Evangelicals: What They Believe, Who They Are, Where They are Changing.* Grand Rapids, Mich.: Baker Book House, 1975.

Welsh, Herbert, *The Indian Question: Past and Present.* Philadelphia: The Indian Rights Association, 1890.

Welter, Rush. *The Mind of America, 1820–1860.* New York: Columbia University Press, 1975.

Whitehead, Alfred N. "Science in the Nineteenth Century." In *Science and the Modern World.* New York: Free Press, 1953.

Williamson, Harold F., ed. *The Growth of the American Economy.* New York: Prentice-Hall, 1964.

Wogaman, J. P. *The Great Economic Debate.* Philadelphia: The Westminster Press, 1977.

Youmans, Edward L. *The Culture Demanded by Modern Life.* New York: D. Appleton and Company, 1867.

Zuidema, S. U. "Common Grace and Christian Action in Abraham Kuyper." In *Communication and Confrontation.* Toronto: Wedge Publishing Company, 1972.

Zylstra, Josina Van Nuis, ed. *Labour of Love: Essays on Work.* Toronto: Wedge Publishing Company, 1980.

Published Articles and Mimeographs

The following articles and mimeographs are relevant to this work but were not necessarily extensively used.

Ahlstrom, Sydney. "Scottish Philosophy and American Theology." *Church History* 24 (January 1957): 267–68.

Ames, Michael. "Missionaries Toil for Souls and Survivals." *The American West Publishing Company.* Edited by Donald E. Bower. 10 (January 1973): 28–33.

Beecher, Henry Ward. "Tendencies of American Progress." In *The Original Plymouth Pulpit.* Vol. 1. Boston: Pilgrim Press, 1871.

Brownson, Orestes. "The Rich Against the Poor and the Laboring Classes." *Boston Quarterly Review* 3 (July 1840): 11–16.

Carnegie, Andrew. "Wealth and its Uses." In *The Empire of Business.* New York: Doubleday, n.d.

Goudzwaard, Bob. "Incomes and Their Distributions." Toronto: Association for the Advancement of Christian Scholarship, n.d. (Mimeographed.)

————. "Toward a Reformation in Economics." Toronto: Association for the Advancement of Christian Scholarship, 1980. (Mimeographed.)

Guest, Robert H. "Scientific Management and the Assembly Line." In *Technology and Change.* Edited by John G. Burke and Marshall C. Eakin. San Francisco: Boyd and Fraser, 1979.

Holmes, Oliver W. "An Oration Given Before the New England Law Society." *Harper's New Monthly Magazine* 33 (June 1866): 27–35.

Olthuis, James. "The Reality of Societal Structures." Toronto: Institute for Christian Studies, n.d. (Mimeographed.)

"Rail System." *North American Review* 104 (December 1867): 16–35.

Smith, Edward P. "Memorial on the Treatment of Indians." *House Miscellaneous Document.* Number 29, 4th Congress, 3d session, Serial 1385. (January 1869).

Smith, Timothy L. "Righteousness and Hope: Christian Holiness and the Millennial Vision in America, 1800–1900." *American Quarterly* 31 (Spring 1979): 21–43.

Tyndale, William. "A Parable on Wicked Mammon." In *Doctrinal Treatise and Portions of Holy Scripture* (1527). Cambridge, England: Parker Society, 1848.

Wolters, Albert, "The Centre and the Circumference." *Vanguard* 10 (April 1980): 5–8.

————. "What is the Gospel?" Toronto: Institute for Christian Studies, 1982. (Mimeographed.)

Wright, Carroll D. "Factory System as an Element in Civilization." *Journal of Social Sciences* 16 (Spring 1882): 110–35.

Zylstra, Bernard. "Dooyeweerd on Economics and Industry." Toronto: Association for the Advancement of Christian Scholarship, 1972. (Mimeographed.)

Unpublished Materials

Ahearn, Marie. "The Rhetoric of Work and Vocation in Some Popular Northern Writings Before 1865." Ph.D. diss., Brown University, 1965.

Chaplin, Jonathan P. "Dooyeweerd's Theory of Public Justice: A Critical Exposition." Master of Philosophy thesis, Institute for Christian Studies, 1983.

Douglas, Ruth. "The Protestant Doctrine of Vocation in Presbyterian Thought of the Nineteenth Century." Ph.D. diss., New York University, 1952.

Ellis, Walter E. W. "Social and Religious Factors in the Fundamentalist/Modernist Schisms Among Baptists in North America, 1895–1934." Ph.D. diss. University of Pittsburgh, 1974.

Gilbert, Alan D. "The Growth and Decline of Nonconformity in England and Wales, With Special Reference to the Period Before 1850." Ph.D. diss., Oxford University, 1873.

Michaelsen, Robert S. "The American Gospel of Work and the Protestant Doctrine of Vocation." Ph.D. diss., Yale University, 1951.

Smith, Gary. "Calvinism and Culture in America, 1870–1915." Ph.D. diss., Johns Hopkins University, 1981.

Wenger, Robert E. "Social Thought in American Fundamentalism, 1918–1933." Ph.D. diss., University of Nebraska, 1973.

Index

Abell, Aaron, 20–21
"Acres of Diamonds," 155–56
Adversial system, 174, 196, 197–98; defined, 195
"Americanism," 42, 220
Augustine, Saint, 34, 100 and passim; and dualism, 101; and labor, 193; and meaning, 101; and private property, 240n.10
Aulén, Gustaf, 183–84
Autonomy: and creation, 162, 166; and "Free Will" in Finney, 132; and freedom, 69; and natural law, 39, 116; as presuppositum, 71; and profit, 202; and "Reason", 68; and salvation, 119; as sin, 178; and work, 92

Bacon, Francis (and the Baconian Ideal): 63, 68–69
Banking, 208–9; and Calvin, 112
Barnum, P. T., 43–44
Beecher, Henry Ward, 51, 52
Bentham, Jeremy, 234nn. 5, 36, and 37
Berkouwer, G. C., 172
Bible and economics, 154–55

Calling, 192 and passim; and corpus Christianum, 103; and John Calvin, 110, 193; and Martin Luther, 110, 193; and sphere sovereignty, 207; and vocation, 110, 192–93
Calvin, John, 110 and passim; and banking, 112; and class relations, 114; fundamental economic dictum, 111; and human evil, 172–73; and stewardship, 111–12
Capital, 83 and passim; and Calvin, 112; and capitalism, 210; as creational good, 177, 186; defined, 201, 209; and

machinery, 53; meaning of, 209; and medieval credit, 106; and progress, 55; and "savages," 149; and social content of, 201, 202; structure of, 201–10; and technologies of scale, 86; and working class, 149
Carnegie, Andrew, 52, 174; his worldview, 239n.114
Caughey, James, 122–24
Chartists (British Union Movement), 123
Common Sense Realism, 62–63, 160; and dualism, 142; and Francis Wayland, 138, 141–45; and individualism, 142; and secularization, 222
Conwell, Russell, 150 and passim; and Francis Wayland, 150; Grace Baptist Temple, 152, 156–58; and Progressive Movement, 155; and Samaritan Hospital, 153; and Temple University, 153
Cook, Jay, 83–84
Corporation, economic and industrial, 53
Corpus Christianum, 103 and passim
Cort, Henry, 73
Costs of business, 204–6

Darwin: and progress, 34
Deism, Deistic, 161–62
Dichotomy, 28; and religion, 29. See also Dualism
Dispensationalism, 58
Dooyeweerd, Herman, 34–35
Dualism (dichotomy), 21, 28–29, 30; and Charles Finney, 131–33; and corpus Christianum, 103; and Francis Wayland, 131–33; and law for creation, 166–67; and Martin Luther, 110; and medieval economics, 66, 67–68; and

"religion" and economics, 60; and social control, 221; and social service, 59

"Ecclesiasticism," 156–58. *See also* Grace Baptist Temple
Economic Growth, 205
Ellul, Jacques, 179
Evangelical: American-English relationship, 121–25; basic beliefs, 18; and Common Sense Realism, 141–42; as conservative, 30, 56, 221; and dualism, 28; and "great reversal," 60; and secularization, 221; and "sin," 56, 173, 175, 187–88; social accomplishments in Britain, 119–20; as world force, 9–10. *See also* Fundamentalists
Evangelical-Industrial liaison: as "isomorphism," 18–19
Executive Salary, 205–6

Faith: as active envisioning, 33, 219; and riches, 71
Finney, Charles G., 124–25, 126 and passim; and business mores, 129–30; and definition of sin, 127–28, 129–30; and Oberline Institute, 127; revivals relationship to culture, 128–29, 134–38; and "stewardship," 130
First Great Awakening (1735–1750), 120
Fisk, John, 39
Frank, Douglas, 19
Fulton, Robert, 74
Fundamentalists: defined, 61; and law, 60–71; and "liberals," 58, 61; and Southern textile capitalism, 63

Galbraith, John K., 98, 231 n.71; and "countervailing powers," 201
"Gold": as ethical imperative, 18, 31
Goudzwaard, Bob, 13–14, 30
"Great Reversal," 60
Gutierrez, Gustavo, 181

"Happiness": and consumption, 72; and economics, 41; and neoclassical economics, 72, 194–95; and obedience to moral law, 133; and objectification of labor, 51; and Utilitarianism, 71–72; and utility, 145–47
Hargreaves, 73

Hays, Samuel, 29, 33
Homo Economicus, 35, 70, 98–99; and Industrial Revolution, 72, 169–70

Incorporation: and capital, 85; defined, 54, 74; and John D. Rockefeller, 89–90; and labor, 239 n.119; and medieval life, 106; and monopolies, 85–86; and railroads, 78–80; and sin, 178
"Indians," 80 and passim; and Evangelicals, 80–82; and exploration, 75; and "Manifest Destiny," 82; and Native American rights, 216–17; and private property, 81, 82; as "savages," 76, 80
Individual(ism), 68 and passim, 114, 128, 140–41, 159; and capital, 202–3; and collectivity, 136, 144–45; and conversion, 120; and cultural pessimism, 141; and Enlightenment, 69; and medieval life, 104, 106; and redemption, 182; and sin, 171–76; and slavery, 141; and unions, 97, 202–3; virtues of, 69–70
Industrial(ism): and English origins, 72, 116–18; and incorporation, 50 and passim; and meaning, 52; process as world view, 10; and requisite patents, 73; Rochester, New York, Charles Finney, and revivals, 134–38; and values, 716; as not *per se* evil, 169
Investment, 207
"Irony," defined, 252 n.66

Johnson, Paul, 19, 136
Just Price, 106

Kansas-Nebraska Bill, 141
Keynes, John M.: and "presupposita," 32
Kuhn, Thomas, 159
Kuyper, Abraham, 35, 36–37; and "common grace," 179

Labor, 92 and passim; and American Federation of Labor, 97; and codetermination, 197–99; consumption of, 148; as disunity, 148; and emigrants, 95–96; as "factor of production," 192; and individualism, 93; and John Calvin, 113, 194; and Martin Luther, 108; and medieval life, 67, 105; related virtues, 92, 93; and socio-economic conservatism, 97; and theory of value, 146; and unions, 93–99; as "very good," 180–81, 193–94

Land, 74 and passim; abuse, 214–16; economically defined, 211; and Native Americans, 216–17; religiously and biologically defined, 211–14, 215; view of in Middle Ages, 67

Laws of Nature, 69, 143, 163–66; and Divine law, 168–69

Lewis, Meriwether, and William Clark, 74–75; and Jefferson's agrarian ideal, 235 n.46

Lincoln, Abraham, 153–54, 212, 247 n.105

Luther, Martin, 107 and passim; and commercial monopolies, 108–110, 220; and physiocratic economics, 107; and private property, 108

Machen, J. Gersham, 58

Mahan, Asa, 127

Malthus, Thomas, 38–39, 228 n.1

"Mammon": and the church, 238 n.113; as ethical imperative, 18, 31; and materialism, 234 n.26; and "repentance," 50

Management: alternatives to traditional views of, 254 n.95; international influence of, 254 n.98; and the nonunion workplace, 253 n.95

Manifest Destiny, 42; and divine providence, 220; and "stewardship," 44, 52–53, 162

Markets: morality and consumption, 234 n.38; and stewardship, 44

Marsden, George, 19

Marx, Karl, and Marxism: 194 and passim; and capital, 201; and theories of society, 203

Maschen, J. Gresham, 58

May, Henry F., 20

Meaning, 31–32; and creation, 160, 164–66; as "modal," 29, 114, 226 n.9; and reductionism, 165

Millennial(ism): and social optimism, 46, 48, 121, 140. See also Postmillennialism and Premillennialism

"Moralism," 174–75

National Labor Union: as first modern union, 93–94. See also Labor

Naturalism: 39–40; as worldview, 71, 159

"New Measures" Revivalism, 120–21

New School Presbyterianism, 45, 122

Niebuhr, Reinhold, 182

Pentecostals, 58–59; and Keswick, 58–59

Perfectionism: and Charles Finney, 126; defined, 45–46; and Pentecostals, 58

Pietism, 118–19

Postmillennial(ism), 48; and social optimism, 48, 220

Powderly, Terrance, 97–98

Premillennial(ism), 58; and Dispensationalism, 57; and social pessimism, 56–57

"Presuppositum": defined, 32, 227 n.22; and evolution, 39; and law for creation, 165–66

Private property, 70–71; relationship of labor and capital, 144

Polanyi, Michael, 159

Progress, 39; and Civil War, 50; and faith, 42; as imperative, 41; as presuppositum, 33, 47–48; as theme in painting, 77; and Whigs, 43

Radnitzky, Gerald, 160

Reagan, Ronald: and "enterprise zones," 207

Reductionism, 29–30; and economics, 70; and laws for creation, 167–69; and structure of capital, 210

Religion: and "autonomy," 31; as "exclusivist," 31; in John Calvin, 114; and meaning giving, 32; and "Origin," 32; and politics in pre–Civil War, 49; and "revivalism," 29; as ultimate commitment, 17, 29, 30, 32; as "well spring," 29

Revival(ism): and benevolence, 47; and British social reform, 117; and class alienation, 136–137; defined, 44–46; and definition of sin, 173; and social optimism, 46 and passim, 117; and Wall Street, 48

Ricardo, David, 145, 194

Ridderbos, Herman, 175, 176

Rockefeller, John D., 88 and passim

Salvation Army, 56, 220
Sandeen, Ernest, 19
Scientific method: as "gospel," 51; as imperative grid, 40–41
Scofield, C. I., 61–62
Second Great Awakening (1800 and following), 120; "New Measures Revivalism," 120–21
Sheldon, Charles, 28
Smith, Adam, 31, 69, 145, 194
Smith, Timothy, 19, 46
Social Darwinism, 39, 53
Soteriology, 170–71, 190–91
Spencer, Herbert, 38–39
Sphere sovereignty, 167; and salaries, 207–8
State and economics, 198–99, 202, 216, 224
Steam engines, 70; and mass production, 71
Stewardship, 162; defined, 211, 249 n.20; John D. Rockfeller's definition of, 238 n.102; and legal statutes, 215–16
Sumner, William G., 40–41

Tappen, Benjamin and Lewis (brothers), 127, 129
Tawney, R. H. 28–29, 60
Taylor, Frederick, 86–88, 94, 180; and organized labor, 195
Technology: and calling, 193; as imperative for control, 69, 233 n.15; and improvements in rail, 53, 78; and Industrial Revolution, 72–73; and "machine age," 51–52; and revivals, 134–36; and social optimism, 51–52; and steel production, 86
"Theologism," 44–45, 230 n.36
Thomas, George, 18–19
Tillich, Paul, 30, 31–33
Transportation, 72–73; and "dominion," 76; and railroads, 76, 77–80
Tull, Jethro, 73

Unions, 195–99. See also Labor
Usury, 105; and Aristotle, 241 n.17; and Calvin, 242 nn. 42 and 47
Utilitarianism, 71–72, 138; and Frabcis Wayland, 146–148. See also "Happiness"

Wall Street Revival, 48
Wanamaker, John, 158
Ward, Lester P. 41
Watt, James, 73
Wawrynski, Anton, 239 n.128
Wayland, Francis, 138 and passim; and Anthony Drexel, 152
Wealth: and utility, 145
Wesley, John, 121, 123
Whig, 43, 49, 61, 131
Wolters, Albert, 36
Worldview: defined, 35–36; and incorporation, 54

Youmans, Edward, 39